Selling Covered Calls
The Safest Game
in the Option Market

To **JAMES P. SHEEHAN**

friend since long-gone
school days:

A gentleman in all
situations and a friend
for all seasons.

Selling Covered Calls
The Safest Game
in the Option Market

Charles J. Caes

LIBERTY HALL
PRESS™

This publication is designed to provide accurate and authoritative information in regard to the subject matter covered. It is sold with the understanding that the publisher is not engaged in rendering legal, accounting or other
professional service. If legal advice or other expert assistance is required,
the services of a competent professional person should be sought.
                    —*from a declaration of principles jointly adopted by a committee*
                           of the Bar Association and a committee of publishers.

LIBERTY HALL PRESS books are published by LIBERTY HALL PRESS,
a division of TAB BOOKS Inc. Its trademark, consisting of the words
''LIBERTY HALL PRESS'' and the portrayal of Benjamin Franklin, is registered in the United States Patent and Trademark Office.

First Edition
First Printing

©1990 by TAB BOOKS Inc.
Printed in the United States of America

Library of Congress Cataloging-in-Publication Data

Caes, Charles J.
    Selling covered calls : the safest game in the option market / by
Charles J. Caes.
        p.   cm.
    ISBN 0-8306-3038-4
    1. Stock options. I. Title.
HG6042.C34   1989
332.63'228—dc20
                                                          89-12656
                                                          CIP

TAB BOOKS Inc. offers software for sale.
For information and a catalog, please contact:
TAB Software Department
Blue Ridge Summit, PA 17294-0850

Questions regarding the content of this book
should be addressed to:
Reader Inquiry Branch
TAB BOOKS Inc.
Blue Ridge Summit, PA 17294-0214

Vice President and Editorial Director: David J. Conti
Book Editor: Barbara B. Minich
Production: Katherine Brown
Book Design: Jaclyn B. Saunders

Contents

Preface

To begin with, this book can pay for itself the first time you write a covered call because you don't have to buy a covered call before you sell it, and you do not have to buy it back anytime after you sell it. Great isn't it, just to be able to sell something even if you do not own it.

The first sentence might sound like an outrageous claim, but the truth is, anybody who shows you how to write a covered call can make the same claim. It's not really this author and this book that are special; it is covered call writing that is special. "Hey!" your broker will say, "The author hasn't said anything new. I could have told you about covered calls, and I can make the same guarantee about my advice." And he can indeed. The entire investment community knows what is in this book, but you and the average stock investor do not. You just buy stocks and hope they will go up—that's what you call stock investing.

Most books dealing with the trading of *puts* and *calls*, which are only two types of stock options, try to educate and instruct the reader on the entire options game all at once. This one takes a very different approach. It first introduces you to a very popular way in which astute investors greatly increase the income from their stock portfolios. This unique and relatively safe way of squeezing more profit from stock holdings entails simply selling covered calls. Because an investor does not need to buy the calls before he sells them, and never needs to buy them back, his income is immediate and irrevocable.

Once this very simple way of producing income is detailed through the use of examples based on real stocks and their price movements, you are introduced to other aspects of option trading. Throughout the text, the concentration is on covered call writing—how to realize capital gains and increase income through the technique.

This approach to teaching option trading eliminates much of the usual confusion investors suffer when trying to understand puts and calls. Stock options are a confusing game to investors who have not yet developed a history of experience about, or a working experience in, the marketplace. Option markets function differently than stock markets. There are more decisions to make before each trade, and there are many combinations to consider in order to reduce risk and ensure profit or income. Additionally, a covered call writer is also a stock trader because the success of the options that he or she chooses to write depends on what happens to the stock on which they are based.

Trying to grasp the entire option investment game all at once can be defeating as well as exhausting. Mistakes may be made during initial attempts at trades if the investor has not taken the time to thoroughly study and understand the types of orders, the way options move according to their money positions, time decay factors, intrinsic value, and market and economic forces. Each trader has a choice of options on different underlying securities and a menu of options with different expiration dates and striking prices for the same security. On top of having so many options to choose from, the harried investor also must decide whether he or she should take a chance on in-the-money, out-of-the-money, or at-the-money options, and whether to be a writer or a buyer.

The entire game, however, is easily understood when approached from one single perspective; in this case, the perspective is that of the covered call writer.

Introduction

IT IS VERY HARD TO MAKE MONEY IN THE STOCK MARKET. DO NOT LET ANYBODY tell you differently. It is also very hard to make money in the option market—that is, unless you write covered calls. Covered call writing necessitates that you own stock. Because of this you must manage both stock and option trading in order to reduce the risk of capital losses as the owner of the stock, while trying to earn additional income from call premiums.

Basically, covered call strategy is very simple and can bring you five-year average returns of 10 to 20% for basic writing strategies, and possibly more, for frequent writing strategies on top-performing stocks. These possible returns include income from dividends and premiums as well as small profits on the underlying securities serving as the basis for call writing. Most of the income comes in the form of premiums from writing the calls.

The simplest strategy entails writing calls on your stock and just letting them expire. The frequent writing strategy entails writing the calls, buying back equivalent calls when it is advantageous, and then writing new calls. The increased turnover results in a lower return on each individual call, but more "paychecks" over the same period.

A call is, in the very simplest terms, a contract that gives the holder the right to buy stock at a certain price within a certain time. If you happen to be the seller of the call, you are obligated to deliver the stock if the holder exercises his rights. If you already own the stock, the transaction is relatively simple because you are already *covered* to meet your obligation. If you do not own the stock, then you must purchase it so you can sell it to the holder of the call.

Suppose you own 100 shares of AT&T. In addition to the dividends you receive from the stock, you would like to earn additional money from your holding. So you write a call.

For example, the call might be an agreement that, for $250, you will give anyone the right to purchase 100 shares of AT&T at $30 per share. (Assume that AT&T is at $28 per share.) As soon as you write the call, you receive the $250 from your broker. If the stock does not move beyond $30 per share by the expiration date of the contract, you keep the $250 and the stock as well.

If the stock goes beyond $30 per share and is called, you still keep the $250 you received for writing the call, but you must sell the stock at $30 per share. Still, that's a $200 profit on the stock. Add that to the $250 in premiums you received for the call, and you have a $450 return (before commissions) in two months on $2,800 worth of stock. That's a 16% return on investment in two months.

It is that simple. Of course, if AT&T goes down in price—perhaps to $20 per share—when the contract expires you have only the $250 from writing the calls to reduce your paper losses on the stock. But the game is not over yet. You can keep on writing calls until you come out ahead of the game. Will you always come out ahead? You can always come out ahead from writing the calls, but how the underlying stock will do in the long run depends on overall market and economic forces and the stock's own dynamics. You had the stock in the first place, however, and would have suffered the loss anyway. Without the income from the calls, your losses would have been greater.

To explain the way in which an investor can take advantage of covered calls, this book looks at the basics of covered call writing, compares the strategy with other types of investments and gives examples of how a writer can play bear and bull markets, as well as what is referred to by this author as a possum market. It then looks at typical investor misconceptions, dangers inherent in option investing, and the option markets.

Investors who are new to either the stock or option markets will want to study the entire book. Investors who are experienced in the marketplace and consistently make money will want to concentrate on chapters 1 through 4 and 7 through 15 in order to learn about options.

Chapter 1 reviews the terminology that must be mastered in order to understand option trading fully, from contract terms to option listings. It begins with an explanation of how common options play an important part in business transactions outside of the marketplace created by the stock and option exchanges and the National Association of Securities Dealers.

Chapter 2 looks at the different money positions that determine whether or not a particular call is worth writing. Basically, there are three money positions: in-, at-, and out-of-the-money. For calls, these positions are determined by the relationship between the striking price (price at which the owner of the call can exercise his rights) and the price of the stock. If the price of the stock is lower than the striking price, then the call is considered out-of-the-money. If it is the same as the striking price, then the call is considered at-the-money. If it is higher than the striking price, then the call is considered in-the-money. In-the-money calls have intrinsic value; this means that if the owner of the call exercises his rights, he will be assured of a profit before commissions are taken into account. The chapter's focus is on the benefits of writing calls in one money position or the other.

Chapter 3 puts on the brakes. It looks at calls in terms of how they compare with other strategies. A call writer expects a limit on the upward movement of the underlying stock and he wants to benefit by guessing what that limit is. As an option trader, the call writer is similar to a short seller. But he is more than that. He is a hedger, an insurer of his portfolio, a person who wants to produce income whether his stock goes up or down or stands still. This chapter compares his call writing campaign with other stock and option strategies.

Chapter 4 focuses on specific examples of just how the call writer can increase his income, while either suffering paper losses or realizing paper or actual gains on the underlying stock.

The ultimate return from a covered call strategy depends a lot on the performance of the underlying stock on which the call may be written. Chapters 5 and 6 look at some of the fundamental and technical aspects of stock and market performance. They show the necessity for researching the underlying stock and knowing when the market is receptive to the call writer and when it is not.

Chapter 7 takes a look at the 1987 stock market crash and shows how a covered call writer, caught in a tumbling stock that seems to be falling forever, can play a strategy that will greatly reduce his losses from the tumbling stock. Then chapter 8 shows how the convenience of a margin account can facilitate the trading of options, although option trading is done only in cash. (*Margin* has different meanings in the investment world. In the case of stock options it means cash or securities on deposit in an account, which a broker can use as collateral when needed. Covered call writers automatically comply if they have the underlying stock in their brokerage accounts.) Chapter 9 looks at how this same investor might improve his earnings picture in the bull market that followed the crash. Using the October 1987 crash and the subsequent stock movements over the next few months as the backdrop for these examples, allows concentrated trading on stock movements that might otherwise take a year or more. But the market often stands relatively still. There are inactive markets as well as bear and bull markets. What does the call writer do in a stagnant market when his stock is not moving one way or another? Chapter 10, ''Playing the Possum,'' explains how a call writer still does very well in this situation.

Chapter 11 looks at those aspects of option trading that can present unusual problems.

Chapter 12 tries to make sure everyone is on the right track by correcting typical investor misconceptions about the option markets. Chapter 13 gives 10 basic rules that all option investors should follow.

Where and what are the option markets? For the most part, they are a number of stock exchanges and a brokerage association that have joined with the Chicago Board Options Exchange to create a fast, efficient market for option trading. Chapter 14 tells all about them.

There is little doubt in my mind that the majority of readers will make their next stock investment part of a covered call strategy long before they are past chapter 8. And no doubt this book will become the most important one they have ever read on stock or option investing. It will more than pay for itself with the first call they write.

1

Understanding
Call Options

THE STOCK MARKET IS ALWAYS AN EXCITING PLACE. WHETHER IT IS GOING UP OR down, there are many ways to profit from it. Even when it is standing still, the stock market offers the investor opportunities to increase capital or income. But *opportunity* is not a *guaranty*. The truth of the matter is that many people lose a great deal of money from stock investments because they have a single strategy: buy low, sell high. That's a good strategy if you know what stocks will be higher in the future than they are today.

It is usually the little guy that comes out the loser, so it is very important for the small investor to know all the possible ways to play the investment game, including the use of covered calls. Exactly why the small investor tends to wind up on the bottom is not always clear. There seems to be a great deal of conflicting data about the abilities of the small investor to know when to buy and when to sell stocks. According to Peter Lynch, manager of the $9 billion Fidelity Magellan Fund and one of the most respected and successful fund managers, small investors usually do not do the proper research. They do not shop for stocks with the same carefulness that they generally use when buying consumer merchandise.

According to other sources, the small investor does indeed have a knack for knowing just when to get into and out of the market, as is often evident from the success of odd-lot traders, who are usually small investors. However, odd-lot traders have not had anywhere near the success during the 1980s that they had in the 1970s.

The small investor also might come out a loser because of a lack of backup money. Generally, the governing rule is not to invest with money you might need

1

in the near future, but the small investor is rarely in a position to follow that advice. He cannot hold onto a stock as long as the big investor can. During downside swings in the market, he is often compelled to sell stock at a loss because he needs the money for a new house, a new car, college tuition, a badly needed vacation, medical bills, or any of the other things in life that sometimes call for a lot of cash all at once.

The small investor often plays a different game than the one books tell him to play. This is mainly because of his or her own impatience, a misunderstanding of what the equities markets are all about, a lack of sophistication and knowledge for making successful investments, and a tendency to panic when choices take a dive (yet it's a rare instance when anyone purchases a stock at its lowest price over the short term).

A lot of monday-morning quarterbacking goes on in the investment community. One of the offshoots of this after-the-fact wisdom is the development of all types of marketing strategies based on past evidence such as historical price earning (P/E) ratio analysis, money to the sidelines in the historically disastrous month of October, or dependence on the usual summer rally. Unfortunately, like political history, market history does not always repeat itself. Things are never exactly the same as before. Investment economics even on a local scale are highly complex, with an ever-changing set of variables resting on a turbulent base formed by human greed, fear, and ignorance. On a national scale, it is even more complex and unpredictable; on an international scale, it is just about impossible to manage. Everything affects the financial communities, from hurricanes to wars to computerized trading.

One of the strategies based on monday-morning quarterbacking is the belief that if the investor just leaves his money in the blue chip stocks, he or she will come out a winner. Cited as proof is the remarkable advance of the Dow Jones Industrial averages in the past eight or more decades. In 1907 the Industrials were at a low of 53; in 1937 the low was 113 and the high 194; in 1947 the low was 163 and the high 186; in 1957 the low was 419 and the high 520; in 1967 the low was 786 and the high 943; in 1977 the low was 800 and the high 999; in 1987 the low was 1738 and the high 2722.

Now, who would argue with such a sound principle, particularly if they have faith in the economy of the United States? Well, this is indeed a great and rich country—rich in resources, in knowledge, and in its citizenry. So it is taken for granted by most of us that if we would leave our money in any of the blue chip stocks that make up the Dow Jones Industrials for the rest of our lives, our capital would increase by leaps and bounds.

But most people do not invest for a lifetime. They expect a return within a shorter time frame. They want to be able to access their profits within a practical time period so they can enjoy their money before the cosmos recalls them. Additionally, some of the blue chip stocks that made up the Industrials in the past have since gone out of business or lost their standing.

So, not all the stocks that make up the Dow Jones Industrials are guaranteed to be successful. In fact, there are no guarantees. The only way an investor can improve his chances for profit is to adopt a number of different strategies. He can't simply be a "buy it now and wait for it to go up" type of investor. He has to be strategic.

Many strategies are available to him, from selling short to making straight income plays on certain debt instruments. The investor who turns to the stock market does so because he is interested in the special types of returns that stocks and stock options can offer. So he looks for those special strategies that can help him beat the odds. For the most part, these strategies entail some amount of risk.

There is, however, one relatively safe strategy that every investor can use—a strategy as safe as anything related to stock investing can possible be. This book is dedicated to this simple income strategy, which many investors choose to ignore or have never been informed about. The strategy is selling options on an underlying stock that they already own.

The name of the game is *covered calls*. You will like the game because of its safety level and because the rules are easy to understand. Most of all, you will like the game because it is a way to increase the income from your stock without having to put up additional money, unless you wish to change your position and buy back your call. Table 1-1 lists some of the basic differences between common stock and call option trading.

CALL OPTIONS

A call is only one type of option available to investors, but it is the only one that will be covered in depth in this text. Basically, a call option gives legal right to the buyer to purchase the underlying security at a fixed price for a period specified in the option contract. Anyone can sell or buy a call.

Buying and selling calls is becoming increasingly popular with investors. Buyers of call options are particularly interested in three very attractive advantages:

1. Tremendous leverage. The price of a call is always much lower than the underlying stock, so the investor has a chance to make a few dollars do the work of many.

2. Great diversity. The low price of calls relative to the price of the underlying stock gives the independent investor the opportunity to expand and diversify his or her portfolio. Rather than tying up thousands of dollars, say in IBM stock, he or she can purchase IBM calls for as little as 10% of

Table 1-1. Basic Differences between
Common Stock and Call Option Trading.

Stock Trading	*Call Option Trading*
Purchase is represented by certificates in buyer or broker's name (street name).	There is no certificate representing ownership. Transaction statements from broker represent the only proof of trade.
No time limit exists regarding ownership of shares purchased; stock can be held for an indefinite period.	Ownership of the rights is limited to the length of time specified in the option contract, after which time the call is worthless to its owner.
Purchasing common stock is the purchase of a percent of the corporation which issued it.	Purchasing a call is simply the purchase of a "right to buy" common stock under certain conditions.
The number of shares available is limited according to the terms of the corporate charter.	The number of calls is unlimited and determined solely by the law of supply and demand.
Purchase of stock entitles the owner to share in any dividend that may be declared.	Owner of a call is not entitled to any dividends declared on the underlying stock.
Price of the stock is always much higher than the call and therefore requires a greater investment for an expected return.	Price of the call is always much lower than the stock and therefore gives the owner greater leverage.
Stock can be purchased on credit.	Calls cannot be purchased on credit.
Stocks can be purchased in odd-lots (less than 100 shares).	A call almost always represents 100 shares of the underlying stock. Stock splits and stock dividends necessitate exception to this rule.
Money owed as a result of a transaction must paid in 5 "working" days.	Money owed as the result of a transaction must be paid the same day.

their value and use the remaining money to diversify into other securities. This does not mean that such diversification is more promising or safer than just buying IBM. Buying calls is always a riskier business than buying stock for a number of reasons that will be discussed throughout this book.

3. Opportunity to ascertain the maximum loss. You cannot lose any more than your investment in the option. Option holders do not have the same risk stockholders have when the stock they own has been purchased at a price below par value (in which case, stockholders can be sued by creditors for the difference to par). In addition, the low price of calls limits the downside risk.

Sellers of calls are particularly interested in these advantages:

- Additional income. If the investor owns the underlying security, he or she can use call options as a means of increasing income from that holding.
- Trading profits. By selling a call option high and buying it low, sellers (writers) of calls can trade their options for profit.

From the viewpoint of the buyer, options are risky business and, therefore, require a great deal of expertise to trade successfully. A good understanding of options arithmetic, a thorough familiarity with the underlying stock, and good market timing are all necessary to successfully buy and then sell call options.

From the viewpoint of the covered seller (writer), dealing in calls is, by comparison, a "piece of cake." It is an almost sure-fire way of increasing income and sometimes capital gains. It is almost sure-fire because the covered seller owns the underlying stock and, therefore, has insured himself or herself to some degree against the usual dangers of stock and option trading. If, however, an investor sells uncovered options, in which case he or she does not own the underlying stock, there is almost imminent danger of excessive losses.

Although there are some very important differences between common stock and call option trading, the name of the game for either enterprise is to buy high and sell low, though not necessarily in that order. Trading takes place in the same way for calls as it does for stock trading.

The purchase of common stock is verified ultimately by certificates registered in either the trader's or the broker's name. There is no time limit influencing the value of the stock or its ultimate retirement; therefore, the owner of the shares does not have to try and achieve his or her investment goals within a given period. The owner of shares actually owns a percentage of the corporation that issued the stock, has a legal right to any declared dividends, and has other rights of common stock ownership, such as the right to vote for directors.

Ownership certificates are not issued for call options. Transaction statements from the broker represent the only proof of trade. The owner of the call options must exercise his or her rights within the time specified in the option contract. Once the time has elapsed, the calls are worthless. A call gives the owner the right to purchase the underlying security and nothing more. The owner has no right to dividends or the other privileges normally allowed shareholders in a corporation.

There are other differences between stock trading and buying and selling calls. The price of the underlying security is always much higher than the price of the call and, therefore, requires a greater investment for the same dollar return. Stock can be purchased on credit (margin) and in odd lots (less than 100 shares), and proceeds from any transaction need not be transferred for five exchange-operating days.

The price of the call, a mere percentage of the price of the stock, always affords the investor large percentage gains—if the price of the call moves sufficiently in the right direction. However, calls cannot be purchased on margin and almost always represent 100 shares; an investor cannot deal in fractions of a call. Proceeds from option transactions must be forwarded the day of the transaction.

COMMON BUSINESS PRACTICE

Calls and other options are not unusual in business. They may be offered for the purchase of art, automobiles, real estate, or any valuable goods.

In all cases, the option contract will specify these basic components: the underlying security or merchandise on which the contract is based, the price at which the owner of the option may buy the security or the merchandise, the length of time during which the owner of the option may exercise his option to buy (or sell), and the price of the option.

As an example of how options work, let's say that you own a valuable piece of art that you wish to sell. You have had the painting appraised and have been informed that it should have a market value of about $10,000.

"I'd like to have that painting," I tell you, "but I haven't got $10,000 right now. Besides, I think I would like to look around to see if there is a better opportunity from another art dealer. So will you hold this painting for me? If I do not get back to you in three months, you can sell it to whomever you please."

You are willing—but for a price. What have you got to lose, since there are no other buyers in sight? So you draw up a contract that states that for $500 you will not sell the painting to anyone else for three months, and that during that time I may purchase the artwork from you for $10,000.

Your painting has now brought you $500 in income and it is still yours. I have three months to purchase it from you. You haven't made such a bad deal. The premium you received ($500) is 5% of the value of the painting. So in three months you are getting a 5% return on the value of your holding; annualized, that return is 20%.

If I decide to purchase the painting, you will have actually received $10,500 for it—the purchase price plus the premium. The premium you get to keep whether or not I exercise my option to buy.

To be redundant for the sake of emphasis: you are willing to make the deal because there are no other buyers in sight and you get $500 from me whether or not I buy the painting. If I do exercise my option and buy, you receive $10,000 on the sale and have already made $500 in premiums. Your prized painting has produced $500 in income for you just because you own it.

However, there is a caveat. The contract that we signed says I have three months to make up my mind. That means that during this period you cannot sell the painting to anyone else. If someone else offers you $12,000 during the period covered by the contract, you cannot sell the painting unless you buy the option contract back from me. You can bet I'm not going to sell it back to you for the same price that I paid for it.

Once you understand what has just been explained, you can also comprehend that any of the following scenarios can take place as a result of our contract in which you are the seller (writer) of the option and I am the buyer.

1. I decide to keep my option on the painting. Just before the contract expires, I exercise my option and give you $10,000 for the painting.

Sale price of painting:	$10,000
Premium paid for option:	+ 500
Total income:	$10,500

2. Knowing the new value of the painting ($12,000), I decide that my option is worth more than $500 because the painting is now worth 20% more than when I first acquired the option. You know this also. So you offer to buy back the option from me for $1,000. In this case, we both profit handsomely at the expense of a third party.

Buy-back price of option:	$1,000
Original sale price:	− 500
Your loss and my profit:	$ 500

This transaction summary is related only to the trading of the option. The business you conducted was actually more compound and complex, as the following summary indicates.

Cost to purchase back option:	$ 1,000
Premium received from sale:	− 500
Your loss from option trading:	$ 500

Sale price of painting to third party:	$12,000
Original value of painting:	−10,000
Additional Income	2,000
Less loss from option:	500
Your total gain:	$ 1,500

3. I decide I can gain more by exercising my option, then reselling the painting to the third party. You will note that in this example I receive $1,500 in profits and you forego as much.

Proceeds from sale to third party:	$12,000
Cost to purchase painting from you:	−10,000
My profit:	2,000
Less cost to purchase option:	− 500
My total profit:	$ 1,500

4. I fail to exercise my option in time and fail to sell my contract to someone else. In this case, you can sell the painting to the third party and profit both from your dealings in the option and the sale of the painting. I, as a result of my failure to act, lose all my privileges.

Sale of painting to third party:	$12,000
Original value of the painting:	−10,000
Your profit:	$ 2,000
Income from sale of option:	$ 500
Your total gain:	$ 2,500

5. I may sell my contract to another—a fourth party who knows you have been offered $12,000 for the painting—at a price above what you offered me. Even if that person paid me as much as $1,800 for my option, he would still come out ahead by $200 when he bought the painting from you for $10,000 and then sold it for $12,000.

In the previous examples, the word *profit* is used a bit loosely, for whether or not you actually profit from the sale of the painting depends on the price at which you purchased it. For the purpose of simplifying the examples, it is assumed that you had paid at least the offering price for the painting.

There are two other principles worth noting here. The first has to do with the type of option you sold. The second has to do with the value of the painting.

Because the option represented the right to purchase the painting under certain restrictions, it is referred to as a *call*. The restrictions were time and price. I had to exercise my option within three months, and I had to purchase the painting for $10,000. Because you held the underlying item on which the option was based, what you sold to me was a covered call.

What is the value of a painting? What is the true value of a share of stock in a corporation? The value of either is not what price is fixed to it, but what someone else is willing to pay for it. The same goes for a call or stock option. It is worth only what someone else is willing to pay for it after taking into account its speculative value based on current interest rates and the potential for the underlying security to behave one way or another during the term of the contract.

You now have a very basic idea of what options are all about and a general idea of what is meant by a covered call. You must remember, however, that the types of options dealt with in this text use corporate stock as the underlying merchandise.

While there are indeed a number of types of option contracts, there is only a need to master one of them at this time in your career as an option trader (part or full time) in order to increase the safety and income from your portfolio. This is the call option.

In the painting examples, the underlying security was the art work. In future examples it will be corporate stock. Bear this in mind: the incentives to both the buyer and the seller of the option on the painting will be just as applicable to buyers and sellers (writers) of stock options.

CONTRACT TERMINOLOGY

Table 1-2 lists a few terms that you must understand to allow quick and dependable comprehension of call contracts. *Exercise price,* or *striking price,* is the price at which the buyer of the call has the right to purchase the underlying stock. The *expiration date* is always the Saturday following the third Friday of the month designated as the expiration month. The *premium* is the price at which the call is traded. The *underlying stock* is the corporate stock on which the call option is based.

Exercise Price

The exercise price, usually labeled the strike price in the listings in your newspaper, is one of the criteria that greatly affect the amount of the call premium. If the price of a stock is higher than the exercise price of the call, the call will probably command a low premium. However, if the price of the stock is lower than

_____Table 1-2. Options Terminology._____

Call Writer	Seller of the option. He or she may or may not own the underlying stock. If not, the writer must be prepared to purchase any stock required to cover the terms of the contract should it become necessary.
Call Buyer	Buyer of the option. He or she will probably deal mainly in the call itself, hoping to buy it at a low premium and sell it at a higher one. But he or she may also exercise his or her right to buy the underlying stock, conditions permitting.
Exercise Price	The price at which the buyer of the call has the right to buy the underlying interest. This is also known as the striking price.
Expiration Date	The date on which the call expires. Calls expire on the Saturday following the third Friday of the month designated as the expiration month.
Premium	The price at which the call is traded. The price represents ''per-share.'' So if the premium is $1/8, as all calls are generally for 100 shares, the true price of the Call is $12.50 before broker commissions.
Underlying Stock	The corporate stock on which the call option is based.

the exercise price of the call, the premium will be higher. The exercise price never changes during the length of the contract, although both the price of the underlying stock and the premium for the call may change.

Example. You own 100 shares of IBM. Each share is worth $200. You sell a call that gives the buyer the right to purchase the stock at $210. The exercise price is $210. If the stock never increases beyond $210 before the expiration date of the contract, then the call expires worthless. Your IBM stock remains yours to keep and write another call against, if you so wish.

As you might imagine, if the exercise price is $210 and the stock is only $200 per share, the call would command a very small premium. However, if the exercise price were $200 and the stock were $210, then the call would have a great deal of value. The buyer could exercise his option at any time and realize a profit of $10 per share on the stock. He can purchase the stock from you for $200 per share and immediately turn around and sell it at $210 per share.

Premium

Regardless of whether or not the call you write is exercised by the buyer, the premium for which you sold the option is yours to keep, as in the example of the painting. Under no situation are you obligated to return the premium. Any dividend declared by IBM is also yours to keep. Selling the call does not sell your rights as a stockholder in the company because you still own the stock. You are the stockholder in the corporation, not the owner of the call. As long as the option is not exercised by the buyer, any dividend IBM declares must go to you. You are the one with the legal right to it, the one with partial ownership in the corporation!

Example. You sold a call option on 100 shares of IBM stock currently listed at $200 per share. The exercise (striking) price is $210 per share. You received $500 in premiums. Within 24 hours of the sale, the broker sends the premium to you. That $500 is yours. If IBM reaches the striking price or goes beyond it and the buyer of the call exercises his option, you must sell the stock (or other IBM stock of equal value) to him for $210; if IBM does not reach the striking price by the expiration date, then the call will expire worthless and you will not have to sell your stock. In either case, you keep the $500 premium. Any dividends declared by IBM, whether or not distributed by the time of exercise, still belong to you.

Expiration Date

The expiration date of the call contract is very important because once the contract expires, the call is worthless. The day before it might have been worth $100, but now that the expiration date has passed, it is worth nothing. Nothing at all! It needs little emphasizing, then, that it is important for both the writer and the buyer of a call to pay special attention to the expiration date.

In most cases, if the price of the underlying stock remains exactly the same and does not increase, the value of the call probably will depreciate because the call will lose value as its expiration date approaches. This time-value erosion is always most pronounced in the last month of an option's life. If the price of the underlying stock remains steady as the expiration of the option approaches, only rising interest rates might be able to hold the value of the call where it was. The likely effect of rising interest rates, however, is declining stock values, so in all probability the call will still depreciate in value.

The expiration date for the IBM calls in the previous example (and most other options) will be the Saturday immediately following the third Friday of the expiration month. The date will be on the transaction statement you receive from your broker after writing (or buying) a call, so you do not have to worry about counting Fridays and Saturdays. Nonetheless, pay special attention to the fact that the expiration date can be the second, third, or fourth Saturday of the month. The day will depend upon the date of the first Friday of each month. (At this writing, the expiration date rule cited holds for all stock options.)

This does not mean, however, that all stock options expire in the same month. Different options have different expiration months, as you will immediately realize by glancing at the sample listings reproduced in this text or by referring to the option listings in your favorite financial or major city newspaper.

Underlying Stock

"What about the underlying stock," you may ask. "Is it of any importance in deciding what calls to write?" Any broker will tell you that you need to know a great deal about the underlying stock because you don't want to write a call against a stock that may skyrocket tomorrow or anytime before the expiration date of the call. If the value of the stock is going to increase rather quickly, you are much better off playing the stock and not the call options. If the value of the stock should decrease just as quickly, dump the stock even though the premium from the call could offset some of the paper loss. Remember, however, that no advice covers all situations and you may have to break the rules to achieve your goals.

OPTION LISTINGS

Available options can be found by checking the listings in any financial newspaper or in the financial sections of the large dailies. The *Wall Street Journal*, *Investor's Daily*, the *New York Times*, and most of the big-city daily newspapers have sections listing options that were traded or available the previous day.

Like any listing for stocks, commodities, or options, the option listings in your newspaper are only a snapshot of yesterday's activity (see Fig. 1-1). Your selection of what contract to enter into should not be determined solely on the information contained in these listings. You must know much more about the underlying security and the factors that may affect the short-term movement of the underlying stock.

The illustration that follows is from the *Wall Street Journal*. It lists trading of some calls offered on a particular day. Option listings also contain information on put trading. *Puts* are the opposite of calls. They are contracts that give the buyer the right to sell instead of buy.

A glance at one of the listings readily indicates the many different option contracts that might be available for any given stock. The prices of these different options vary depending on their expiration dates and striking prices in relation to the price of the underlying stock.

Month

The months listed here represent the expiration month of the contracts being offered. In each case, the specific expiration day will be the first Saturday after

PACIFIC

Option & NY Close	Strike Price	Calls—Last			Puts—Last		
		Oct	Nov	Dec	Oct	Nov	Dec
A M I	15	2	2 5/16	2 1/2	r	r	r
17 1/8	17 1/2	1/4	1/2	1	7/8	r	r
17 1/8	20	r	s	5/16	r	s	r
Bevrly	5	r	r	1 1/8	r	r	r
5 3/4	7 1/2	r	r	1/4	r	r	r
Bowatr	25	3 7/8	r	r	r	r	r
28 7/8	30	3/8	1	1 1/4	1 3/4	r	2 3/8
28 7/8	35	r	r	1/2	r	r	r
CasCke	25	r	r	r	r	r	5/8
26 5/8	30	r	r	5/8	r	r	r
CombEn	25	s	s	r	s	s	1/4
30 3/4	30	r	r	2	r	1	r
30 3/4	35	r	r	3/8	r	r	r
Cray	65	r	r	r	1	1 1/2	2 1/4
69 1/4	70	1 5/8	2 7/8	3 3/4	2 3/8	3 1/4	4 1/8
69 1/4	75	3/8	r	2 1/2	6	6 1/8	6 3/4
69 1/4	80	3/16	r	1	r	r	10 1/2
69 1/4	85	r	s	3/8	r	s	16 3/4
DataGn	17 1/2	1 5/8	r	2 7/8	3/16	1/2	r
19	20	1/2	r	1 3/8	r	r	r
Echlin	17 1/2	r	r	3/4	r	r	r
Lockhd	40	1 1/8	1 3/4	2 1/4	1/2	r	r
40 5/8	45	1/8	5/16	1/2	r	r	r
40 5/8	50	s	s	1/8	s	s	r
PerkEl	22 1/2	r	r	r	r	r	3/4
23 1/2	25	1/8	1/4	3/4	r	r	2
SciAtl	10	r	r	2 1/4	r	r	r
12	12 1/2	3/16	r	r	r	r	r
SmkB	40	5	r	5 3/4	1/16	r	r
45	45	1 3/16	r	2 7/16	7/8	r	2 1/16
45	50	1/8	3/8	15/16	r	r	r
45	55	s	s	5/16	s	s	r
45	60	s	s	1/16	s	s	r
StoneC	25	s	s	10	s	s	r
35 3/8	35	1	1 3/8	2 1/8	1	r	1 3/4
35 3/8	40	1/16	r	1/2	r	r	r
US Air	30	r	s	9 3/4	r	s	r
39 3/4	35	5	r	5 1/8	1/8	r	1/4
39 3/4	40	3/4	1 1/8	1 5/8	r	r	r
Veeco	15	s	s	5	s	s	r
19 1/2	20	3/4	7/8	1 1/2	r	r	r
19 1/2	22 1/2	1/4	s	3/4	r	s	r
VistaC	50	r	r	r	1	r	r
51	55	r	1	s	s	s	s
Wendy	5	r	1 11/16	1 11/16	r	r	1/16
6 5/8	7 1/2	1/16	1/8	5/16	r	r	r
6 5/8	10	s	s	1/16	s	s	r
		Oct	Nov	Jan	Oct	Nov	Jan
Acuson	25	r	r	1 1/2	r	r	r
AdobeS	40	3 7/8	r	6 3/8	r	r	r
43 3/4	45	1 1/2	2 3/8	r	r	r	r
A M D	10	1/8	5/16	11/16	1 1/8	1 1/4	1 3/8
9	12 1/2	1/16	1/16	5/16	3 1/2	r	3 3/4
9	15	1/16	s	1/16	6	s	r
Alza	20	2 5/8	r	3 3/4	r	r	r
22	22 1/2	5/8	r	r	r	r	r

Fig. 1-1. A typical stock option listing from the *Wall Street Journal*. Notice that the listings contain striking prices and expiration months for both calls and puts. The expiration day in each month is always the Saturday after the third Friday, though this may change in the future. Puts give the right to sell a stock at a certain price. Calls give the right to buy at a certain price. The owner of a put hopes the underlying stock will decrease in price and the owner of a call hopes the underlying stock will increase in price. (Reprinted by permission—*The Wall Street Journal*, ©Dow Jones & Co., Inc. 1987.)

the third Friday of the month. Some cycles may be monthly, some quarterly, and some may be a combination of the monthly and quarterly cycles. If at any time the underlying stock increases or decreases markedly, new option contracts may be introduced.

Exactly how much a stock must advance before additional options become available is determined by its trading plateau. High-priced stocks generally have to move about 10 points before a new option becomes available. The lower-priced stocks may only have to move two or three points. In some cases, not all the available options are listed and you should check with your broker for clarification. As one expiration month is deleted from the listings, another is added. Here we see the same expiration months in all cases, but a glance at your financial newspaper will reveal many different expiration months for groups of stocks on each option exchange.

If the stocks do not change in price as the expiration dates approach, the calls should decrease in value. The amount of the decrease, however, is not predictable and will vary considerably depending on whether the options are six months or one month away from expiration. Another factor influencing the decline of the price of the option as the expiration date nears is the relationship between the striking price and the price of the stock. If the striking price is high, the call will decrease more rapidly; if it's low, it should decline at a slower pace.

The prices here are the last prices at which the options traded. If you were to phone your broker to find out the premium at which you could buy or sell a call, you would receive a reply indicating the bid and ask prices of the selected option. These bid and ask prices may differ by as much as a $1/2$ point. If you wish to sell or buy a call option, and would like the best price rather quickly, go for the middle price. If the spread is $2^1/2$ bid and $2^3/4$ ask, offer to buy or sell at $2^5/8$ and you will generally make a trade. There are no guarantees, however!

Option & Close

This column lists the underlying stock for the call contract and the price at which the stock closed the previous day. The closing price is important because it tells traders whether or not they should buy or sell the option—if they are interested in it at all. For instance, if the price of the stock is higher than the striking price and you were to write that option (because of the very high premium), you can expect the buyer to "call the stock."

A general rule of thumb is to write a call if the striking price is higher than the stock price and to buy only in-the-money calls—calls with a striking price lower than the stock price. In and out of the money strategies will be discussed in the second chapter of this book. For now, it is important to remember that the relationship between the striking price and the stock price influences the level of the premium and, therefore, investor interest.

Strike Price

This is the price at which the buyer has the legal right to purchase the stock from you, the writer of the call option. It is important to remember that the closer the striking price is to the price of the underlying stock, the more likely the chance of the stock being called.

As the seller (writer) of a covered call, you should be interested in the striking price and the length of the contract. For instance, if you write a call even at a relatively high striking price but with a four-month contract, the chances of having to sell the stock will increase unless the market is in a bear phase or not going anywhere at all. In six months anything can happen in the stock market. A stock can easily double in that time period or become a takeover candidate. It can also head south like wild geese in winter in which case you do not have to worry about the buyer calling. Instead, you will have other worries,such as, will the stock ever climb back up, etc.

As a rule of thumb, a writer of covered calls wants close expiration dates and high striking prices. Sometimes, however, the premiums offered for other contracts will make you want to break that rule and take a chance on lower striking prices with longer expiration periods. You, like every other investor, will have both short-term and long-term objectives and will have to play the stock and option combinations that best suit your financial situation.

Calls-Last

Here it is: the premium information. These are the columns that tell you whether or not the game is worth playing. Remember that these are yesterday's prices so you will have to double-check with your broker to find out the current day's trading spread (bid and ask prices).

Option contracts are almost always for 100 shares of stock. A listing of $1/4$ in these columns actually represents a premium of $25.00. If you wanted to sell 10 covered calls on IBM you would have to own 1,000 shares of IBM stock—not 10.

Generally, your broker will check your account to see if you own enough of the underlying stock to cover your sale of the call options. If you do not own enough stock, then you are going to have to put up a lot of money in your account. Brokers know the losses that can be incurred from dealing in uncovered calls. In other words, they do not want to have to cover your position if you renege. Since the stock market crashed in October 1987, brokers want as much as $100,000 in equity in your account before they will even consider letting you deal in uncovered calls.

Although your broker will probably check to make sure that you have enough of the underlying stock to write a covered call, be sure you understand that each call is for 100 shares of stock, except in very unusual circumstances (like splits and stock dividends).

OPENING AND CLOSING TRANSACTIONS

When an option trader purchases or writes an option for the first time, he or she has, technically speaking, "opened a position" or "made an opening transaction."

Example #1. You own 200 shares of IBM. The July calls are selling for $2. If you write those calls against your stock, you will receive $400 ($2 × 200). As you are not expecting the stock to reach the striking price, the calls look like a good investment. You call your broker and make an opening transaction. He subtracts about $40 in commissions and puts the rest in your account (or sends it to you).

If the stock remains at almost the same value as the expiration date nears, the calls depreciate in value. They are now worth $1. Therefore, you decide to take your profits while you can and at the same time protect your holdings. You decide to close out your position by putting in a purchase order for the calls.

You buy the two calls back at $1 each at a total cost of $240, $40 of which is the broker's commission. You have closed out your position and made $120 in the process. ($360 received for selling, $240 paid to buy the call back.)

In this example you opened and closed your position. You wrote a call against your stock and then bought it back. You made $120 and ensured that no one could call your stock. The writer of a call can also make offsetting transactions. In the previous case the call was written and then purchased. In the case that follows the buyer purchases first and writes later.

Example #2. You buy two IBM calls for $2 ($2 × 200) because you expect the stock to go up, thereby making the calls all the more valuable. The broker charges you $40 in commissions. The purchase price of the calls is $440.

As the expiration date nears the stock remains in a tight trading range, never exceeding the exercise price. The calls, as one would expect in this scenario, begin to depreciate rapidly. You decide to sell before they depreciate any further. You sell at $1 and receive $160 after deducting the $40 broker's commission. You have made a closing transaction that, unfortunately, cost you $280. It is better, however, to lose $280 than $400, which is what it would have cost you if the calls had expired.

There are two lessons to be learned from the above examples. The first, of course, if what is meant by opening and closing transactions. The second is that it is generally riskier to be the buyer of a covered call. In the situations described above, the underlying stock hardly moved one way or the other, but the writer still came out with a profit. Even if the stock had substantially increased, the writer would have enjoyed the premium at which he sold his call, although he could not participate in the stock's marked advance. If the stock price decreased, the premium from writing the call would have offset at least some of the paper loss. The buyer of the call was not as well positioned. Whereas the writer could benefit from movement one way or the other, or even from no movement at all, the call buyer needed to see an advance in the underlying stock to profit.

The lesson: for safety's sake, write calls, don't buy them.

BUYING CALLS

If selling covered calls is such an attractive strategy, why would anyone want to buy calls? Why would anyone be interested in being on the other side of the contract?

People who buy stock options are basically high risk traders. They are interested in quick profits and a high return on their investments. Calls offer an opportunity for quick profits—as well as quick losses—and a high-percentage return on investment. Because of their low price and movement in relationship to the underlying security, options, in general, offer a trader something that is very important to anyone who wants to strike it rich: leverage.

Leverage in the world of finance means getting one dollar to do the work of many dollars. Traders and speculators always think leverage. Stock options offer them the perfect tool. The covered call you sell might increase by many percentage points over the life of the contract. Traders in stock options want to be there if that happens.

The rate at which a call may move up or down in price depends upon the factors mentioned earlier, including, among other things, the usual influences on price that supply and demand forces exert. The low price of a call, however, automatically gives leverage. For instance, a stock selling at $20 per share has to move up $10 before the investor can realize a 50% return, but a call on that same stock selling for $1/8$ of a dollar need only move $12^1/2$ cents for an investor to double his money.

Example. You can purchase a call for 100 shares of IBM. The premium is $5 (total cost: $500) at a time when IBM is selling for $200 per share. Market factors are such that with each movement of one point, the call moves $1/2$ point. In the first three days, IBM jumps 5 points. That means the call will jump $2^1/2$ points. The stock has increased by only $2^1/2\%$ but the call has increased by 50%.

Do you now understand the leverage call options afford the investor and why someone would chance buying those that you make available? The above, of course, has been a very simple example of the relationship between a call's movement in price and the movement in price of the underlying security. There is much more to this relationship, as you will begin to realize in coming chapters. Suffice it to say that the buyer of a covered call is interested in reselling his stock option at a higher premium than that which he paid for it, whereas the seller wants to pay a buy-back price that is lower than the original sale price, or wants the contract to expire.

What the buyer wants is quick and substantial profit on his money. He hopes to get it from the calls he is buying and selling. Rarely is he interested in converting his options into stock. It is usually more profitable for him just to deal in the options.

There is always the possibility that the buyer of your call actually wants the underlying security, but does not have the money to make an outright purchase. He does, however, expect to have the dollars he needs within a short period of time. But, as a cautious person, he is afraid that the underlying security will jump in price because his analysis of its prospects is highly favorable. He does not want to chance missing out on the advance. So he looks to the marketplace for calls that will assure him some position. The calls will give him the right to buy the stock at a lower price than he expects the stock to be at when he finally has the finances to make his purchase.

TRANSACTION STATEMENTS VS. CONTRACTS

The call option, in the most simplest terms, is a right to purchase. The conditions for that purchase will be set in the option contract. The contract will specify these conditions explicitly: the premium, the underlying security, the expiration date, the striking price, and who is the writer and the seller.

Option trading is handled as quickly and efficiently as stock trading. Option transactions are cash, so payments are made the same day. If you sell stock, there is a five business-day waiting period.

When you deal in stock options you never actually see a contract. All you see is a transaction statement from your broker that specifies the terms of the legal agreement. Because the option contracts are standardized it is perfectly legal, as well as uncomplicated and advantageous to both brokers and traders, to avoid getting involved with formal contracts. It is this standardization that makes it possible for you or me to deal in stock options in the first place.

When you buy and sell stock options, you are doing so in the secondary market provided by the exchanges dealing in options. Do not let the term secondary market mislead you into thinking that the purchase and sale of stock options is less than a forthright enterprise. Even when you buy and sell stocks and bonds through your broker, you are almost always dealing in a secondary market. The stock exchanges themselves are secondary markets. When corporations issue stock, for instance, they first sell it to investment bankers who, in turn, make it available to the general financial community.

With few exceptions, if you buy AT&T stock, for instance, you are not actually making a purchase that will result in money being put in AT&T's treasury. The company sold the stock you just purchased a long time ago. Now, you are purchasing it on the secondary market created by the exchanges and their member brokers. You are buying the stock from broker accounts.

SELLING AND BUYING

To sell an option, contact your broker and specify:

- The number of options
- The particular option
  a. the striking price
  b. the underlying security
  c. the month of expiration
- The premium
- The type of order
  a. all or none, or partial
  b. opening or closing

For instance, if you want to sell 5 calls on Warner Communications, simply say to your broker: "I'd like to sell 5 Warner Communications June 30 Calls at $2^{1}/_2$, all or none. This is an opening position." The broker will ask if you own the underlying stock. He needs to know if you have enough equity in the account to cover your position if it becomes necessary.

There are other types of instructions that the exchanges will accept. These are listed and defined in the chapter on option markets under the subsection entitled, "Types of Orders and Trading Rules."

If you want to buy, give the same information. Remember that a buy can be an opening or closing transaction as can a sell. If you sell a call and later buy it back, then the first transaction was an opening one and the buy was the closing transaction. If you buy a call and later sell it, then the sell was the closing transaction.

Once you are in the option market as either a buyer or a seller, you must realize that you are playing a game different than one you might play if you were just dealing in the stock market. Options require your undivided attention. Your first dozen or so trades should be made under the guidance of a skilled broker or financial counselor.

2

Money Positions

THE VALUE OF A CALL IS PRIMARILY AFFECTED BY THE RELATIONSHIP BETWEEN the underlying security and the striking price, and by the amount of time remaining until the expiration date. The first of these relationships is based on a true dollar value (or guaranteed profit) and is referred to as the intrinsic value. The second is based on the lifetime of the call and is referred to as the time value.

The intrinsic value and the time value for calls are not always the same. A call on Warner Communications and a call on Dow Jones may have the same difference between strike price and stock price and the same exercise date—yet the calls will have different premiums. This is because demand for the options will influence the price of the calls, and that demand will reflect bullish or bearish interest in the underlying stock. Many other factors also affect the price of an option, including the volatility of the underlying stock and interest rates.

Examples of the three types of calls are shown in Table 2-1. Calls are separated according to how their values are derived: in-the-money, at-the-money, and out-of-the money. At any given time, it is possible to have in-, at-, and out-of-the-money calls available for any given stock, as well as more than one option in any given money position. (See Table 2-2).

In-the-money calls are those having an exercise price that is below the current market price of the underlying stock. If you owned these calls and wanted to sell the stock immediately after exercising your options, you would be assured a profit because you could buy the underlying security at the striking price and immediately sell it at the higher market price. Bear in mind that buy and sell

_____Table 2-1. Types of Calls._____

A. In-the-Money: A call having an exercise price below the current price of the underlying stock.

Stock	Current Quote	Exercise Price
AT&T	$13^1/_2$	12
Bell Atlantic	75	70
Colgate	$41^1/_2$	40
Caesars World	$25^3/_4$	20
Hershey	$25^1/_2$	25

B. Out-of-the-Money: A call having an exercise price above the current price of the underlying stock.

Stock	Current Quote	Exercise Price
Hitachi	$118^1/_4$	120
IBM	115	125
Lehman	$12^1/_2$	15
MCA	$44^7/_8$	45
Seagram	54	55

C. At-the-Money: A call having an exercise price equal to the current price of the underlying stock.

Stock	Current Quote	Exercise Price
Tyco	25	25
Zenith	30	30

commissions on the stock and the commissions for the option transactions will cut steeply into your profits; these commissions will be determined by the actual price of the call and the number of calls bought or sold.

At-the-money calls are those having an exercise price equal to the current market price of the underlying stock. If you owned these calls and wanted to sell your stock immediately after exercising your rights, you could only be assured of breaking even on the stock before commissions, and showing a loss on the stock after commissions. So, it is hardly practical to exercise at-the-monies.

Out-of-the-money calls are those having an exercise price above the current market price of the underlying stock.

Table 2-2. Sample Securities with Many Different Calls.

A. Merck

Stock Price	Strike Price	May	June	July
152$^{1}/_{8}$	140	13	14$^{1}/_{2}$	17$^{1}/_{2}$
152$^{1}/_{8}$	145	8	9$^{1}/_{2}$	12$^{1}/_{2}$
152$^{1}/_{8}$	155	2	4$^{1}/_{2}$	6$^{1}/_{4}$
152$^{1}/_{8}$	160	$^{1}/_{2}$	2$^{1}/_{2}$	4
152$^{1}/_{8}$	165	$^{1}/_{4}$	1$^{5}/_{16}$	2$^{2}/_{8}$
152$^{1}/_{8}$	170	$^{1}/_{4}$	$^{1}/_{2}$	1

B. Disney

Stock Price	Strike Price	May	June	July
57$^{1}/_{8}$	55	2$^{3}/_{4}$	3$^{3}/_{4}$	4$^{1}/_{2}$
57$^{1}/_{8}$	60	$^{1}/_{2}$	1$^{1}/_{4}$	1$^{3}/_{4}$
57$^{1}/_{8}$	65	$^{1}/_{2}$	$^{3}/_{4}$	1$^{1}/_{4}$
57$^{1}/_{8}$	70	$^{1}/_{4}$	$^{1}/_{2}$	$^{5}/_{8}$
57$^{1}/_{8}$	75	–	–	$^{1}/_{4}$

These stocks are on the Chicago (Merck) and American (Disney) exchanges. Note that they are only two of very many stocks offering a number of different call contracts. Depending on how much you wish to invest and what you feel the price movement of the underlying stock will be until the contract date, you may select one or more contracts on each stock.

IN-THE-MONEY CALLS

Note that in all cases the calls with intrinsic value are those that have prices above the striking (exercise) price. They are in-the-money because the buyers of the calls on these underlying stocks are in a better position to profit after exercising their rights. The stock can be purchased at the striking price and immediately sold at the market price. As the market price is higher than the striking price, the calls on the underlying stock have intrinsic value. Table 2-3 lists the pros and cons of writing in-the-money calls.

While in-the-money calls represent a worthwhile opportunity for buyers who purchased the calls at lower prices or are considering such a purchase, they are more often than not very disadvantageous for writers. Although in-the-money calls may command higher premiums than calls (on the same underlying security) that have similar exercise dates, they are subject to exercise immediately, in which case the writer must scramble to cover his position. See Table 2-4 for write advantages for in-the-monies.

_____Table 2-3. Pros and Cons of Writing In-the-Money Calls._____

Advantages	Disadvantages
Premiums are relatively higher.	Broker fees are relatively higher.
If the stock is volatile, you might be able to realize a great deal of income from continually writing and buying back, if you catch the price swings right, and if these swings are impressive during the term of the contract.	The stock may be called at anytime, and the premiums are taxable income so if the stock falls below the striking price during the term of the contract, you have taxable income but a nondeductible paper loss.
	There is no chance to benefit from any increase in the value of the underlying stock while at the same time there is the continued danger of suffering a decline in the value of the underlying stock.
	Usual risks of writing detailed in chapter 9.

_____Table 2-4. Write Advantages (In-the-Money Calls)._____

Example	Stock	Current Price	Premium	Strike Price	Write Advantage
#1	Avon	22½	2½	20	0
#2	Avon	25	4½	20	−½
#3	Avon	30	11	20	+1
#4	Avon	35	7	20	+2
#5	Avon	35	20	20	+5
#6	Avon	40	20	20	0

Do not be fooled by the size of the premium. When writing in-the-money calls, you must remember that if your stock is called, which it most surely will be, you must sell at the striking price. So to determine your true advantage to writing a call, always match the loss (that will result if you must sell the stock) against the premium you earned from writing. And remember this: related commissions from writing the call and selling the stock will probably wipe out any gain. You could buy in and sell out as the call falls and rises, but then you are playing a very chancy game. There are few good reasons to write in-the-money covered calls. Even in example #5 where there is clearly a write advantage, you must ask yourself if the return on investment is worth the gamble.

There can be profit in writing in-the-money covered calls, however. Profit can be made if the premium exceeds the intrinsic value of the option by enough points to assure a gain if the stock is called. In other words, the premium on in-the-money calls must always exceed the difference between the striking price and the price of the underlying stock by enough to cover all transaction fees and ensure a substantial profit, otherwise it is not attractive to a writer. When the premium is in such a profitable range, it could be said that the in-the-money call has an advantage for the writer.

In the examples that follow, you will see how you can win and lose by writing in-the-money calls. Please note that there is some repetition in the presentation of these examples for the purpose of simplifying and reinforcing the lessons to be learned, and that exercise dates have been left out to avoid undue complications.

Example #1. You own 600 shares of Warner Communications. Calls are available with a striking price of $25. The stock is selling at $30 per share putting the related calls in-the-money. The premium for each call is $6 (meaning each call will command $600). You write six calls (each representing 100 shares of W.C. stock) and receive $3,000 in premiums; the money is yours to keep. Sometime afterward, the option is exercised. You must sell your 600 shares at $25 (the striking price) for a loss of $5 per share. You have profited from the call, but have lost on the stock transactions.

Transaction Summary

Sold 6 calls at $6 each:	$3,600	
Sold 600 shares at $5 per share loss:	− 3,000	
Gain:	600	

Once you wrote the in-the-money call in the example above, the buyer could have exercised his option immediately, one month later, or at any time before the expiration date. That is the danger of selling (writing) in-the-money calls. At any time you may be required to deliver the underlying stock in the amounts required by the contract. However, you did make a profit after all the transactions were tallied.

Example #2. You own 500 shares of Warner Communications. The stock is selling for $30 per share. You write 5 calls (each representing 100 shares) on the stock, each call bringing in premiums of $600. The striking price is $25. The stock climbs to $50 per share before the exercise date and the calls advance 1 point for each 1 point advance in the stock, as in-the-money calls may sometimes do if the exercise date is not too close. The buyer of the option exercises his rights and now you must cover your position by selling your 500 shares of Warner Communications stock. Again, you win on the sale of the option, but this time you blow the chance to ride the 25 point advance in the stock. (See Table 2-5.)

In the above example you made a $500 gain, even though you had to cover your position by selling your 500 shares of Warner stock. Again, you win on the sale of the option, but this time you must forego the additional profit you would have received from the 25 point advance. The $500 in premiums is far less than the $12,500 in profits you could have made from just trading the stock—if you sold it at its highest points.

Premiums are relatively higher for in-the-money calls, but you can expect that the proceeds from writing them will be greatly reduced or wiped out by your having to sell the underlying security at the striking price. Do not forget that in this example, the commissions for writing the option and selling the stock have not been included, and they would come to about $175.

Example #3. You own 500 shares of International Telephone. You write 5 in-the-money calls on the stock at $600 each. The stock is selling for $30 and the striking price is $25. The calls are in-the-money. You feel that while this is ordinarily a bad position for a writer, you have a hunch that the stock has just made an incredible and unwarranted climb and might start to fall below the striking price rather quickly. Your strategy is to have a position in the stock, but to get some immediate income and downside protection. By gosh, you call it right for a change! The stock climbs a bit more, then falls below the striking price at the expiration date. The option expires and your stock is not called. You make $3,000 from the sale of the calls and get to keep the stock. You may write additional calls now if you so desire, or you may just play the stock. It's your choice.

In this example, you took a risky chance. You got a bit speculative and decided to try a long shot: the stock would fall below the striking price before the exercise date, or it would fall close enough to it to depreciate the call so that you could buy it back at a lower price. In either case you would make a profit, in the first from the premium, in the second from the closing transaction.

This was a rather unusual strategy and one that is rarely recommended. Yet, under certain circumstances, the strategy can work. It represents a technique which, in effect, brings a great deal of speculative flavor to working with covered calls. If you were forced to cover your position, the result would be similar to those in the first two examples, or you might realize a small loss.

Generally, Example #3 represents a strategy you might take when you are doing some writing as part of a long-term income play, wherein you have been writing calls on the underlying stock for some time, have already made a substantial income from premiums as well as a strong paper profit from the stock, and feel a gamble such as the one just described is worthwhile.

Now, pleased with your success, you are ready to write a new call on another stock. You figure if you can make money writing an in-the-money call one time, you can do it again. Fools rush in where angels fear to tread! Happens all the time.

Example #4. You own 1,000 shares of Golden Nugget, currently selling at $10 per share. You write 10 calls on the stock. These calls have a striking price of $7.50. Premiums are $3. You receive a total of $3,000. The stock jumps to $12 per share and the calls to $5. You decide to change your position because it appears the stock is going to skyrocket, so you buy back your calls for a $200 loss per call, or a total of $2,000. You feel the loss is offset by the paper gain from the stock. For all practical purposes you are even: $2,000 gain from the advance in the stock, $2,000 loss from the closing transaction on the option.

Now let us assume that the market value of the stock begins to head in the other direction. The stock continues to fall and fall and fall until it drops to $7.50 per share. Based on your evaluation of reports on the stock, you decide to sell it at $7.50 because you no longer feel sure of the stock's performance. You lost $2,000 when you bought back the calls. Now, you sell the stock for a $2.50 per share loss. This means a $2,500 loss on the price of the stock before commissions.

Ouch. You are running far into the red. The stock and option play cost you $4,500 in this example, which has been given to underscore the extent to which an investor can be wrong. The safest way to play this game, once you wrote the call, would have been to hold on to the stock even when it started going up. You would have had at least $3,000 as a result of writing the call. This would have put you ahead of the game even if you had decided to take the $2,500 loss on the stock.

In the last example, you became anxious about the underlying stock's movement and decided to change your position by closing out your calls. The result proved disastrous because you were still playing with in-the-money calls that could be exercised at any time. You gave a speculative flavor to your covered call writing, but that is not what covered call writing is about. Covered call writing is about getting extra income with greater safety from your portfolio.

Let's review the previous transactions. To simplify Table 2-5, it is assumed that all stocks were originally purchased at the market price in effect at the time the calls were written. This makes it easier to calculate the gain or loss. Additionally, note that in the case of the calls, the sale must necessarily be first, then the purchase.

_____Table 2-5. Transaction Review #1 (In-the-Money Writes)._____

Example	Security	Purchase Price	Sale Price	Gain	Loss
1	6 calls, W.C.	—	$ 3,600	$ 3,600	
	600 sh., W.C.	$ 18,000	15,000		3,000
2	5 calls, W.C.		3,000	3,000	
	500 sh., W.C.	15,000	12,500		2,500
3	5 calls, IT&T		3,000	3,000	
	(Option expired)				
4	10 calls, G.N.	5,000	3,000		2,000
	1000 sh., G.N.	10,000	7,500		2,500
			Totals	$ 9,600	$10,000

There are stories to be told in this summary, as well as a missing piece in one of the stories. The missing piece has to do with Example #2. In this example, you may remember, there was a rather large increase in the price of the stock. While you, the writer, enjoyed a $3,000 premium from the sale of the calls, you would have made much more if you had ignored playing with the calls and just rode the stock.

The other stories to be told are all about an investor who wrote $9,600 in calls, but wound up losing $10,000—before commissions—on the underlying stock as a result of his trading. All this writing of calls and selling of stock—only to come out a loser. The reason: you were writing in-the-money calls that command high premiums but put the underlying stock in danger of being called at the striking price at any time.

A closer look at Example #3 reveals that you managed a taxable gain from writing the calls, but suffered a paper loss. In the long term, this may well work out in your favor, but for the present your tax situation is hardly the best.

Look again at the transaction summary. Wouldn't it be nice if you could enjoy the premiums and greatly limit the chance of your stock being called? Well, this is possible when you move away from writing in-the-monies to writing out-of-the money calls.

Writing the covered calls in the previous examples brought you $9,600 in premiums, almost all of which was wiped out because your stock was called and because at one point you became greedy and tried to switch positions. After all that work, a $400 loss!

You might also note that in all the examples but #2 the premiums were at what might be referred to as a ''write advantage.'' This means that the premiums were higher than the difference between the stock price and the striking price. Why is this important? Well, it allows a slight profit to the writer in case his stock is called, which it will most likely be if it remains in the strike zone.

AT-THE-MONEY CALLS

Table 2-6 gives the pros and cons of writing at-the-money calls. Table 2-7 provides additional examples of at-the-money calls. They are at-the-money because the striking price is equal to the price of the stock. Actually, if broker commissions were taken into account, these calls would really be out-of-the-money. However, it is common not to consider commissions before defining the money positions of stock options. Always bear in mind the impact of broker commissions on the intrinsic value of a call.

At-the-money calls are borderline opportunities for a writer. Given a neutral rating for the underlying stock (neither bullish nor bearish) before the expiration date of the call, the greater risk is with the buyer than with the writer.

Before writing an at-the-money consider the prospects for the underlying issue and the size of the premium. If the underlying security is about to increase in value, do not chance writing an at-the-money because you will do much better

_____Table 2-6. Pros and Cons of Writing At-the-Money Calls._____

Advantages	*Disadvantages*
Premiums are relatively higher than those for out-of-the-money calls.	Broker fees are relatively higher than those for out-of-the money calls.
If the stock is volatile, you might be able to realize a great deal of income from continually writing and buying back, if you catch the price swings right, and if these swings are impressive during the term of the contract.	A slight upward movement of the stock will put the call in the money and in danger of being called
The chances of the underlying stock being called is less than that for in-the-monies, though more than that for out-of-the-monies.	There is no chance to benefit from any increase in the value of the underlying stock.
The value of the call will depreciate rather quickly as the expiration date nears, allowing you to possibly buy back the option at a lower price than that at which you sold it—as long as the underlying stock has not advanced much beyond the striking price.	Usual risks of writing detailed in chapter 9.

_____Table 2-7. At-the-Money Calls._____

Stock	Current Price	Exercise Price
Avon	25	25
Bell Atlantic	75	75
Colgate	41	41
Caesar's World	$27^1/_2$	$27^1/_2$
Hershey	30	30

In each of the above examples, the price of the underlying stock is below the exercise (strike) price of the call.

---

just riding the stock. Who can predict stock movements, however? Thus one of the reasons for calls—the premium is, at least, a sure thing.

If the premium is high enough to cover a substantial advance in the stock through the expiration date, then you have the second deciding factor you should consider before determining whether or not to write an at-the-money call.

The buyer of the contract is interested in the call because he hopes to sell it later at a higher price. You, however, are interested mainly in income, and therefore you have written a call that you believe to be in your favor. You have written a call on an underlying stock that you do not expect to climb above the specified exercise price. The premium will be the same one that excited you to write the call in the first place. If the premium is too low, you are not going to be interested in writing the option and gambling on whether or not you will have to sell the underlying security on the short term. If the premium is high enough, however, and the striking price is at least high enough for you to break even on the stock if it is called, then you may decide the gamble is worth it. So, all things considered, it is the premium that excites the option markets and that make the game worthwhile for the writer. Table 2-8 gives examples of write advantage for at-the-money calls.

In the examples that follow, you will see how you can gain or lose money by writing at-the-money calls. Please note again that there is some repetition in these examples for the purpose of reinforcement, and that exercise dates are left out to keep the examples simple. In addition, tax considerations will not be taken into account. Remember that when dealing with stock options you can easily wind up with a taxable gain on the option and a non-deductible paper loss on the stock. This reduces the true return from your writing adventures.

Example #1. You own 1,000 shares of Harcourt Brace, currently selling for $10 per share. You write 10 at-the-money calls selling at a premium of $1. Your premium income, therefore, is $1,000. As it turns out, the stock climbs to

_____Table 2-8. Write Advantages (At-the-Money Calls)._____

Example	Stock	Current Price	Premium	Strike Price	Write Advantage
#1	Avon	22¹/₂	2¹/₂	22¹/₂	+2¹/₂
#2	Avon	25	4¹/₂	25	+4¹/₂
#3	Avon	30	6	30	+6
#4	Avon	35	7	35	+7
#5	Avon	35	¹/₄	35	+ ¹/₄

In each of the cases above, there is advantage to the writer and always the possibility that the underlying stock may not be called. In example #5, however, while the calls are technically at-the-money, broker commissions put them out-of-the-money. When do you want to chance at-the-money writing? The answer is when the premiums are relatively high and you expect that the stock will trade in a very narrow range at and below the striking price.

$15 per share before the expiration date and the options are exercised. You must (a) forego the profit to be realized by the $5 per share jump in price, and (b) sell your stock at the striking price of $10 per share.

As it turns out, this was a rather safe play. The premium commanded by the calls when you sold them had a write advantage, and at worst you would have had to sell the stock at its market price when you wrote the calls. On the sale of the stock you broke even, if we assume that the original price you paid for the stock was the same as the striking price. On the sale of the calls you received a premium income of $1,000. In short, you made $1,000 but had to unload the underlying shares. (See Table 2-9)

Using hindsight, you would have been better off if you did not deal in the calls and, instead, just held onto the stock. Your game plan, however, was based on your projections that the stock would not move very far into the strike zone during the length of the option contract. How could you know that it would advance with the strength that it did?

Because at-the-money calls are so close to having intrinsic value, just the slightest move upward in the price of the underlying security can make the writer sorry he sold them. Whether or not it is worth writing at-the-money calls depends on the write advantage of the premium and the length of time before the contract expires.

For instance, two months remain until the expiration date and you can write an at-the-money covered call for a premium that is 10% of the value of the underlying security. You decide that 10% on your money for a two month period is an impressive enough return to write the calls. You will have to write a number of calls to take advantage of the reduced commissions that come with quantity orders and assure that most of that 10% goes to you and not to the broker.

Example #2. You own 1,000 shares of Harcourt Brace. You write 10 at-the-money calls on the stock for total premiums of $1,000. The striking price is $10. The stock drops $1 per share and remains at $9 through the expiration date. The call, therefore, expires and you never have to cover your position.

In this example, you get to enjoy both the premium income from writing the call and continued ownership of the underlying stock. You may continue to write calls over and over again on this same stock as long as there remains a market for them. If you never have to cover your position because the stock does not move into the strike zone and the option is never exercised, you will continually enjoy premiums, plus any dividends that may be declared in the future. The underlying security can become a money tree for you.

Example #3. You own 1,000 shares of Harcourt Brace. You write 10 at-the-money calls against the stock for total premiums of $2,000 ($200 per call). The striking price is $10. The following day the stock drops to $9 per share and the respective calls also fall in price from $2 to $1. Immediately, you buy back the calls for a total price of $1,000. Remember, you sold them for $2,000. That means you have made a profit of $1,000, still have your stock, and still have the opportunity to write a call again if the stock goes up.

As it turns out, the stock climbs again to $10 per share and at-the-money calls are again available for $2. You sell 10 of these calls, receiving another $2,000 in premiums. The stock price and the call price drops a few days later. Using the same strategy as before, you buy the calls back for $1,000 and once more realize a profit of $1,000, get to keep your stock, and have the opportunity to write more calls when they appreciate, if you so desire.

In less than a week, you have produced $2,000 in income from the underlying security. What's more, you still have the stock. The $2,000 in income represents a 20% return based on the striking price of the underlying stock, which, for purposes of this example, is assumed to be the purchase price of the stock. If you had paid less than the striking price for the stock and waited until it advanced before selling an at-the-money, your rate of return would be much more.

Example #4. You own 1,000 shares of Harcourt Brace, currently selling at $10 per share. You write 10 at-the-money calls on the stock and receive $100 for each call. Total premiums are $1,000. The stock jumps to $12 per share and the calls to $3 per share. You decide to change your position because you believe the stock is going to skyrocket, so you buy the calls back for $3,000. You are expecting to ride the stock to new highs and are willing to absorb the loss from buying back the calls. You made this mistake once before when playing with in-the-monies, but you feel this time you are doing the right thing.

However, the stock drops to $11 per share and the calls to $1 before the expiration date. You are now unsure of the stock's potential and you decide to unload it. Assuming that $11 is $1 more than you paid for each share, you will show a $1,000 profit on the stock transaction, but you will have lost $2,000 on the calls.

You will note that this example is similar to the fourth example for in-the-money writing. It has been constructed to illustrate the dangers of changing your position with an at-the-money call that has changed into an in-the-money.

"I've got the point," you might say. "Changing horses in mid-stream is not very strategic, nor is buying back calls when a stock starts to advance."

"Good," I reply. "The point cannot be drummed home often enough."

Table 2-9 summarizes the transactions in the previous four examples. As before, it is assumed that the underlying securities were originally purchased at the striking price.

Table 2-9. Transaction Review #2 (At-the-Money Writes).

Example	Security	Purchase Price	Sale Price	Gain	Loss
1	10 calls, H.B.J.	-	$ 1,000	$1,000	
	1000 sh., H.B.J.	$10,000	10,000		
2	10 calls, H.B.J.		1,000	1,000	
3	10 calls, H.B.J.	1,000	2,000	1,000	
	10 calls, H.B.J.	1,000	2,000	1,000	
4	10 calls H.B.J.	3,000	1,000		$ 2,000
	1000 sh., H.B.J.	10,000	11,000	1,000	
			Totals	5,000	2,000

Remember that in the summary in Table 2-9 above the sell transactions took place first, then the purchase transactions. Notice too, that the stories told in this transaction summary differ somewhat from those used for the in-the-money writing examples. Also note that the premium income is not as high in the above summary as it was in the earlier writing examples because at-the-money premiums are rarely higher than in-the-money premiums.

Now, take a look at Example #1. Here you received $1,000 in premiums for writing the calls, but were forced to sell the underlying stock because it advanced into the strike zone and the option to buy was exercised.

In Example #2, you received another $1,000 in premiums and a special bonus: your stock never advanced into the strike zone far enough to make exercise worthwhile, so the call expired and you were able to keep the underlying stock.

In Example #3, you attempted successfully to trade in the calls to squeeze out as much as you could in premiums, a strategy that works a bit better with at-the-monies than it does with in-the-monies. Your strategy: write calls and buy them back if they depreciate. Then if the calls advance again, sell once more at the higher price with the intention of buying back the calls if they depreciate in price again. Bear in mind that this strategy rarely pays off well when you are writing at-the-monies. You need to know a lot about the underlying stock to chance playing this game. You also have to know that the stock will not move into the strike zone and that its trend is downward or, at worst, stable.

In Example #4, you used the same poor judgment you made earlier when you tried to change your position with an in-the-money write on a call that had accelerated in price. You got greedy, and therefore careless, and made a gamble out of covered call writing rather than a safe bet. The rule of thumb is to avoid losing money by buying back a covered call unless you have some inside information, which never comes easy to the small investor, and which is absolutely illegal to act upon anyway.

OUT-OF-THE-MONEY CALLS

This is the type of call you should be interested in as a writer. Out-of-the-money calls are nice income plays that also guarantee you additional profit if your stock is called. This does not mean that every out-of-the-money covered call is a good write. You still need to evaluate the size of the premium, the amount that the call is out-of-the-money, the time remaining until the expiration date, the volatility of the underlying stock, current interest rates, other short-term investment opportunities, and whether or not you want to chance giving up the underlying stock under any conditions. Table 2-10 summarizes the pros and cons of writing out-of-the-money calls.

Table 2-11 gives examples of out-of-the-money calls. Table 2-12 shows the write advantage to out-of-the-monies. The calls are out-of-the-money because the striking price is higher than the price of the stock. Broker commissions, including buy and sell commissions on the stock and the options, must be taken into account when you make your profit projections. Once again, in the examples that follow broker commissions are not counted and tax considerations are ignored.

Example #1. You buy 1,000 shares of Dow Jones stock, currently selling at $40 per share, $5 below the striking price for June calls. You immediately write 10 of these calls. Your total premiums are $1,000. The stock climbs to $49 per share—$4 above the $45 striking price. Your stock is called. You must sell the required number of shares in the underlying stock to cover your position.

You were called, but there is no real damage. You made a rather handsome profit because you are dealing with out-of-the-money calls. The transaction

_____Table 2-10. Pros and Cons of Writing Out-of-the-Money Calls._____

Advantages	*Disadvantages*
The chance of the underlying stock being called is far less than that for in-the-monies, and better than that for at-the-monies.	There is little chance to benefit from any increase in the value of the underlying stock if it advances above the striking price.
The value of the Call will depreciate rather quickly as the expiration date nears, allowing you to possibly buy back the option at a lower price than that at which you sold it—as long as the underlying stock has not advanced much beyond the striking price.	Usual risks of writing detailed in chapter 9.
There is plenty of opportunity to realize a great deal of income from continually writing and buying back, if you catch the price swings right.	
You will almost always realize a profit if your stock is called and you must sell it at the striking price.	

enabled you to (a) receive $1,000 in call premiums, and (b) receive a profit of $5,000 even though you had to sell the stock at $45 instead of $49. The $45 sale price still represents a $5 per share profit, or $5,000 to you.

Your return, before commissions, from the combination play of stock and call writing was $6,000 on a $40,000 investment. That is a 15% return over the short-term. Not bad. If this were an in-the-money write you would have lost

_____Table 2-11. Out-of-the-Money Calls._____

Stock	Current Price	Exercise Price
Avon	25	30
Bell Atlantic	75	80
Colgate	41	50
Caesar's World	$27^1/_2$	30
Hershey	30	35

In each of the above examples, the price of the underlying stock is below the exercise (strike) price of the call.

Table 2-12. Write Advantages (Out-of-the-Money Calls).

Example	Stock	Current Price	Premium	Strike Price	Write Advantage
#1	Avon	22$^1/_2$	8	30	+15$^1/_2$
#2	Avon	25	7	30	+12
#3	Avon	27	5	30	+ 8
#4	Avon	28	4	30	+ 6
#5	Avon	29$^1/_2$	1	30	+ 1$^1/_2$

In each of the cases above, there is advantage to the writer and always the possibility that the underlying stock may not be called. In all cases, you will notice, there will be a profit if the underlying security must be sold at the striking price.

money on the sale of the stock. If it were an at-the-money, you would have broken even. Since this is an out-of-the-money transaction, however, you get a nice little capital gain on the turnover. (See Table 2-13)

Example #2. You buy 1,000 shares of Warner Communications at $35, a price $5 below the striking price for August calls. You write 10 of the calls for total premiums of $1,000. During the length of the contract the stock drifts between $30 and $40 per share, finally settling at $30 per share at the expiration date of the call.

Your stock plummeted so you did not make out very well in the above example. In fact, you lost $5 per share on paper. However, you did earn $1,000 in premiums, which offset some of the loss. If your long-term objectives were to hold on to the Warner stock, your strategy paid off. Stocks like Warner will fluctuate up and down, so selling calls against them in the early periods of your ownership will produce short-term income while you are waiting for possible long-term capital gains.

Example #3. You own 1,000 shares of Karen Rigg Cosmetics currently selling at the original purchase price of $35 per share. You write 10 out-of-the-money calls on the stock for total premiums of $1,000. The striking price is $40 per share. When the call expires, the stock is sitting at $39 per share.

You have made out well again. You received $1,000 in premiums and have a $4 paper profit in the stock. You can make that potential profit actual by selling the stock, or you can write another out-of-the-money call to increase your income. It's your choice. How do you want to play it?

Example #4. You buy 1,000 shares of AT&T at $35 per share. You write 10 out-of-the-money calls against the stock for total premiums of $2,000. The striking price is $40 per share. The stock fluctuates between $30 and $40 per share, but never moves into the strike zone. Meanwhile, the calls fluctuate between $1 and $2. Each time the calls depreciate to $1, you buy them back. When they advance to $2, you sell them again. You do this five times during the term of a four-month contract. Your total premiums for the period are $5,000.

In this example, if your stock was ever called, you would still realize a profit because the striking price is $5 above the per share price you paid. In such case, you would have made $5,000 in capital gains as well as the $5,000 in premiums.

Example #5. You buy 1,000 shares of Harcourt Brace at $10 per share. You sell 10 calls against the stock for $500. The striking price at $12.50. The stock and calls advance in price. You decide to buy back your calls when they are $2 above what you paid for them (for a total loss of $2,000). The stock does not continue its advance, however, and its price falls back to $10.

Once again, you changed horses in midstream. The damage is less now than what you previously experienced in other examples because the striking price kept the stock from being called. Even if the stock were called, you would have realized a $2.50 per share profit. As it stands, your only loss (though it is a hefty one) is on the calls. You sold them for 50 cents, then later purchased them back at $2.50.

Table 2-13 reviews these transactions for out-of-the-money calls.

Table 2-13. Transaction Review #3 (Out-of-the-Money Writes).

Example	Security	Purchase Price	Sale Price	Gain	Loss
1	10 calls, D.J.		$ 1,000	$ 1,000	
	1000 sh., D.J.	$40,000	45,000	5,000	
2	10 calls, W.C.			1,000	
	(Paper loss on stock)				
3	10 calls, K.R.C.		1,000	1,000	
	(Paper gain on stock)				
4	10 calls, AT&T	1,000	2,000	1,000	
	10 calls, AT&T	1,000	2,000	1,000	
	10 calls, AT&T	1,000	2,000	1,000	
	10 calls, AT&T	1,000	2,000	1,000	
	10 calls, AT&T	1,000	2,000	1,000	
5	10 calls, H.B.J.	2,500	500		$2,000
			Totals	$13,000	$2,000

The summary is a bit misleading because it infers that there will always be substantial profit if you deal with out-of-the-money calls. This is not always true. The amount of profit will depend upon the write advantage (Table 2-12). It will also depend upon your trades in the underlying stock. If you make a great deal of income from writing the calls, then wind up with excessive trading losses in the underlying security, you are getting nowhere fast. Do not assume that you will profit just because you are writing out-of-the-money calls. There are no guarantees in the stock and option markets other than the premium for writing options.

In Example #5, there was indeed a loss of money, but this was because you attempted to switch positions and changed from being a writer of calls to a bull in the underlying security.

The total premiums gained from writing the calls is indeed impressive: $8,000. (Remember that $5,000 of the $13,000 gain came from selling 1,000 shares of stock in Example #1.) Depending upon the amount of time it would have actually taken to acquire that income, your tax situation, and whether or not there were offsetting paper or cash losses, you can make out fairly well writing out-of-the-money calls.

3

Shorts, Puts, and Other Strategies

"THERE IS SOMETHING THAT HAS ME A BIT CONFUSED," SOMEONE ONCE SAID when the writing of covered calls was explained. "I understand that I own the underlying stock, so it makes sense to me if you ask me to sell the stock. I do not own the call, however, so how can I sell it?"

This very same thing may be troubling you. Remember, however, that the stock and option markets are simply a game. A serious game, because your money is at stake, but a game nonetheless. The rules of the game allow you to sell something before you own it. When you do this, you are short selling. Selling short is the selling of a stock or option you do not own with the hope you can buy it back later at a lower price. Table 3-1 explains some of the confusing terms associated with option trading.

SHORT SALES

The short seller expects the price of the option or security to fall. He is actually planning and hoping for that stock or call option to take a dive. His profit will be the difference between the selling price and the purchase price, as it would be in any normal stock transaction. The only difference is that in the case of short selling, the sequence is reversed.

One of the nice things about the stock and option markets is that you do not have to wait for the market to take off. You can try to make a profit by writing calls if you expect the stock price to stand still, or you can sell short the underlying security if you feel the market is going to fall. If you expect the market to go

_____Table 3-1. Confusing Terms._____

Term	Explanation
Bull	A bull is someone who is hoping or expecting the stock market or individual stocks to go up. That is, someone may be bullish about the market in general or bullish about specific issues. The bull is usually long in stock or calls or short in puts.
Bear	A bear is someone who is hoping or expecting the stock market or individual stocks to go down. That is, someone may be bearish about the market in general or bearish about specific issues. The bear is usually short in stock or calls and long in puts.
Selling short	Selling a stock or option before you own it, through arrangement with a broker. An investor shorts when he expects the target stock or option will decrease in value, allowing him or her to buy it back at the lower price. Profit or loss is determined as usual: by the difference between the purchase and sale prices, even though the sequence is changed.
Buying Long	The standard transaction: buying the stock or option with the hope of selling it later at a higher price.
Put	An option which gives the buyer the right to sell the underlying security at a fixed price during some time period.
Call	An option which gives the buyer the right to purchase the underlying security at a fixed price during some time period.

up, there are many things you can do from buying stock or calls to selling short other types of options.

Example #1. You inform your broker that you want to sell short 100 shares of IBM at $150 per share. He borrows the stock from another account so that you can sell it. Your account is credited with $15,000. Later, IBM falls in price to $120. You call your broker and tell him you want to cover your short position. He buys the shares back for you. Your profit before commissions: $30 per share ($30 × 100 shares).

This example involved a buy and a sell transaction the same as if you were buying then selling stock (buying long). Only here the selling was done first. You sold shares at $150 then bought them back for $120—a profit of $30 per share.

Short selling gives the investor a way of profiting from the market even if it goes down. Some investors do nothing but sell short. They look for securities that will go down in price just as others search for stocks that will go up in price.

Selling short has its pitfalls, however. A stock selling at $20 can only fall to zero, but there is no limit to how high it can increase. Thus, the amount of money that can be lost from selling short far exceeds that which can be lost by buying long.

Example #2. You sell short 100 shares of IBM at $100 per share. The stock climbs to $150 per share, at which price you sell it. Your loss before commissions: $50 per share.

This time the strategy did not work. You wound up with a 50% loss. You sold the stock for $10,000, then bought it back for $15,000. You lost $5,000. In some cases, a 50% loss means the short seller was lucky. Why? Because if he is not careful, he can lose a lot more.

In the above examples, you sold short a very wealthy company that was not likely to be taken over. Suppose you sold short stock in the Gorilla Collection Agency and a takeover started.

Example #3. You sell short 1,000 shares in the Gorilla Collection Agency for $10 per share. Suddenly the stock rises in price to $15 per share. You do not sell, however, because you feel there is no justification for the rise in price. You decide to wait things out and hold your position. Six months later another corporation offers $25 per share for the stock and the market price climbs to $30. You decide you have no choice but to sell before things get worse.

In this example, you lost 200% of your original investment, which is another way of saying you lost twice what you invested. You are out $20 per share or $20,000.

Smart investors will usually only short sell optionable stocks—stocks that are listed on the option exchanges. By doing this they can insure their short positions by buying calls on the stock. If the stock plummets, they make out on the short sale. If the stock climbs, they may make out on the calls they bought. As you may now realize, there are many tricks investors use to help them profit in the marketplace. Few of these tricks, however, are as dependable as the writing of covered calls.

Short selling is such an integral part of the stock market game that astute investors keep close tabs on something called the short-interest ratio, which is basically the composite total of issues on the Big Board (New York Stock Exchange) that have a substantial number of their shares sold short. Brokers are required to report the number of shares of each and every stock in which their customers have short positions. The shorts that make up the ratio may be hours or years old because there is no time limit on short sales like there is for stock options. The short-interest ratio is derived by taking the number of outstanding short sales and dividing it by the average daily volume on the Big Board for the preceding month.

As the theory goes, when the short-interest ratio is relatively low, the stock market is near its top, so it is time to switch from long to short positions. When it is relatively high, it's time to cover your short positions by buying into the stock.

When you write a covered call you are actually selling short. You own the underlying stock, so you are not likely to get hurt if you ever have to cover your position to meet contract obligations. This is because the call will increase only if the underlying security increases, so what you may lose on the call you will probably gain on the stock.

There are, of course, some important procedural differences between selling stock short and writing calls. To begin with, if you want to sell a stock short, you must have a margin account with your broker. A margin account is basically an account that allows you to buy stock on credit. Special forms have to be filled out in order to apply for the privilege of opening a margin account. A minimum deposit of $2,000 is required, at the time of this writing, to use the account once it has been opened. The initial amount required to activate a margin account is set by the Federal Reserve Board. The amount required may change from time to time according to the government's monetary policies.

The broker does have a say, however, in the amount of margin required to maintain equity in an account. So there are really two types of margin—one set by the Federal Reserve Board and the other by the broker or the exchange on which he is trading. Brokers are always much more aware of the dangers of margin purchases than their clients. As basic arithmetic immediately reveals, if you are only putting up half the money for a stock purchase, it will take only a 50% decrease for you to lose all your money. The arithmetic is basically the same in the case of short sales, but now a 50% gain in the stock price will wipe out your investment.

UP AND DOWN

Just being able to play a stock to go up and down is too limiting for the sophisticated investor. He or she wants to be able to play the stock to stand still or to go both up and down at the same time. Writing covered calls is one way to play a stock that is standing still. There is always the income from the call, despite the fact that the stock does not head north or south.

Writing covered calls, specifically out-of-the-money covered calls, is also one way of playing a stock to go up and down. Think about it. When you write a covered call you are assured additional income, even if the value of your stock falls for awhile. Then later, when the call has expired and the stock goes up, you can sell the stock at a profit.

Example #1. You buy 1,000 shares of Pepsi stock at $30 per share and write 10 calls on the stock for an income of $3,000. The stock drops to $25 per share through the expiration date of the call. Then, within five months of the original purchase date, Pepsi stock climbs to $37 per share, at which price you sell it. You make $7,000 on the sale of the stock. Total return from the transactions: $10,000.

That $10,000 represents a $33^{1}/_{3}\%$ return on your investment—not bad for five months, but there are a lot of ifs here. You can see a profit like this if your stock does indeed increase in value after the call expires, if you are able to get a sizable premium from writing the call, and if your stock does not temporarily move into the strike zone and is called.

Some will argue that there are better ways to play a stock to go up and down, but "better" is a tricky word in the investment community. It is always taken for granted that if there is a better way to make a profit, there is also a better way to lose more money.

Two of these better ways involve dealing in puts: (1) buy the stock and buy a put, (2) buy a put and a call. In each of these cases you are putting up money, which you can lose. When writing a covered call you must put up money for the stock purchase, but the writing of the call brings in money that can offset any paper or cash loss if it does not add to your profits.

Let's look at these other two ways in order to give further insight into comparative market strategies and to learn about this thing called a put. First, the put.

PUT OPTIONS

A put option gives the buyer the legal right to sell the underlying security at a fixed price. It is the opposite of a call, which gives the buyer the right to purchase the underlying security. Investors prefer to deal in puts rather than calls when they expect the underlying security to go down in price. When this happens, the premiums for puts increase, allowing the investors to make a profit from the sale of the put.

Just as someone may be either a writer or a buyer of a Call, so can they be the writer or buyer of a Put. The put buyer is a market bear, just like the short seller in the stock market. The only differences are that the put buyer does not sell first then buy. He has to put up money on his first transaction, he has limited risk, and he is not dealing directly in the underlying security. He may change his position at anytime by selling the put and dealing only in the underlying security.

Most importantly, the put buyer does not have the tremendous risk in the underlying security that the short seller does. This is because the amount of money the put buyer can lose is limited to the premium he paid for the put plus brokerage commissions. The short seller, however, runs the risk of unlimited loses.

There are many other pluses to buying puts rather than selling stock short. These include the generally lower transaction costs for dealing in options (particularly with discount brokers), the minimal amount of money needed to get the same dollar return because of the high leverage in dealing in any stock option, whether put or call, and the freedom from liability if dividends are declared on the underlying security.

In addition to buying a put or selling short a stock, an investor may also sell short a put, just as he may sell short a call. The investor who sells short a put is actually bullish on the underlying security. This is because the premium for a put generally increases as the underlying stock price decreases. If you sell short a put with the expectation of buying it back at a lower price, you are assuming that the value of the underlying security will increase. See Table 3-2 for the relationship between stock and put/call movements.

_____Table 3-2. Stock and Put/Call Relationships._____

Puts and calls will generally move in opposite directions if the underlying security makes any noticeable movement one way or another. This may be illustrated by the following symbolization (in which the arrows represent price movement).

$$STOCK\uparrow \quad then\ CALL \uparrow$$
$$and\ \ PUT \downarrow$$

$$STOCK\downarrow \quad then\ PUT \uparrow$$
$$and\ CALL \downarrow$$

If the stock moves in a very narrow range, just the approach of the next expiration date will probably put downside pressure on both the puts and the calls.

Example #1. You sell short 15 June Pfizer puts at $2. The stock goes up and the puts fall in price to $1. You buy back the puts in a closing transaction. Your profit is $1,500 (15 puts × $100).

Shorting a put, then, is another way of profiting from a rise in the price of the underlying security. Buying a call is another, safer way of doing the same thing. The put premiums, however, may make them worth the gamble. Also, when you sell short a put you do not pay out money as you must when you buy a call. Instead you receive money on the first transaction, or at least your account with the broker is credited for the amount of the premium less commissions.

Example #2. You sell short 15 June Pfizer puts at $2. The stock falls $10 per share and the puts increase in value by that amount. You buy the puts back at $12 to cut your losses. Your loss on the investment is $15,000 (15 puts × $1,000).

Example #2 shows you the dangers of shorting puts. The losses can mount up. You can easily lose 5, 10, or 15 times your original investment. Remember that the advantages of writing uncovered puts are greatly reduced when you consider the losses you may realize.

Whether a put is in-, at-, or out-of-the-money depends on which is higher—the exercise price or the current quote. An in-the-money put is one that has an exercise price above the current price of the underlying stock. An out-of-the-money put is one that has an exercise price below the current price of the underlying stock. An at-the-money put is one that has an exercise price equal to the current quote. In all cases, of course, adjustments must be made for brokerage commissions (see Table 3-3).

Table 3-3. Put Money Positions.

Stock	Current Quote	Exercise Price	Money Position
Amdahl	47	45	Out-of-the-money
CBS	160	155	Out-of-the-money
Ford	50	50	At-the-money
General Electric	45	45	At-the-money
Hitachi	109¼	115	In-the-money
Lehman	15¼	20	In-the-money

If the exercise prices were for calls instead of puts, then Amdahl and CBS would be in-the-money and Hitachi and Lehman would be out-of-the-money.

UP AND DOWN AGAIN

Understanding puts allows you to understand two of those "better" strategies that were mentioned earlier: buying stock and selling a put, and buying a put and a call. Each of these strategies allow you to play the market to go up and down—not up or down, but up and down.

Example #1. You are expecting that Digital Equipment stock will increase in value. However, the stock has been swinging wildly lately and you are not sure you can catch it near its bottom. So you purchase 100 shares of the stock at $90 and a July put at $5. The stock falls $20 per share and the put increases in value to $20 per share. You sell the put for a profit of $1,500, which offsets your paper loss of $1,000 on the stock and puts you $500 ahead. Then you find an October put for $5 and purchase it (total cost: $500). This time the stock increases to $100 per share, so you take your profits of $10 per share on the stock and let the put expire. As it turns out, the stock continues to rise and the put decreases to a nominal amount.

A close look at the transactions in this example indicates that you made $1,000 on the sale of the stock plus $1,500 in premiums from the first put, and that you lost $500 on the second put. Your total gain was $2,000. If you hadn't purchased the second put, you would have another $500, but how could you know that Digital stock was not going to go down even further in price? That is why you insured yourself with another put.

Example #2. Your friend, Bob Cotter, was playing Digital stock both ways at the same time you were. His strategy was a little different. He purchased both a put and a call, each for $5. Total cost to him was $1,000 before commissions. When Digital went down to $20 per share, he sold his put for $20 and realized a profit of $1,500 just like you did. Later, when Digital went up to $100 and the call increased in value to $15, he sold the call for a gain of $1,000.

Bob made a profit of $2,500 by investing in both a call and a put. He bought the call so he could profit if the stock went up and the put so he could profit if the stock went down. He got back $2^{1}/_{2}$ times what he had invested.

You, on the other hand, had to invest $9,000 in the stock plus $1,000 in puts to secure your profit. The dollar return was the same, but not the rate of return. Bob indirectly played the same stock with only 10% of what you had to put up, and made a greater percentage on his money.

In these examples, things went right. In the real world they rarely go right. Any number of things could have happened to keep you and Bob from making a profit. The stock could have stayed in a narrow trading range and neither the put nor the call would have advanced significantly for Bob to profit. Both options could have expired worthless as he waited too patiently for the stock to move one way or another. You could also have lost some or all of the money you invested in the put, and taken paper or cash losses on the stock.

On the other hand, if you had decided to write a covered call, you would have had at least some premium income. Of course, in comparison to what could have been realized by either of the two strategies mentioned above, playing the covered call does not seem exciting, but at least it is safer.

IN HARM'S WAY

Covered calls are probably the safest way to engage in the strategy of short selling. Covered calls are safe short sales because if the underlying security skyrockets you can sell the underlying stock to cover your position. For maximum safety, write out-of-the-monies and be sure of the underlying stock's ability to stay in a narrow tracking range.

Many investors are turned off by covered calls because they feel covered calls are mainly an income play. They would rather speculate in the underlying security or speculate in uncovered puts or calls and make big money. Despite the fact that covered calls are indeed an income play, the income can be somewhat substantial when you add a little speculative fervor to the game. The income from covered calls can far exceed what others may average from speculating in stocks or uncovered options over the course of a year.

Playing it safe is always a good strategy. If you can stay out of harm's way, do it. To illustrate, let's take a look at what can happen to someone selling uncovered puts short.

During the stock market crash of 1987 there was a woman who had given her broker the right to trade her account as he saw fit. She had sufficient equity to qualify to sell uncovered options. Many people who are not interested in the market, but are interested in making money, give their broker such authority. This is called setting up a discretionary account.

Her broker had close to $250,000 invested in the option markets. Most of the investments he was making involved writing puts. The market had reached new highs and there was a segment of the financial community that believed things were about to take off. Some market forecasters were predicting that the Dow Jones Industrial averages, which had reached 2722.42 the previous August, would reach 3500. Some even thought it would climb to 4000. A very few super-hopefuls saw 5000 on the horizon. If all this were to come true, then there would be big profits for all those taking bullish positions such as going long on stock or calls, or selling puts.

To make money in the market, an investor has to be aggressive. Being aggressive means dealing in large quantities. So, the broker sold a great many puts. Then, as you well know, the market took a dive. It seemed it was heading for the center of the earth. Stocks plummeted, calls plummeted, but puts increased as though they were just launched from a rocket pad (see Table 3-4).

Rising put prices were not limited to just a few stocks or a few industries. The market plunge was so drastic that almost every put listed climbed. Even worse was the fact that no one realized that the plunge would be so deep, so they kept putting up money to cover their positions instead of selling and taking their losses. Their money continued to disappear—as did this woman's.

As it turned out, the broker managed to lose every last cent of the woman's money, and then some more. As a matter of fact, when everything was totaled the woman lost her retirement income of $60,000 and incurred a debt to her broker of nearly $250,000.

Can this really happen in the option market when you are selling short on puts? Table 3-4 illustrates just how easily this can happen. Selling calls short also can produce disastrous results if the underlying security surges. In reality, many of the more careful investors who decide to sell short on some stock will also buy calls on it. Then if the stock which is expected to go down in price, increases in value, some or all of the losses will be offset by the corresponding increase in the value of the calls purchased.

Table 3-4. Put and Call Premium Movement in Relation to Stock Price Movement.

Date	Stock Price	Strike Price	January Calls	January Puts
Oct 19	$33^3/8$	30	s	s
		35	$2^3/8$	$2^1/2$
Oct 20	$29^3/4$	30	s	s
		35	$^7/8$	$7^1/8$
Oct 21	30	30	$3^1/8$	r
		35	$1^3/8$	$6^1/2$
Oct 22	33	30	r	$1^7/8$
		35	$2^1/8$	4
Oct 26	$31^3/8$	30	r	$2^3/4$
		35	$1^3/8$	5
Oct 27	$26^3/8$	30	2	$5^1/4$
		35	1	9

r = Not traded
s = No option

In the above examples, the stock and option movements for Marriott Corporation during 1987 are listed, but only for the January 30s and 35s. This was the period following the famous crash of October 19, thus the reason for the wide fluctuations in price. Imagine if at the end of the day on October 19 you thought there would be a turn-around and so you sold short 10 January 35 Puts for $2,500, hoping to buy them back later at a lower price! By October 27, those puts climbed to $9. Writing uncovered options, puts or calls, can be dangerous.

Example #1. You sell short 1,000 shares of Chrysler Corporation at $30 per share. To cover yourself in case there is an extraordinary advance in the issue, you also buy 10 low-priced calls listed at 50 cents. As it turns out, the stock advances to $45 on takeover rumors, setting your paper losses at $15 per share. At the same time, however, the low-priced out-of-the-money calls you purchased have increased substantially in value, to the point that they are now in-the-money and selling at $9.50 each. This means a profit of $9 each ($900 for each call) for a total profit of $9,000. So while you lost $15,000 on the stock, you recovered some of it on the advance in the call premiums.

It is not unusual to find investors using stock and call or stock and put combinations as insurance against unexpected moves. The kind of fiasco that occurred on October 19, 1987 can be damaging to a covered call writer's account, but if he is alert, he can make the best of an otherwise disastrous situation. Studying Table 3-4 reveals not only what can happen to writers of puts, but also how a covered call writer might play the market during the same period, assuming he or she wants to hold on to the underlying security.

Example #2. Assume that on October 19 you owned 1,000 shares of the underlying security Marriott Corp. Fearing further decline or narrow movement of the stock for the short term, you decide to write 10 January 35 calls on it. You choose the 35s because they are out-of-the-money. As a result of the write, you receive $2,375. The next day, the calls fall to $7/8 when the stock heads south. Guessing that a stock with such solid fundamentals as Marriott will bounce back, you close out your position by buying back the calls. Your profit on the options for one day is $1,500 ($2,375 less $875).

On October 21 the stock moves to $31³/₄. You do nothing. The January 30 calls look tempting, but they are in-the-money now. If you write them your stock might be called. Your intention is still to hold on to the stock if you can. On October 22 the stock jumps three points and the January 35s reach $2¹/₈. You debate whether or not the stock will stay above 35 until the January expiration date.

Example #3. You decide to short 10 of the January 35s again. You feel the three-month range for Marriott will be between $30 and $35 per share. Writing the calls brings you another $2,125. On October 27 the stock declines markedly and rests at $26³/₈. The calls, of course, follow the slide and drop to $1. You decide to buy them back and do so, paying total premiums of $1,000. Your profit from writing and buying back the calls is $1,125.

During these days of erratic stock movement, the put writer lost 3.6 times her investment while you brought in $2,625 in premiums. An erratic market can be an ideal place for a covered call writer, as the example shows, if the calls are written or bought at the correct time. In the final analysis, what happens in the trading of the underlying issue must be taken into account before the success of the call writer can be determined. It could be years before the final tally can be made, as you will realize after reading the next chapter.

KEEPING COVERED

It is because of the inherent unpredictability of the marketplace that the more astute investor is interested in ways to cover himself. For instance, a cautious investor is not likely to go long on a stock without buying a put, no matter how sure he is that the stock will go up. The purchase of the put provides him with the downside insurance he needs in case his stock falls.

He is also not likely to sell short on a stock without purchasing a call, no matter how certain he is that the stock price will decline. Selling the stock short sets him up to benefit handsomely should the price of the shares go down, while the purchase of the call allows him a certain protection should the stock increase in value. To effectively cover himself, however, the investor must pay attention to the expiration dates of his options and switch to new ones at or near the expiration date.

COMPLEX STRATEGIES

There are other, more complex strategies that investors will use. For instance, there is a strategy called *spreading* that is designed to take advantage of the price relationship between two or more options. Here the speculator is not gambling about the market value of one specific stock or option, but is gambling about the future relationship between the options.

There are a number of different spread strategies. There are bull spreads, bear spreads, butterfly spreads, and calendar spreads. Once an investor begins fooling around with these complex strategies, however, he is getting further and further away from the safety afforded by playing covered calls. Complex strategies like spreads, straddles, and strangles are not guarantees of success. Speculators probably lose with these techniques more often than they gain.

These strategies are worth mentioning so that you can develop a history of experience in option trading techniques that will help you appreciate the simplicity and safety of out-of-the-money covered call writing, if anything that has to do with stock or option trading can ever qualify as "safe."

The bull spread, as its name would imply, is a strategy for those who have a rather positive outlook on the market or on a specific stock. The speculator buys and sells calls with the same expiration date (though not always) at the same time. The striking prices on each of the calls is different. The call that he buys will have a lower striking price than the call that he sells. Having taken his positions, he now waits for the market to go up.

The strategy is popular because it limits the investor's risk. Once again, he is trying to stay out of harm's way. In stock or option trading, however, everyone must realize that when one limits risk, one also limits potential. So it is with the bull spread. It works as the following example illustrates. Please note that the figures here are selected so that the arithmetic can be easily followed. They do not represent the kind of price spread one would ordinarily expect to see.

Example #1. Suppose the underlying security is selling at $27. The June 25 calls are at $4, the June 30s at $2. The speculator can make the bull spread by purchasing the 25s and selling the 30s. After the purchase and sale, he has a $200 ($2 × 100) debit in his account. Therefore, his break-even point on the spread is $27, because the $2 debit must be added to the lower strike price. If the stock reaches or passes the $30 strike, he'll be able to maximize his profits. If the stock moves below $25, he'll be taking a maximum loss.

The bear spread is executed in the opposite way of the bull spread. The bear spread is a strategy for the speculator who anticipates that the value of the underlying stock will decrease. He sells the higher-priced call and buys the lower-priced call. The first will have the lower striking price.

Example #2. Suppose he sells the June 25s for $4 and buys the June 30s for $2. His account is credited for $200. Now, he sits back, anticipating that both options will expire worthlessly. If they do, he's up $200. Best of all, he never really had to put up any money, did he?

In the calendar spread, the speculator buys and sells calls with different expiration dates, hoping that when he makes his closing transactions the credits to his account will exceed any debits. The buy and sell transactions are simultaneous.

In the butterfly spread, the speculator is combining both a bull and a bear spread. This is a very complex strategy that involves the buying and selling of three separate calls. The speculator buys two calls with two different striking prices, and sells two calls with a striking price between those of the first two. He has taken these positions because he is trying to make some money in a flat market. The money he makes will be dependent upon what happens to the options at the middle striking price.

In each of the above strategies, the speculator bought and sold the same kind of option. In something called a *straddle*, he deals in both a call and a put, but this time he is selling them. The strategy works only if each option has the same expiration date and the same striking price. The straddler wants to squeeze as many dollars as he can from an underlying security that probably won't move much one way or another. He receives premiums from both the put and the call. He's not putting up money, but getting it instead. He'll pay dearly later, however, if the underlying security takes off. In effect, he is selling short a put and a call at the same time—a rather risky enterprise.

There are indeed many strategies for squeezing profits out of the stock and option markets. High-powered investors with a good head for math like playing the more complex games. Most of these games are not for the casual investor who cannot possibly stay tuned to the market every minute of every day. The casual investor, like you, can get in on the better plays by writing covered calls.

PROFILES

A lot of people own stock. They buy stock for dividends or try to buy low with the hope of later selling high. That is the extent of their knowledge of what can be done in the marketplace. Most of these individuals are not very familiar with even the simplest market strategies.

Actually, the number of people who own stock is startling. Over 50 million people are shareholders in publicly-traded corporations. Just about as many women as men are stock owners. Most stock is held by individuals in the 35-44 age bracket with 21-34 years old second. Most stockholders have four or more years of college and incomes between $30,000 and $60,000. A vast number of shareholders in corporate America, perhaps 4 million, have incomes less than $15,000 per year.

Many stockholders are retired and trying to live off the stocks in which they have invested all or part of their savings. They depend mostly on the dividend income from their investments. They ride their stocks high and low and rarely ever sell them. They are interested in the income from common or preferred dividends and are willing to just let the stock they own go any way the market pulls it, as long as the dividends continue.

Most stockholders who depend on dividend income invest in very solid companies with histories of continued and rising dividends. Many of these companies are listed also on the option exchanges, which means these income-interested investors have additional opportunities to bring in extra dollars. They often pass by the opportunity, however, because they are not willing to take the chance to investigate the advantages of dealing in covered calls.

DIVIDENDS

Dividends are never guaranteed. Legally a company is only required to pay a dividend if it has actually declared that dividend. The use of covered calls, when practical, is a simple strategy that allows a measure of insurance against skipped dividends and the usual subsequent depreciation in the market price of the stock after a dividend is skipped. The fact that dividends are not guaranteed is as much a surprise to the average stockholder as the fact that they can increase the income from their portfolios by writing covered calls.

Dividends are the portion of a corporation's net earnings that are distributed to holders of stock in that corporation. Dividend payments, from the accountant's point of view, are simply a return of a stockholder's money to him. Each penny of a dividend actually reduces the value of the share of stock on which it was earned. So, in effect, when a stockholder receives his dividend, he suffers a resulting depreciation in each share of stock that he owns.

Some companies have no dividend policy. Their board of directors prefers to reinvest all earnings and continue to lift the net worth of their company's stock. Shareholders in these corporations cannot expect any periodic income, so income-oriented investors usually shy away. Yet, these are often solid companies listed on the major exchanges and the option exchanges. Because these corporations are on the option exchanges, the smart income-oriented investor can write covered calls to replace the missing dividends. The annual rate of return from the covered calls will probably far exceed what dividend-paying companies offer.

There are a number of factors that boards of directors must weigh before they decide whether or not to pay dividends. Some are legal considerations; others have to do with financial and managerial decisions.

The legal and financial concerns can be tied together in one untidy package. A company running in the red cannot distribute dividends without first making important amendments to its corporate charter. This means adjusting the value put on its capital. If it does not do this, it is misleading both its shareholders and any individual or institution that has lent it money.

People and institutions lend money to a corporation based on accounting records that clearly illustrate its capital position. Therefore, any corporation will run into legal problems if it arbitrarily makes adjustments to its recorded capital just to pay dividends to its shareholders. The shareholders themselves will be cheated when this happens because the payout they receive reduces the market value of their holdings.

Other financial concerns that may inhibit a dividend policy have to do with current tax laws, the Internal Revenue Service's treatment of dividends as ordinary income (which actually means double taxation for shareholders), and the board of directors' evaluation of how much of the company's earnings will be needed for investment capital.

Managerial concerns necessarily include all of the above plus other business concerns, such as the need for maintaining the market price of the stock so that new issues can be brought to market successfully, and the need to use earnings for corporate expansion, product development, or even takeovers.

Covered call writers, however, generally are unconcerned about dividend policies, except that the dividends represent a few extra dollars above and beyond what their call writing squeezes out of the underlying security.

Increasing Income

NO ONE WILL EVER GET RICH WRITING COVERED CALLS, BUT THEY WILL CER-
tainly increase the income from their portfolios and, in the long run, will probably
do much better than investors who prefer to simply trade the underlying security, either by buying long or selling short.

When you deal in the stock market, the first thing you must remember is
that you are a businessman. You own an investment business. True, it is a single
proprietorship, but it is, nonetheless, an activity that you manage solely for the
purposes of producing additional income and capital appreciation.

The trading activities of three separate individuals are detailed in the examples that follow. In the first case, an investor buys three stocks long with the
intention of enjoying the dividend income while he waits for the stock to appreciate. He has little concern or pressure to ever sell. In the second case, an investor buys the same three stocks, but she is just as concerned with short-term
capital gains as with income. In the third case, the investor is you, but you are
going to play a different game than they do. You are going to squeeze every possible dollar you can out of your investment. You are interested in income from
covered calls as well as from dividends and capital gains.

Before you study the following sets of transactions, bear in mind that the
stocks used in the examples are simply arbitrary selections and are by no means
singled out because they are the best with which to trade shares or options. Also
bear in mind that there are numerous combinations of events that can alter your
profit and loss (P&L) or income statement. Stocks may move up or down by many
points and the time periods for these movements can range from seconds to
to decades. Therefore, the examples that follow cannot possibly cover every sit-

uation that may be encountered by an investor, but have been selected only for the purpose of developing a better understanding of covered calls.

When you attended grammar school, your math teacher did not teach you how to multiply every number that exists. The task is impossible. He or she did teach you to multiply many numbers up to 12 and possibly to memorize the multiplication table up to 10 or 12. Once you were well exercised in the basic skills necessary for this type of arithmetical operation, you were able to understand how to multiply any whole number in existence. Well, the following examples are presented with the same educational and instructional goals, though you must understand that arithmetic is a subdivision of the science of mathematics. When you deal with stock and option investing you are in the arts rather than the sciences. So, there are no guarantees.

BACKGROUND FOR EXAMPLE STUDIES

In the examples that follow, each investor buys the same three securities at the same time and at the same price. What we (you and I) will do is track the total return on their investment for a one-year period. In the beginning, each receives capital gains. You will note that in this case covered calls are not necessarily the best way to go, although they are always profitable. Each investor will also have capital losses on the stock trades. Here you will note the advantage of having covered calls to cushion your losses.

The underlying securities are AT&T, Warner Communications, and Dow Jones. These three stocks were selected mainly because they have been rather sound investments in the past, have listed options, and have price movements that are markedly different. The different price movements will help you develop a greater history of experience about the market and gauge the kinds of stocks that might be more beneficial to a covered call writer.

AT&T stock generally represents a long-term investment. There are usually no wide changes in its price from month to month. Investors generally do not expect to buy and sell the shares frequently. Speculators who like to go in and out of a stock, sometimes on a daily basis in order to turn a profit, have much better prospects.

Warner Communications has been less predictable. It is a well-managed company with a good track record and its stock sometimes moves in spurts. (Warner Communications since this writing has merged with Time, Inc.)

Dow Jones, among other things, is the New York-based publisher of the *Wall Street Journal*, and owner of domestic and overseas wire services. Many people often confuse the stock of Dow Jones with the Dow Jones averages. The averages are just a guide to help investors determine general market direction. If the Dow Jones averages go up, it does not mean that the stock of Dow Jones has gone up. Remember that in the examples that follow, reference to Dow Jones is reference to the common stock of the company and not to the averages.

The reasons Dow Jones was selected as one of the underlying securities for the following stock and option transactions is that employees of certain rank in the company are restricted in terms of the frequency with which they are allowed to trade their stock in the company. This is true of some other companies also, which makes this an even more ideal example. As it has turned out, the company has been a rather consecutive winner. Over the long term, these employees have made out well. Additionally, many other employees not bound by the same trading rules do not trade their stock because they realize the long-term possibilities of holding on to their shares and enjoy the psychic satisfaction of owning part of the company.

This presents a rather unique dilemma. People generally want short-term as well as long-term rewards from their investments. In the case of Dow Jones, the short-term reward comes in dividends, which are declared four times per year. However, the dividend yield on this stock is usually very low, sometimes under 2%.

Employees, therefore, are often tempted to take advantage of the 15 to 20% short-term swings in the stock. Corporate rules or long-term goals, however, restrict them. So, how can they increase their income from the stock without frequent trading? You guessed it: covered calls.

To buy at least 100 shares of the stocks at the arbitrary price selected for the following examples, an investor would need roughly $9,000. "Roughly" means that this is the total cost based on what the shares of these stocks were selling at when this was written rounded to the nearest $5, and excluding broker commissions. The current price of the related calls may also be different. When this book finds its way into your home or office, the price of these same stocks may be at completely different levels. Please understand that you are reading history—edited history at that. Some adjustments in related option prices have also been made to simplify the math and speed you along.

The purchase price for each of the stocks would be as follows. (The dividends are listed in Table 4-1.)

100 shares, AT&T @ $25 per share = $2,500
100 shares, W.C. @ $30 per share = $3,000
100 shares, D.J. @ $35 per share = $3,500
Total = $9,000

Table 4-1. Dividend Payouts.

Stock	Price	Dividend	Div. Percent
AT&T	$25.00	$1.20	4.80%
W.C.	30.00	.56	1.87%
D.J.	35.00	.68	1.94%

COMPARATIVE TRANSACTIONS—Capital Gains

While the following investors each selected the same stocks, they did so for various reasons. The first likes to buy and forget, the other to buy and sell when practical, and the third—you—to substantially increase income.

Tom Cameron. The first investor you will meet is Tom Cameron. Tom is interested in finding ways to increase his capital while securing some income from his investments. He has about $9,000 to invest, so he decides to buy some AT&T stock, mainly for income. He then spreads the rest of his money between two stocks that he feels may turn out to be winners over the long term—Warner Communications and Dow Jones.

A glance at Table 4-1 reveals the annual income he may expect to receive from his investments, if the dividend payout continues on each stock. He will receive $120 from his shares of AT&T, $56 from his shares of Warner, and $68 from his shares of Dow Jones.

This comes to $244 on a $9,000 investment before deducting buy and sell commissions. This is a 2.6% return on Tom's total investment, but he is hoping that price appreciation in the underlying securities will increase his total return to around 30%.

As the year progresses, the stocks move up and down in price. Warner Communications dances between $30 and $40, Dow Jones between $30 and $40, and AT&T between $25 and $30. Tom is not one for going in and out of a stock, so he simply holds on to them and collects the dividends. After one year, he decides to sell all his holdings because he either needs the money or finds some other investment better suited to his short- and long-term goals. The stocks were not at their peak when sold and only one of them had actually moved more than 20% during the time period.

When he sells, each stock is up $5 (see Table 4-2). This means capital gains of $1,500 on top of dividend income of $244 for the period. His total return was a respectable 19.38%, but short of the 30% return he had hoped to receive.

Table 4-2. Tom's Transactions.

Quant.	Security	Purchase Date	Purchase Price	Sell Date	Sell Price	Gain	Dividend
100 sh.	AT&T	1/7	$2,500	1/4	$3,000	$ 500	$120
100 sh.	W.C.	1/7	3,000	1/4	3,500	500	56
100 sh.	D.J.	1/7	3,500	1/4	4,000	500	68
					Totals	$1,500	$244

Percent return on original investment of $9,000: 19.38%.

Janet Lupton. Janet pays close attention to her investments and buys and sells on swings. She chooses to build the same portfolio as Tom Cameron, but her incentives are a bit different. Janet selects all three stocks because they are optionable, and therefore give her a great deal of flexibility. She can cover her positions with puts if she gets scared about short-term prospects and still play for the upswings.

Although AT&T is paying a respectable dividend, Janet feels the real value of the stock is in its price potential. She thinks it has the potential for strong upward movement within the year, and so she buys in at the same time and at the same price as Tom.

She buys both Warner Communications and Dow Jones because she likes to take advantage of price swings when they are extensive enough to make the strategy worthwhile. She is willing to sell at the first unusual jump in price, then buy when the stock settles back. If it doesn't settle back, she'll just buy something else.

Janet's stocks move, of course, as they did for Tom. Janet, however, takes advantage of swings in the Warner Communications and Dow Jones stock, and goes in and out as the situations warrant. She sells Warner Communications at $40, buys it back again at $33, and then sells it once more at $35. She uses the same strategy with Dow Jones, selling first at $38, then buying back at $32, and finally selling at $40. She simply sells the AT&T stock after holding it a year. She gets the same closing price as Tom: $30 per share.

She also received $244 in dividends because she kept the stock for the same length of time as Tom. Her in-and-out trades on two of the issues did not affect dividend receipts. She was only out of the securities for a very short time and always held the stocks on the date of record in order to receive forthcoming dividends.

Janet made $500 in capital gains from her investment in AT&T, $1,200 from her investment in Warner Communications, and $1,100 from her investment in Dow Jones (see Table 4-3). She received a total of $244 in dividends from all three companies, giving her a net return of $3,044 or 33.82% (before commissions).

You. Your incentives for buying these same stocks are quite different. You want income and a relatively safe place to put your capital. You feel the option markets on Warner Communications and Dow Jones offer you plenty of opportunity to achieve both goals. You like AT&T because you feel the stock is near its low for the next couple of years and both the dividend payout, plus the covered calls on the stock, make it even more attractive.

You establish a different strategy for each stock you hold. AT&T is paying a nice dividend so you plan to hold the stock for the long term. When calls are

_____Table 4-3. Janet's Transactions._____

Quant.	Security	Purchase Date	Purchase Price	Sell Date	Sell Price	Gain	Dividend
100	AT&T	1/7	$2,500	1/4	$3,000	$ 500	$120
100	W.C.	1/7	3,000	9/12	4,000	1,000	42
100	W.C.	9/26	3,300	1/4	3,500	200	14
100	D.J.	1/7	3,500	9/26	3,800	300	51
100	D.J.	10/14	3,200	1/4	4,000	800	17
					Totals	$2,800	$244

Percent return on original investment of $9,000: 33.82%.

worth selling against the stock, you do so. You purchase AT&T and immediately sell a covered call. Many investors do this, using the logic that one never buys a stock at its low. Most investors expect some price decline in the first stages of their position. Others see the combination of stock and call purchases as a way to insure minimum income if the stock is called or remains stationary. Speculators, however, would not chance playing this game, as they are in and out for the fast dollar and do not want to be trapped because of their covered call positions. Besides, speculators would probably prefer to buy the calls long, rather than play the stock.

As it turns out, within a month after you purchase the stock it goes to $29. Checking the paper, you notice that the April 30 calls are valued at $1.25, so you sell a covered call and receive $125 before commissions. The stock hits $30 per share, then falls back to $27. As the expiration date approaches, the calls drop a mere 1/8 of a point, so you close out your position by buying the call back at Y8 (12.50). You closed out the position in order to cover yourself in case the stock surged in the final period of the contract. The market had been bullish and you were wary.

Remember that we are dealing in 100-share lots in these examples just to simplify the math. After commissions, it is often impractical to sell low-priced calls except in quantity. Imagine, however, the advantage of dealing in quantities of 500 shares or more. The returns are compounded and the commissions represent a smaller percentage of the money being invested.

You do not expect the AT&T stock to go beyond $30, so you sell a June call. Given the price of the stock and relative interest rates, it is assumed the call commands a premium of $125. The stock moves between $25 and $30, but never goes beyond $30. In June the call contract expires. You have now made another $125. You do the same with the October 30 calls, and make another $125! You just ride the stock and continue to collect dividends, until you decide to sell it after a year for $30 per share like Mr. Cameron and Ms. Lupton.

With Warner Communications, which is a little more volatile than AT&T, you never let the covered calls you sell expire. Instead you buy them back for safety's sake.

You buy Warner on January 7 at $30. When the stock moves to $37, you sell a May 40 call for $100. You think that the stock has made a nice upward swing in price and may retreat. Selling the $40 call brings in $100 in income for you. If you do have to sell the stock to meet your obligation to the option contract, you need only sell it at $40. If called, you are assured a $10 per share profit on the stock, plus the $100 in call income. As it turns out, the stock never goes beyond $40 and you buy back the call a couple of weeks before the expiration date for $25. That's a $75 profit. We'll assume, for purposes of simplifying these examples, that you do this same thing four times during the course of the year and then finally sell the stock at $35 per share. When all the transactions in Warner are totaled you realize a $300 profit from the covered calls and $500 from the sale of the stock.

You play the same game with Dow Jones that you did with Warner Communications. Again, to simplify the example, we will assume that you sell and buy the covered calls four times during the year and make the same amount of profit each time ($100). When you sell the stock, your income statement will show a $500 gain from selling the stock and a $500 gain from playing the covered calls. (Table 4-4 summarizes your transactions.)

In Table 4-5, you will find a comparative summary for the trading transactions of Mr. Cameron, Ms. Lupton, and yourself. Note how the three strategies resulted in a different return for each of you. Also bear in mind, however, in these examples we've all been playing in a bull market. In a bear market the strategies would not result in such profitable undertakings.

You will also note that in these contrived examples, selling the covered calls was not necessarily the most beneficial way of participating in a bull market. It rarely is. You did much better than Tom who just sat on his investments, but not quite as well as Janet who was willing to go in and out of her stocks as opportunities presented themselves. In reality, however, her technique is somewhat questionable because her timing and knowledge of the underlying security must be close to uncanny to assure profit. When does she buy? How high will the stock go? How far will it retreat? Will it go back up again? She's gambling money each time on hair-splitting, closely-timed decisions. Selling covered calls, however, does not require putting up additional money. You are only selling. As long as you are dealing with out-of-the-monies, you are relatively safe.

"Do I buy a stock just so I can deal in the calls?" you may ask. The answer to this question is "no, definitely not." You purchase stock because you feel it's a good investment—the dividends are impressive and/or the chances for capital appreciation are tantalizing. Play the covered calls when you are in a long-term

Table 4-4. Your Transactions.

Note: Dates for call transactions have been inserted for consistency, though they were not mentioned in the text in order to keep the written examples as uncluttered with detail as possible.

Quant.	Security	Purchase Date	Purchase Price	Sell Date	Sell Price	Gain	Dividend
100 sh.	AT&T	1/7	$2,500	1/4	$3,000	$ 500	$120
1 Call	AT&T	4/4	12½	2/7*	125	112½	
1 Call	AT&T	N.A.**	N.A.	4/25	125	125	
1 Call	AT&T	N.A.	N.A.	7/25	125	125	
100 sh.	W.C.	1/7	3,000	1/4	3,500	500	56
1 Call	W.C.	3/14	25	2/14	100	75	
1 Call	W.C.	5/14	25	4/14	100	75	
1 Call	W.C.	7/14	25	6/14	100	75	
1 Call	W.C.	11/14	25	9/14	100	75	
100 sh.	D.J.	1/7	3,500	1/4	4,000	500	68
1 Call	D.J.	N.A.	N.A.	2/7	100	100	
1 Call	D.J.	N.A.	N.A.	4/7	100	100	
1 Call	D.J.	N.A.	N.A.	7/7	100	100	
1 Call	D.J.	N.A.	N.A.	10/7	100	100	
					Totals	$2562.50	$244

Percent return on original investment of $9,000: 31%

*The covered calls are sold before they are purchased, thus the sell date is always earlier than the buy date. In the case of the stock, of course, the sell date is in the following year.

**N.A. = Not Applicable. Remember that the contracts expired.

_____Table 4-5. Comparative Summary._____

	Capital Gains	Dividends	Total Return
Tom Cameron	$1,500	$244	$1,744
You	$2,562.50	$244	$2,806.50
Janet Lupton	$2,800	$244	$3,044

investment situation and you want to increase your income. Or, play the calls when you see that a stock and call combination will assure an exceptional return over a short period of time. For instance, if by purchasing a few hundred shares of Warner Communications and then selling an equal number of calls on the stock you can assure an 8% return in three months, then the strategy clearly has its advantages—if, of course, the stock remains stationary or is called. If you can find these same unique combinations four times a year, that's a 32% return on your money before commissions.

In the previous examples, the stocks were held for one year. Your return from dividends and call premiums was almost 15%. You received $1,062.50 in premiums and $244 in dividends for total income of $1306.50. Remember, however, that only AT&T was paying a relatively substantial dividend (4.8%), yet you were able to squeeze out almost 15% in income from the covered calls. At the same time, you did not cancel the potential for future and additional capital gains. You were selling out-of-the-monies, which meant that even if the stock was called it would be called at a profit for you. If the stock wasn't called, you were still in a position to ride it to higher levels or to sell additional calls, depending upon your evaluation of the benefits of either strategy.

COMPARATIVE TRANSACTIONS—Capital Losses

Covered calls are more attractive in a sliding market. If you are really betting on a downturn, however, you might be better off selling short or investing in puts. Assuming that you usually buy long and want some downside protection without putting up additional money, then covered calls are a nice side play. They are an especially nice play when they expire shortly before a rising stock reaches the striking price. It is impossible to know before hand, however, whether or not a stock will reach the striking price.

In the example transactions, we witnessed a $1,500 capital gain for Tom, a $2,800 capital gain for Janet, and a $2,562.50 capital gain for you. Now suppose that each of you were caught in a bear instead of a bull market, and that your stocks decreased $5 per share over a one-year period. Each of you, having 100 shares in each of the three stocks, would show paper losses of $1,500. Janet would not have gone in and out as she did because there would not have been any temporary surge in price to offer the opportunity for profit. Tom, just sitting on his investments, would simply be a victim of his original strategy.

Each of you, however, would enjoy the $244 in dividend income over the period. You would also enjoy income from selling covered calls, although you would sell the calls at a different striking price than you had in the previous examples. For instance, instead of selling AT&T 30s, you would probably be selling 25s over and over again. The calls on both Warner and Dow Jones would be the 30s instead of 40s. The striking price you select will, of course, be determined by the price of your stock (you prefer only out-of-the-monies) and where you estimate the price per share will be at the expiration date of the call contracts.

In your case, the sliding price of the stock would be offset by the premium income from selling the covered calls. As long as you own the stock, which you still do, any dividends declared are yours. Thus, you also enjoy the $244 total annual payment that Tom and Janet have received.

STRIKING PRICES

The striking prices you select will be higher if you are bullish and lower if you are bearish. In Table 4-6, you will see a past listing of calls for Digital Equipment. $109 is the stock price listed on July 12. Expiration dates for the contracts are July 16, August 20, and October 22. Notice that the calls command rather high premiums when compared to the price of calls for lower-priced stocks. You will find, however, that the ratios between premium and stock prices are rarely consistent, with some favorable allowances for more bullish issues, and tighter ratios for more bearish issues.

_____Table 4-6. Digital Equipment (Dig Eq) Call Options._____

Option & N.Y. Close	Strike Price	July	August	October
Dig Eq	95	$14^{1}/_{4}$	s	r
109	100	$9^{3}/_{8}$	$10^{1}/_{2}$	$13^{1}/_{2}$
109	105	$4^{1}/_{2}$	7	$9^{3}/_{4}$
109	110	1	$4^{1}/_{4}$	7
109	115	$^{3}/_{16}$	$2^{1}/_{8}$	5
109	120	$^{1}/_{16}$	$^{1}/_{2}$	2
109	130	$^{1}/_{16}$	$^{1}/_{4}$	$1^{3}/_{8}$

r - Not Traded   s - No Option Available

Assume that you purchased 200 shares of Digital Equipment on July 12, and are considering selling covered calls.

- You can sell two July 95s and receive $2,850 in premiums, but if your stock is called you must sell it for $95 per share. It will surely be called because the price has passed the striking price at which the option owner can exercise his rights. There is indeed a $50 spread in your favor between what you make on the call premiums and the selling price of the stock. This spread is favorable only because commissions are not being taken into account. The commissions for selling the stock would actually be over $100, thereby canceling out any meager profit you would otherwise realize.

- You can sell the July, August, or October 100s, but once again you are selling in-the-monies and the rule we have been following is *only sell out-of-the-monies*. The October 100s might look attractive at first because you are looking at a 12% return before commissions in a three-month period. Notice, however, that the stock is deep into the strike zone, meaning it can depreciate almost nine points and still be called. So you may sell two October 100s and receive a total of $2,700 in premiums, but wind up losing close to $1,800 on the stock, if a declining market leaves it callable·

- You may consider the 105s, but again you are dealing with in-the-monies. The dangers are similar to those you would face if you sold any of the 100s. The stock can be called at anytime. In a declining market, it may mean a loss on the sale of the stock that might greatly reduce the advantage of having gone after the call premiums.

- You can sell the July 110 and play it relatively safe, though, not relatively smart. This is because the premiums are low and the striking price is close at hand. If your stock should be called, you will only gain $1 per share. Add that to the $200 in call premiums and your total return is less than 2%. It's hardly worth the gamble .

  Your philosophy would be entirely different if, say, you had originally purchased Digital at $100 per share. After a nine point advance, any of the 110s might look like a chance to assure additional profit or offer some downside protection. Here your decision must be based on what you feel the stock will do in a one- to three-month period and what your rate of return has been to date. If you see a nine point advance in the stock shortly after purchasing it, then the calls assure an additional and attractive return on your investment, or some downside protection that may be needed after a quick advance. If the nine point return has been a long time coming, the premiums for the 110s may still be worthwhile. If you anticipate a continued or accelerated advance in the price of the stock, however, just hold on to the stock and forget about selling the calls.

- You may sell the August or October 115s and 120s. These make a great deal of sense because in each case, if you are called, you realize multi-point gains on the stock. In the first case, it is 6% and in the second, 10%—on top of which you receive another $200 to $650 from the calls. The October 120s are the most practical investment because there is less chance that Digital will reach the price in the three months before the contract expires. In this case, you might find yourself in the enviable position wherein the calls expire and the stock increases $10 per share in price. You can sell the 200 shares of stock you own for a profit of $2,000 after already receiving $650 in premium income.

It is impossible to cover all the different possibilities that exist in selling calls at different striking prices and expiration dates. Perhaps the scenarios just described will trigger an understanding of some of the considerations that must be weighed before any calls are written on an underlying stock. In any case, you must by now realize that selling only out-of-the-money calls gives you the best protection. Just how far out-of-the-money you may want to go will depend upon the immediate income you need or want, and the chances of the stock reaching the striking price.

LONG-TERM STRATEGY

Some investors may consider writing covered calls a long-term strategy, in which case they choose striking prices and dates that will increase the chances that they will never have to give up the underlying stock. As one call expires, they sell another, or as they make one closing transaction, they take advantage of another contract. To understand the perspective that guides these investors, consider first a businessman who decides to start his own print shop.

He will spend a large amount of money to rent space for his shop and office, and for supplies and equipment. Let's say, for purposes of example, that his start-up costs are $100,000. He hopes that his business will increase in value, but his main objective is to produce as much income as possible.

The type of investor who takes a long-term interest in playing covered calls on the same underlying stock is much like the printer. Instead of investing in equipment and office space, he invests in the stock of a corporation listed on the option exchanges. By constantly watching the stock and call option price movements on a stock that has an established trading range in which the fluctuations are five or more points in either direction, he can probably easily achieve double-digit returns on his investment just by selling the calls. Add that to whatever dividend the stock is paying and he may be able to average a much better annual return than many small-money speculators.

Such a strategy is easier planned than executed, thus the reason for the next chapter, which explains some basics every investor needs to know before he buys and sells stock, as well as whether or not he's going to insure his positions with covered calls. It's a strategy that can make sense over the long term, though it is one that requires constant attention to one's investments.

Just as our printer may one day sell his business, so will our investor sell his stock. Either may show a loss on the sale of the underlying merchandise, in the case of the latter, but hopefully the percent of return after a period of five or more years will more than cover the loss. Of course, either may show a profit on the sale, in which case they have done even better.

"Do the pros play this game also?" you are probably wondering, "or are you just showing alternatives to usual strategies?" If you work closely with a broker who has had experience and success in the option markets, you will quite often find him recommending the purchase of a particular stock and the immediate sale of a covered call. You will not usually find such recommendations in the newsletters that investment counselors often publish because stock and covered call combinations must be executed on the very latest information. Prices change so quickly that a half-point move in the price of a stock as the contract nears termination can greatly effect the value of the related call.

There are investment newsletters or programs that you can subscribe to that offer telephone hotlines and options recommendations. On the weekends you can pick up a copy of *Barron's* and read a column called "The Striking Price," which often interviews financial analysts and others in the investment community who recommend stock and call combinations that offer special opportunities such as those discussed above. For instance, in one column there was a report on the recommendations of a Paine Webber broker who was suggesting the purchase of "500 shares of Marion Labs at 19\frac{1}{4}$ and the sale of five October 20 calls at 1$\frac{1}{2}$ for a 7.8% return to expiration whether the stock is called or remains unchanged." All recommendations, however, must be thoroughly evaluated. In this case, the projected return included an expected dividend of seven cents per share and was net of commissions, as the article responsibly reported. The special caveat, of course, was the clause "whether the stock is called or remains unchanged." If the stock plummeted, the paper losses could wipe out any advantage from having sold the call. Recommendations like these from respected members of the financial community take into account the fundamentals of the underlying security. While they are never guaranteed, they are often worth considering.

If you were to take advantage of the above recommendation, then in October you could consider new calls and play the game over and over again. The option game is considered short-term because of the length of the contracts, but that does not mean a long-term strategy that considers consecutive contracts cannot be put into place.

The bottom line is that the underlying security is important to your success. You've got to know it and the marketplace.

5

The Underlying Stock

YOU WANT TO PICK WINNERS AT ALL TIMES. JUST BECAUSE YOU ARE PLAYING with covered calls does not mean you can enter into a stock carelessly. You want stock that will move up in price, yet stay below the striking price, or at worst, remain in a very narrow trading range. It is better to have your stock called than see hundreds of dollars in call premiums wiped out by thousands of dollars in paper losses that may one day become cash losses. So, how do you find the winners? It is by no means an easy task, particularly for the independent investor.

Picking winners when you are dealing in covered calls means determining how much they will win by as well as whether or not they will win. Fortunate for the covered call writer, however, is the fact that he will receive premium income whichever way his stock goes.

Timing is still the most important factor. When do you write the call? Certainly not when the stock is ready to take off. What striking price do you choose? Certainly not one that the stock will reach during its next price leap. What expiration date do you choose? Certainly not one that offers the stock the opportunity to reach the striking price, unless of course the guaranteed rate of return if the stock is called or stands still is impressive enough to leave you unconcerned.

STOCK PICKING—Basic Strategies

Because the success of your covered call strategy always depends upon the movement in price of the underlying stock, it is important to understand two fundamentals of investing: what makes stocks move up or down and how you can determine whether they are going to go up or down. The most successful investors are those who, through practice and some special skill developed over years of consistent attention to the stock market, are able to effectively time when it is advantageous to go into an investment and when it is time to pull out.

Unless you are a short seller or put buyer, you always want to make sure that the stock you buy is issued by a company that is financially sound, well managed, entrenched in its market, and has continued profit potential. Once upon a time the advice on Wall Street was ''the right stock at any price.'' Those were the days of blue chip stocks when the nation was new at gambling on stocks and learned the hard way that even the giants can lose or go under completely. Today, the motto is a lot different. Brokers, especially since the late 1960s, have been advising ''any stock at the right price.''

This should be the guiding motto of the covered call writer with one more rule attached. Options on the stock must also be listed on one of the option exchanges.

The problem that every investor faces is determining at what price it is worth gambling on a stock. Gamble is an appropriate word because the stock and option markets are always risky. Profit guarantees are impossible. Guarantees of premium income from covered calls are possible, but this does not mean that your total investment program will be profitable. What you make on the covered call premium you could easily lose on the stock.

''Just what makes a stock go up or down?'' Asking this question sets an investor far apart from many, believe it or not. You would be surprised to learn how many novice investors take for granted that a stock will eventually go up in price simply because it is listed on an exchange and people are buying it. The quickest way to learn about all the misconceptions that people have about stock price movements and the market in general is to join a stock club, often formed by employees of a company as both a learning and investment experience. Most of these clubs can be best entitled, ''The Keystone Cops Invest in the Stock Market.''

There is an economic seesaw that makes stock prices go up and down. On one seat is something called *supply*. On the other seat is *demand*. Supply and demand are the governing forces for all stock price movements. When there is more supply than demand, the stock goes down in price. When the demand goes up, the stock goes up in price. Stock exchanges are nothing more than auction markets. A stock is only worth what someone is willing to pay for it—just like a painting.

Knowing this fundamental truth does not guarantee investment success. You must understand the factors that affect the economic relationship between supply and demand in a free market such as the exchanges offer and the U. S. government allows. (Not all markets operate like the U. S. stock exchanges.

Some are much more regulated.) These factors include national and international economic outlooks as well as such individual stock fundamentals as earnings projections, dividend schedules, takeover prospects, etc.

There are a lot of variables to consider before judging which end of that supply-demand seesaw is going to move up. It is important to realize that whatever the position of the seesaw yesterday it could change today because when people invest in a stock, they invest in tomorrow. They buy based on what they anticipate the price of the stock will be in the near- to long-term future. This is often why current news about a company may be positive, even though its stock is reacting negatively, or vice versa. The good or bad news is already reflected in the price of the stock. What the astute investor must do is evaluate what prospects a company has that will motivate others to go after its stock.

There are two basic approaches to determining the value of a stock: technical and fundamental. There are those who would argue that there is also a third—the psychological approach—in which anything goes. If it has any practical value, the psychological approach is more in the timing of a particular investment rather than the actual selection. The psychological approach is the most chancy and hardest to evaluate without taking into consideration fundamental factors, but once the stock has been singled out the psychological approach can help you decide when to make your move.

The psychological approach is based on the thesis that good things come out of bad and bad things come out of good. Its strategy is called *contrarian,* for it entails going against the news. When the news is bad, buy. When the news is good, sell. The best bargains, according to this approach, are when things are bad. When things are good, they can only get worse. There will be more on the psychological approach later.

The technical approach is hailed by many as the most likely to succeed, but many does not mean majority. Many professional investors and securities analysts would dispute the high recommendations it receives. Even technical analysts themselves will often look at a stock's fundamentals before publishing their recommendations. To the technical analyst, price movement and volume are all important. He or she cares mainly about investor interest and the way a stock is moving.

Price movement and volume by themselves tell little, so the technical analyst is mainly interested in comparisons. He wants to know how the stock is moving in relation to some indice, such as the Dow Jones averages or Standard and Poor's 500 average, as well as whether there is a definite trend one way or another. The analyst wants to know what a stock's volume is in relation to the rest of the stocks in its industry group and other industry groups. Clearly, a stock with an upward trend in price over a predefined period that also has unusually high volume relative to its past and the other stocks in its industry is sending a ''buy me'' message, according to technical analysts. High volume means great demand. Great demand means higher prices. Often the signals are right, but sometimes they are wrong. In some cases, they are a trap. In 1986, Golden Nugget began to show a marked increase in volume and eventually the price moved up. The movement was in anticipation of a takeover by Donald Trump, so the fundamentals for the move weren't there to hold the price at each new plateau. When Trump purchased only the Atlantic City casino and not the entire corporation, investors lost interest and the stock retreated. When the October 19 crash occurred, the stock was hit even harder, although it recovered nicely.

What are the fundamentals that can hold the prices at each new and higher plateau? Well, those in the know have extensive lists of factors that must be analyzed in order to determine whether or not a stock is fundamentally sound. The six most influential factors are discussed below. As an independent investor without sophisticated computer programs to rely on, you should confine yourself to these fundamentals, which are easily researched and evaluated.

1. Assets and liabilities—current
2. Assets and liabilities—projected
3. Projected earnings
4. Historical and projected price-to-earnings (P/E ratio)
5. Management
6. Labor relations

The first two fundamentals are extremely important because, in the final analysis, the strength of any company is measured by its relative debt. One of the ways you can determine the soundness of a company in which you want to invest is to look at its current assets to liabilities ratio. The ratio is obtained by taking the dollar value of a company's current assets and dividing this figure by the total liabilities. If a company has current assets of $30 million and current liabilities of $15 million, the current ratio is 2 to 1. A 2 to 1 current ratio means that a company is quite capable of meeting its short-term obligations because it has $2 for every dollar it owes. Therefore, if it were suddenly required to pay off all its debt, it could do so.

Many analysts would argue that only a 3 to 1 ratio indicates the company is out of harm's way, but this depends upon the nature of the company's business. For example, real estate developers or the hotel industry may have many loans secured by buildings and land that may offset a lower ratio. A company's current assets and liabilities may be extracted from its balance sheet. Generally, as an independent investor you will not have the very latest report data. If you have your account with a full-service broker, however, he can give you the latest information.

In addition to determining whether or not the company you are interested in is relatively sound, you will also want to know if there are any future projects or anticipated business events (in the area of marketing, research, competitive demands, or over-all economic outlook) that may effect this ratio in the future. Keeping up on the financial news and having continued access to your broker's information systems will keep you informed on future prospects, but, of course, no one has a crystal ball. If you know of severe labor problems, product failures, or declining sales volume for the company in which you are interested, then you know that its balance sheet is probably going to change. This makes it very important to keep tuned in to the marketplace.

Earnings, the third factor, hardly needs to be explained. A company has to have continued earning power to make it worthwhile to investors. Balance sheet information is simply a snapshot of where a company is at the moment the report is completed. This is true of all financial statements. They are a snapshot of the company's financial image for a given moment. As the reports are being prepared, events are already underway to change the next series of financial statements. In some industries, it is relatively easy to project short-term results, but in the media industries, for example, it is particularly difficult. What's important to realize in terms of a company's earnings is that no one is interested in what the company was doing yesterday or is doing today. Investors want to know what it will be doing tomorrow. For this reason, projected earnings are especially important.

The problem with earnings forecasts, however, is that they don't necessarily influence future share prices, even if they come true. This is because the marketplace may have already anticipated the forecasts or the achievement and the stock prices are already where they should be for the future.

One of the ratios that analysts use to determine how future earnings will effect the current price of a stock is the price-to-earnings (P/E) ratio, which is calculated by dividing a stock's market price by its earnings. If a stock is earning $2 per share and selling for $10, its P/E ratio is 5. P/E ratios are available from all stock tables listed in financial sections of newspapers and, of course, in the financial dailies and weeklies like *Investor's Daily* or *Barron's*. By taking the P/E ratio listed in the stock columns and then dividing that number into the price of the stock, you can determine the earnings per share, which have no column heading in the tables and are not calculated for you.

The P/E ratios listed in the stock tables are current. It is necessary to determine the effect future earnings will have on the current price of a stock by spending a little time travelling—to the past, present and future—in order to evaluate possible price ranges. Thus, the importance of item four on the list of fundamental factors.

Suppose that a stock called Power Tech traditionally sells between $5 and $7 per share and its P/E ratio has traditionally fluctuated between 5:1 and 7:1, as given in Table 5-1. Now, suppose that a new product and increasing market strength has led analysts to predict that earnings will increase $4 per share in

_____Table 5-1. Reading P/E Ratios._____

Stock: Power Tech

Year	Earnings Per Share	Current Price	P/E Ratio
1984	$2.00	$10.00	5
1985	1.50	7.50	5
1986	1.50	10.50	7
1987	1.00	7.00	7
1988	2.00	10.00	5
1989	1.50	9.00	6
1990	1.00	7.00	7

Here is a stock that has an historical P/E ratio range of 5 – 7. If earnings per share of $4 were to be projected, it would be reasonable to assume the value of each share would eventually rise to $20 to $28. And one might also assume that if the projections were 10 cents per share, the shares would trade under $1. All this is true, of course, *if* investor interest does not vary the relationship between earnings and price.

1993. What price might you expect the stock to reach some time before 1993?

If the stock has traditionally sold between 5 and 7 times earnings, you might assume that the stock might trade in the future between $20 and $28 per share, if investor interest or confidence remains at past levels as indicated in the P/E ratio. There is no guarantee that these P/E ratios will be maintained. They might increase or decrease drastically. The ratio is designed to give you some measure by which to evaluate future stock prices.

P/E ratios are tricky signals. Sometimes their relative values clearly signal whether or not you should get into a stock. At other times, they say nothing at all until they are used with a whole list of other analytical factors. For instance, if a P/E ratio is relatively high, one might assume that future advances in earnings are already reflected in the price of the stock. If the ratio is low, it may reflect the fact that investors believe the stock is in harm's way. It is important to realize that different stocks trade at different ratios. Growth stocks usually trade at higher P/E ratios than, say, utility stocks. It is also important to look at relative P/Es within and across stock groups and to be aware that the P/Es for cyclical and noncyclical stock groups send out different messages. The point is, as in most things related to stock forecasting, P/E ratios can give mixed signals. Do not make any decision based solely upon the P/E ratio.

Management, the fifth fundamental, is an extremely important element to consider when analyzing the future possibilities of a stock. A corporation is a highly complex organization. The men and women at the top do not have to get involved in the nitty gritty of everyday operations, but they do have to set an example, show leadership, and protect the image and markets of their company. They do not have to pull the bow back or aim the arrow, but they do have to select the right archers, give them the best equipment, and tell them the target. They must be politically astute, have a strong knowledge of finance and the marketplace, and know their company. Too often top management falls short in many of these traits. Movement to the top of an organization is sometimes accomplished by political or promotional inspirations and not by sound management decisions.

The companies that keep America on its toes and competitive in world markets realize the importance of grooming people for executive positions in their organizations. It takes a long time to develop the kind of street smarts that it takes to run a large department in a corporation. Once around the block does not develop the history of experience or the instincts it takes to be a success in the corporate arena. As an investor, you can tell the strong management teams by the current and past performance of a company, by who's on top and how long he or she has been and probably will be there, and by who is the next likely candidate to replace them.

Even companies with a history of putting the best at the top can run into unexpected trouble. Texaco was an example of one of the largest and most efficiently run corporations. In 1987, however, it became the largest company ever to file for bankruptcy because a very competitive management team unknowingly stepped inches over the law when attempting to prevent a merger between Getty Oil and Pennzoil. As a result, Texaco was ordered by a Texas court to pay Pennzoil $8.53 billion and to post a $12 billion bond during its appeal. Needless to say, the stock went tumbling until Texaco, through ingenious legal, business, and financial maneuvers found its way back into the heart of Wall Street.

Labor relations is the sixth item on the list. A corporation with union problems should be watched carefully because when a union goes on strike the short term implications on the corporation's stock are almost always negative. If you are playing stock and covered call combinations, you never want to be in a spot whereby the underlying security has dropped so far that you have to continue to write calls for an extended period to get back your investment—or wait an extended period for the stock to climb back up.

STOCK PICKING—Other Financial Assessments

In addition to the P/E ratio, there are other ratios that will give you a greater understanding of the stock you are considering. Probably the two that are the most important, and which you can easily calculate yourself with information immediately accessible from your broker, are the price-to-book value ratio and the return on investment (ROE) ratio.

The book value ratio is determined by dividing the number of outstanding corporate shares into the difference between the corporation's assets and liabilities. There is little need for you to determine the book value yourself because your broker should be able to supply you with this information. Market analysts look at the relationship between stock price and book value to help determine whether or not a stock is worth the risk. For some stocks, a 2-to-1 ratio between the stock price and the book value is sufficient to flag the stock for further research. On the other hand, some analysts will not even consider the shares of certain stocks unless they are selling below book value. Present book value is not nearly as important as projected book value, which may be determined if projected earnings are available. Look to your broker or other financial advisor to help you determine whether or not it is worth getting excited about a stock based on its relationship between current and projected book value. The stock price may already reflect future performance.

The ROE may be determined in two ways, though the second way is preferred. The first is to take net income and divide it by ending shareholder's equity (book value). If a company's net income is $10 million and the shareholder's equity is $100 million, then the return on shareholder's equity (the ROE) is 10%. The second way of determining the ROE is to divide net income by average book value. The ROE serves to broaden your knowledge of the stock's financial position and growth potential (where average book value is part of the formula), but it is rarely seen as an important determinant of possible returns. Generally, the more astute investor is concerned with changes in the P/E because a declining price-to-earnings ratio can smother any gains one would ordinarily expect from high profitability.

TIMING

Looking at the fundamentals is one way of determining whether or not a stock is worth buying. The only problem is that the fundamentals give little hint about when a stock may take off. Looking at the stock listings in any newspaper shows the highs and lows over a given year and, of course, where the stock was at market close the previous day. In some cases, the current price is at an impressive high. However, it may have taken one, two, three, four, or five years for the stock to reach that high. Fundamental analysis says this is the stock, but pros usually depend upon technical analysis to know when to buy. A 50% increase in a stock is an impressive move, but not if it takes five years.

There is an important point that must be stressed here. Those who depend upon technical analysis before taking a position in a stock rarely get in near the bottom nor do they have any guarantees. Climbing prices and high volume for an impressive period must be evident before the technician makes his play.

Technical analysis is a "what and when" tool. Investors use it to determine what stock to buy and when to buy it. Short-term investors and speculators like it for this reason, but technical analysis is no guarantee of profit. Investors depending upon this means of stock selection may also lose often and heavily.

The technical analyst is always charting price and volume movements. When he sees they indicate broad involvement by the investment community, which includes the independent investor like you, he sends out his signals. His strategy usually entails both short-term and long-term charting. Long-term movements indicate a candidate for possible purchase; short-term movements indicate the time to strike. The technician (or chartist, as he or she is often called) uses many complex formulas to help determine what and when to buy. In the end, however, a lot depends upon the analyst's instincts because they are basically historians. What they try to do is base their recommendations on what they have learned about the past performance of a stock. What is actually going to happen to any stock tomorrow and the day after often depends on any number of unexpected variables, from legal suits to new investment trends, new product developments, new competition, economic crashes, etc. The charts may have promised wonders for many stocks on October 18, 1987, but all those promises went unfulfilled with the crash of October 19. However, barring any special calamity that may effect stocks in general or one stock specifically, technical analysts frequently spot continued directions and sometimes new trends.

Although covered call writing is a long-term strategy, and fundamental analysis is probably the most important tool to writers, some discussion of technical analysis is necessary. Few small investors realize what it entails, yet some of the investment newsletters or services they subscribe to may be using it to make their recommendations.

The chartist tries to determine major trends by establishing a *trendline* and using it to track relative highs and lows for a given stock. If their graphs show that the price of a stock is continually reaching new highs, then the trendline signals the investment community that an upward trend is forming. On the other hand, if each successive high is lower than the previous one, and each successive low is lower than the previous one, then a downtrend is in the making.

As mentioned earlier in this chapter, price is not the technician's only consideration. He or she also charts the volume of activity. Volume is the number of shares that are traded on any given day for a particular stock. The chartist plots the volume against the average turnover in shares for selected historical periods, thereby determining what the average volume should be for a given stock.

Volume is rarely consistent. There are frequent surges and pullbacks as institutional investors take their positions. Takeovers and other special news items may also lure the independent investor into other industry groups on a short-term basis. The chartist will calculate the rates of average change in order to detect when high volume, in relation to price movement, is signalling or veri- fying new interest in the underlying security. New interest means new demand, which makes the seesaw begin to move. As demand increases and supply begins to diminish, stock prices start to climb.

This does not mean that the rise in price will be steady. Stocks do not go one way or another in a steady manner. As a stock begins or continues its climb, it bounces up and down just like a pulse reading on an oscilloscope. It may start at $25, go to $26, fall back down to $25.50, then go up again, perhaps to $26.75. As a stock climbs to whatever will be its eventual high, you may see extraordi- nary price dips as investors decide to take their profits at various stages.

A declining stock will also bounce up and down, but with the average bounce going a slight bit lower each time. It may start at $25, go down to $24, up to $24.50, and then back down again. One might even see a bullish upsurge that takes the stock to its original price before the downtrend.

Besides technical analysis, there is another method of timing in-and-out positions on a stock—the psychological approach briefly mentioned earlier. The psychological approach is used by some experts to select stocks. There is no real mathematical or scientific basis for its strategy, as with some of the other approaches to stock selection. This approach relies on the theory that stocks are more worthy of investment if the news about them is bad because they will be at bargain basement prices so big money will accumulate them. On the other hand, the time to sell is when the news is good because everyone is interested in buy- ing. Experience has proven that this approach is somewhat successful when buying and selling stock but, again, there is no scientific or mathematical pad from which the approach launches its strategy. It cannot be launched success- fully without a knowledge of the fundamentals inherent in a particular stock and a current reading of the stock's technical factors. Thus, it is treated here as a tim- ing method rather than a selection method.

You are a contrarian when you use the psychological approach because you are acting contrary to public opinion, published news, or investor interest. You are not foolish, however. Instead you have found a stock with all the fundamen- tals in place and a technical reading that says "buy." You don't buy, however, because the uptrend has started and the stock is closer to its ultimate high than you want it to be. You'd rather have purchased the stock when it was 20 to 30% lower. So you wait on the sidelines like Sherlock Holmes stalking a suspect until a news item moves investor interest away from the stock and into other areas. This news might be something negative about the stock, something negative about the industry group it is in, something negative about the market in gen- eral, or something very good about other stock groups. In any event, the news causes the investment community to drop the stock. As the demand temporarily diminishes, the price of the stock falls, maybe 5, 10, 15, or 20%. When this happens you move in and take your position. You later sell when everyone is once again excited about the stock.

The covered call writer should be aware of this contrarian approach, but not bother to include it as one of his or her strategies. Timing is not as important a concern for the option writer as it would be for the speculator who has an investment plan that necessitates both short- and long-term goals from his or her ever-changing portfolio.

TARGET STOCKS

Target stocks for covered call writers should be those that have very sound fundamentals. A call writer wants companies that sell at prices that represent good P/E ratios, are not heavily in debt, are well managed, and have good earnings projections. The covered call writer wants the underlying stock to be a good investment.

He or she also wants to be sure that a technical analysis of the stock does not indicate a strong new trend one way or the other. If technical analysis indicates there might be a strong decline in the stock, stay away from it no matter how attractive the call premiums. If technical analysis reveals that a strong upward trend is approaching, the writer needs to reconsider his or her covered call strategy. If the stock is indeed going to reach new heights, it is better for the covered call writer to be well invested in the underlying stock, without the handicap of calls written against it.

If you are going to purchase a stock for the privilege of a guaranteed income when you write the call, remember that this guaranteed income is contingent upon the stock being called or remaining in a narrow trading range below the strike price. You neither want to unload the stock nor see it tumble in price (in which case paper losses cancel out gains in taxable income from dividends and premiums from calls), so the best thing you can do is find a financially sound company whose stock is on a slow upward trend that will not bring the share prices into the strike zone before the expiration date of the contract. If you have written out-of-the-money calls and are called, you will make money from the stock and the call premiums. (See Tables 5-2 and 5-3.) At worst, you will be complaining that you could have made more money if you did not write the calls. Not making as much as you would have liked is a lot better than complaining about losing.

THE SMART AND NIMBLE

A lot of small investors get squelched in the market. They get hurt mainly because they are ill-informed, have not done their homework, use a simple buy-

Table 5-2. Sample Returns on Investment from Buying Stock and Writing Covered Calls If the Stock Is Called.

Stock	Purchase Price	Sale Price	Call Prem.	Strike Price	Period	R.O.I.*
A (200 sh.)	$26	$30	$1	$30	3 mos.	119%
B (200 sh.)	$26	$30	$1.50	$30	6 mos.	121%
C (200 sh.)	$30	$32.50	$1.25	$32.50	3 mos.	113%
D (200 sh.)	$50	$55	$2.25	$55	3 mos.	115%

*R.O.I.—Return on Investment: Capital gain on stock sale plus premium income added to original investment (cost of stock). Note that the returns from the stock and call combinations are for only three or six months. Annualize these returns and the investor is getting what would be equal to a 60% to 76% dividend.

Table 5-3. Buying Stock and Writing Covered Calls When Stock Is Not Called Until After a Second Call Is Written at the Same Strike Price for Same Period.

Stock = 200 shares

Stock	Purchase Price	Sale Price	1st Call Premium	2nd Call Premium	Strike Price	Period	R.O.I.*
A	$25	$30	.75	.75	$30	6 mos.	126%
B	$25	$25	$2.50	$2.50	$25	6 mos.	120%
C	$40	$42.50	$2.75	$2.75	$42.50	4 mos.	120%
D	$40	$45	$2.00	$2.00	$45.00	6 mos.	123%

*R.O.I.—Return on Investment: Capital gain on stock sale plus two Call premiums added to original investment (cost of stock). Annualize these figures and the investor is realizing what would be equal to a 40% to 60% dividend.

low-and-sell-high philosophy, and put their money in long-term investments when they themselves have liquidity problems that force them to sell too soon.

Things beyond their control often drive the independent investor out of the market for good. These include the Texaco bankruptcy already discussed, the Union Carbide disaster in Bhopal, India, which sent that stock tumbling and, of course, the 1987 stock crash that pointed out to the financial community the dangers of computer-trading, over-leveraging, and other financial games that make the stock market less an investment environment than a casino.

The truth of the matter is that the well-informed independent investor, willing to pay attention to what he or she is doing, can reap exceptional rewards from the stock market. These rewards may come from playing stock and call combinations, or they may come from buying different stock options, selling short, or taking a chance on take-over candidates.

According to some reports, during the decade from the mid 1970s to about the mid 1980s, the individual investor had a better track record than the Standard and Poor's index and most professional money managers. This may have been from simple luck, however, because during this same period it was the secondary and low-priced issues that were setting records, and these are the types of issues on which independents gamble. As time marched us all into the mid 1980s, these same stocks began to lag behind the Blue Chips. With this retreat, the independents began showing a lackluster performance. Then in 1987, the big crash! Many independent investors panicked and unloaded their positions. They took heavy losses from which they are only now beginning to recover.

There are a lot of contradictory reports about investors and the market. A lot of statistics are often made up for self-serving efforts. They cannot be challenged because in many cases there are no exact records on who made how much and how. Regardless of what may have been the truth in the past, if the independent investor wants to make his mark on the future, he or she must understa...d that the stock market is a very different game now than it was during the 1970s and 1980s. One of the major changes is the intensity with which the game is now played. The stock market now is a place of exceptionally heavy volume and erratic price swings. It is unlikely that it will ever return to the type of market it was in the past.

The answer to the question of how to make money in the market is to take advantage of opportunities wherever and whenever they occur. For the small investor this means being nimble and not too diversified. Diversification can spread the independent investor's funds too thin and thereby eliminate all the advantages of being in the market in the first place.

Take the time to select one or two stocks with strong fundamentals. Instead of waiting years for the value of the stock to increase, consider writing covered calls and playing the market in many ways. This at least, puts you in the position to benefit by even opposite trends.

Table 5-2 clearly indicates the way in which the covered call writer gains from an excessive bull market caused by unexpectedly strong market forces that increase the price of the underlying stock so much that the stock is called. Table 5-3 shows another way in which the same stocks are forced upward, but not into the strike zone. The call is rewritten for the same period at the same striking price.

In the case of declining issues, the call writer continues to buy back the earlier options and write new ones, a strategy more clearly defined and explained in a coming chapter on "Wrestling the Bear."

6

The Overhanging Market

THE UNDERLYING STOCK THAT YOU HAVE SO EARNESTLY RESEARCHED WILL NOT move on its own fundamentals. There is an overhanging market that will pull it one way or another, or leave it hanging. Think of your stock as an oceangoing vessel. No matter how powerful or well-crafted the ship is, a storm can send it off course or move it even faster on its way. Similarly, the stock market controls the tide that will handicap or support your stock. This overhanging market does not move on the basis of scientific principles, as many academics would like us to believe. People drive the stock markets—sometimes on whims, by greed or fear, sometimes with sense, sometimes with nonsense.

The underlying stock in which you are interested is going to be tugged along with the market in most cases, though not in every case. Some stocks have a record for moving parallel with the market in general, some move ahead or just behind the market, others move in almost definable ratios to general market movements or to some market index.

ECONOMIC FORCES

National and international economic trends also impact the stock market. The stocks in which you invest are dependent upon forces that go well beyond the company's balance sheet or the stock's trendline. It is not always easy to find direct ties between major economic developments and stock prices because there are so many variables that affect the economic scene. The impacts do not necessarily come where and when expected and sometimes have effects opposite those anticipated.

Despite contradictions that sometimes occur between short-term economic developments and trends, there are some factors that provide dependable, general guidance about the prospects of the stock market. Even an elementary understanding of these economic forces will help you better anticipate when the market will perform well, remain stagnant, or retreat.

The business cycle is the first subject related to the economics of investing that should be understood by everyone involved with the stock market. The business cycle consists of widespread advances or declines in business. Current economic theory divides the cycle into four periods: expansion, settlement, contraction, and recovery. During an expansion period, business enterprise reaches new heights; during a settlement period, business levels off. Although there may be occasional reaches to previous highs, for the most part the opportunity for the wildcat enthusiasm that brought the economy to its current plateau is missing. Business retreats during a contraction period—hopefully not to previous lows—and then returns to or above its previous high during a recovery period.

Business expansions and contractions are measured by the change in the gross national product (GNP). The GNP is the total of all goods and services produced by a country. Since 1948, statisticians tell us, every major business expansion has left the investment community with higher stock prices.

There is an important fact associated with the GNP that you, as an investor, should realize. While there is indeed a correlation between economic upturns and stock prices, the movements are not time dependable. It has sometimes been the case in the past that when the GNP indicated economic settlement or contraction, stock prices swung low. This means that you can sometimes expect economic news and stock market news to be on seesaws of their own, wherein they are headed in opposite directions. The reason is because the stock market anticipates the news and the prevailing prices at any given time probably discount the future.

The market usually moves ahead of the economy. In the example above, when GNP was settling and the market was low, it was because the economy was ready for a downturn after an expansion period and the investment community, anticipating negative results, had driven down stock prices. When the economy starts to move out of a settlement period and into a contraction period, stock prices will move up on the theory that things will eventually get better. This is the basis for the contrarian approach to stock investing.

In the past, one of the key indicators of the health of the economy in general has been interest rates. Interest rates represent the cost of money. When they are too high, money becomes hard to get and the economy suffers. When interest rates fall, money becomes loose, capital investment is encouraged, and the economy starts into its phase of expansion. Economists tell us that interest rates behave according to the following scheme. When consumers begin to hoard their money and spend as little as possible, the flood of money that would otherwise be available for investment purposes begins to swell.

When the cost of money is too high and people have all the cash they need (not want), no one is very interested in buying money from banks or other lenders. Now is the time when the interest rates begin to fall in reaction to the reduced demand for money at current costs. When the price of money becomes cheap enough, people and businesses will again begin filling out loan applications. As interest in borrowing again develops because of the lower prevailing interest rates, the cost of money will begin to rise, and the whole cycle of supply and demand repeats itself.

Interest rates generally rise and fall far in advance of economic swings and act as signals to stock investors about which way the market will be going. Falling rates are generally a buy signal; rising rates a sell signal. Bullish investors prepare to take their positions when they see the prime rate fall. The bears prepare to take their position when the prime rate is on the rise.

The prime rate is the rate banks charge their most creditworthy customers. It is generally affected by the discount rate charged by federal reserve banks. (The discount rate, it should be noted, has recently changed more as a reaction to higher rates than as a signal of higher rates.) The prime rate in turn influences the call money rate. This is the rate banks charge brokers on stock exchange collateral and is usually less than the prime rate. Table 6-1 lists some comparative money rates.

Table 6-1. Comparative Money Rates.

Discount Rate (that charged depository institutions by the Federal Reserve).... 6.0%

Prime Rate (that charged by banks to customers with excellent credit ratings) .. 9.0%

Federal Fund Rate (that charged on overnight interbank loans, and basis for money market rates) 7.81%

Call Money Rate (that available to brokers) 8.0%

Treasury Bill Rate (that available on discounted short-term government securities) 7.04%

Certificates of Deposit (that available on CDs of $100 thousand or more that are issued by money center banks for 6-month periods) 7.78%

Commercial Paper Rates (that available on high-grade corporate promissary discount notes and dealer placed) 7.92%

Bankers Acceptance Rates (that available on short-term negotiable discount time drafts) 7.92%

As interest rates rise, the P/E ratios for the majority of the listed stocks fall. This is because investors are not willing to pay too high a price for stocks and want to see less of an arithmetical distance between the value of shares and the price at which they are being offered. As interest rates pull back, investors are encouraged to return to the market and are willing to pay more for their stocks, causing P/E ratios to increase again.

The investment community usually reacts with great speed to interest rate changes, more so to declines than to advances in the rates. A dropping prime rate will almost always put an upside push on interest rates and a declining prime rate will always create a downside tug. A move of even part of a percent on treasury yields can put a lid on the market, which shows how pessimistic investors are about their chances of really coming out ahead by staying in the market.

When consumer spending appears to be getting out of hand and interest rates are on the rise, it is not unusual to see dropping prices in both the stock and bond markets. For instance, a 10% rise in the yield on treasury bonds can be expected to put downside pressure on both stock and bond prices.

Rising interest rates immediately put investors on the defensive. They switch out of their margin accounts and buy mostly on cash, if they buy at all. They also sell if they anticipate that the rise is just the beginning of a trend, or they begin covering their positions by writing covered calls or buying puts. Finally, if they continue to invest or maintain their investments, they will stick with less volatile issues such as pharmaceuticals and utilities.

Professional investors like to keep their eyes on unemployment statistics as well as interest rates and the GNP. This is another indicator, however, that is not always dependable. Generally speaking, the lower the rate of unemployment, the healthier the economy. In the past, chartists have found that the highs and lows in stock prices usually occur when the unemployment rate is low. This makes reading the value of this indicator a little tricky.

If you wish to use this indicator, you must remember that the stock market does not move in unison with the general economy. Instead it anticipates events and, in the case of unemployment statistics, usually races to its peaks and valleys well ahead of anticipated turnarounds. Investor psychology sometimes takes an unusual attitude toward unemployment statistics, however. When the fear of inflation is hovering over the marketplace, sometimes high unemployment is a positive sign to investors. They fear that with too many employed inflation will run rampant, interest rates will skyrocket, and the market in stocks will tumble like the walls of Jericho.

The investment community fears inflation because it is a period of rising prices, during which time each dollar buys less. Business managers are confronted with some very special problems during inflationary times. Perhaps to the novice investor, it would seem that business and industry could profit handsomely from the rising prices that inflation promises, for they raise the costs of goods and services accordingly. Rather than realize any gain, however, business and industry find themselves caught in a very unique dilemma. Periods of inflation do not mean just the rising cost of goods, but also the rising cost of wages and salaries. Managers find that increases in the costs of their goods and services only serve to feed price increases for labor and other production costs. Even the government cannot gain by inflationary spirals. The value of the national currency becomes so eroded that its position in the international marketplace is greatly diminished. The government must then deal with a balance of payments deficit and increase exports to meet its commitments.

MARKET INDICATORS

Like the 49ers who found signs to tell them where to dig for gold, stock investors can come up with ingenious indicators to tell them what stock to buy.

A commonly used index is the Dow Jones averages. There are three parts to these averages, one for the industrial group, another for transportation, and a third for utilities. The stocks that make up these averages change on occasion in response to new economic patterns and the companies that may actually reflect them. These averages are important because in the past they have served as fairly consistent, though general, indicators of market direction.

The Dow Jones averages are an outgrowth of a theory presented many years ago by Charles H. Dow, the man who founded the *Wall Street Journal*. Dow's ideas were later perfected by his successor, William P. Handon. As the theory is taught today, the stock market is influenced by three types of price movements. These movements are defined in terms of their time span and are either daily, short-term, or long-term. If all three averages reach new highs at the same time for consecutive periods, a bull market is expected. If all three averages fall to new lows for consecutive periods, then a bear market is in the making.

Other indexes help to double-check the signals being given by the Dow Jones averages. These include Barron's 50-Stock averages, the Wilshire Index, the New York Stock Exchange Index, and Standard and Poor's 500 (see Fig. 6-1).

Open to the statistical pages in any financial daily or the financial section of a large daily newspaper and you will find numerous indicators that serve as a quick reference guide for the investor. Two of these indicators are the new highs and the new lows. Bear in mind that any stocks appearing on these lists are not there because they have hit their bottom or reached their top. They may still have a long way to fall or a long way to rise. This is to say that you cannot expect the new low list to give you stocks that you can buy now because they are as low as they will go and are now ready to climb. Remember a stock can always go lower.

Major Indexes

12-Month High	12-Month Low		Weekly High	Weekly Low	Friday Close	Friday Chg.	Weekly % Chg.	12-Month Chg.	12-Month % Chg.	Change From 12/30	% Chg.
Dow Jones Averages											
2791.41	2144.64	**30 Indus**	2711.39	2687.93	2711.39	(28.16)	(1.03)	542.46	19.80	542.46	25.01
1532.01	959.95	**20 Transp**	1158.78	1136.74	1158.78	(11.92)	(1.02)	193.46	20.04	188.94	19.48
235.98	181.84	**15 Utilities**	234.53	233.40	234.53	(1.45)	(0.61)	48.02	25.75	48.25	25.90
1115.15	816.95	**65 Comp**	1021.26	1010.36	1021.26	(9.88)	(0.96)	196.23	23.78	195.32	23.65
337.63	258.45	**Equity Mkt.**	324.42	319.74	324.42	(2.14)	(0.65)	63.98	24.57	63.68	24.42
New York Stock Exchange											
199.34	154.98	**Comp**	191.95	189.40	191.95	(1.50)	(0.77)	35.89	23.00	35.69	22.84
237.76	187.87	**Indus**	228.98	226.44	228.98	(1.87)	(0.81)	39.91	21.11	39.56	20.88
101.31	73.91	**Utilities**	101.00	99.44	101.00	(0.31)	(0.31)	26.12	34.88	26.31	35.23
212.37	145.49	**Transp**	175.16	171.64	175.16	(2.01)	(1.13)	29.02	19.86	28.56	19.48
173.29	127.35	**Finan**	152.76	148.57	152.76	(1.83)	(1.18)	24.90	19.47	24.57	19.17
Standard & Poor's Indexes											
359.80	275.31	**500 Index**	347.42	342.46	347.42	(2.72)	(0.78)	69.55	25.03	70.20	25.32
410.49	318.66	**Indus**	396.35	391.86	396.35	(3.56)	(0.89)	75.07	23.37	75.09	23.37
331.07	226.42	**Transp**	274.12	267.35	274.12	(2.11)	(0.76)	45.78	20.05	45.95	20.14
154.88	111.15	**Utilities**	155.29	151.79	155.29	0.41	0.26	42.37	37.52	42.65	37.86
35.24	24.30	**Finan**	30.49	29.28	30.49	(0.41)	(1.33)	5.92	24.09	6.00	24.50
NASDAQ											
485.73	376.50	**OTC Comp**	444.57	434.35	444.57	0.73	0.16	67.23	17.82	63.19	16.57
472.42	372.71	**Indus**	437.59	426.81	437.59	3.57	0.82	63.57	17.00	58.64	15.47
561.34	424.10	**Insur**	533.14	524.38	533.14	(20.58)	(3.72)	108.69	25.61	104.00	24.23
491.16	375.38	**Banks**	386.52	375.38	386.52	(0.54)	(0.14)	(47.45)	(10.93)	(48.79)	(11.21)
212.43	163.49	**NMS Comp**	194.52	189.90	194.52	0.40	0.21	30.66	18.71	28.87	17.43
185.12	144.95	**NMS Indus**	171.93	167.55	171.93	1.55	0.91	26.49	18.21	24.51	16.63
Others											
397.03	300.33	**AMEX**	370.84	367.95	370.84	(4.66)	(1.24)	68.62	22.70	64.83	21.19
278.98	229.00	**Value Line-G**	254.23	251.05	254.23	(2.42)	(0.94)	24.36	10.60	21.55	9.26
3523.47	2718.59	**Wilshire 5000**	3361.82	3314.70	3361.82	(24.61)	(0.73)	630.17	23.07	623.40	22.76
189.93	145.78	**Russell 1000**	181.89	179.19	181.89	(1.24)	(0.68)	35.11	23.92	34.90	23.74
180.78	144.67	**Russell 2000**	165.20	162.82	165.20	(1.32)	(0.79)	20.32	14.02	17.84	12.11
203.10	156.56	**Russell 3000**	193.84	190.97	193.84	(1.34)	(0.69)	36.45	23.16	36.03	22.83

G-Geometric Index.

Fig. 6-1. Performance of the major indexes is used to measure stock market performance. All indexes do not show the same rate of change from day to day, as this listing from *Barron's* shows. Here, for instance, the Dow Jones Industrials are showing a 9.3% change, but the NASDAQ Industrials are showing a 17.19% change. (Reprinted from Barron's)

You can use the lists over a period of a few weeks to determine the current and long-term market direction. When the list of new lows continues to grow at a steady pace, it is a sign of trouble. When there is a temporary expansion of the list, then what you are seeing is no more than a bear phase in a bull market and you can hold on to your current stocks unless, of course, their individual fundamentals and trendlines are deteriorating.

The new high list will help you determine whether or not the market is indeed in an upswing. It has to be used in conjunction with the new low list, however. If the number of stocks setting new highs is continually greater than those setting new lows, then there are strong possibilities that a bull market is coming. If the new highs begin to grow considerably, reconsider selling those covered calls. Buy them back if it is not too late. It's time to ride the stock or accumulate in-the-money calls on your favorite issues.

Another indicator that investors pay attention to is the advance/decline indicator. It is such a popular indicator that even during radio or television broadcasts that spend just 30 seconds on stock market news, the indicator may be given along with the Dow Jones industrial average, perhaps the most popularly quoted index.

The advance/decline indicator is a nice double-check on the DJ industrials. Very often, you may read or hear that the Dow Jones industrials are down. Bear in mind that this does not necessarily mean your stock is down. It only means that, overall, the stocks that make up the Dow Jones averages are down in price. Secondly, the Dow Jones industrial averages may be down but the advance/decline indicator may show a greater number of stocks advancing than declining. In this case you can divide the impact of the DJ industrial report. However, if the DJ industrials are down and the advance/decline indicator is down, it is time to take note. It could be that this is just a short-term signal, a long-term warning, or nothing to worry about. It is a signal that things might go bearish, so pay heed. If it turns out that this indicator plus the DJ averages, Standard & Poor's 500, the New York Stock Exchange Index, and all the other indicators are down, get ready to jump ship, sell short, or buy puts. Don't react drastically, however, unless all these indicators are pointing the same way for a couple of weeks. One or two days of coincidence among the indicators on occasion may be expected. On the other hand, if the advance/decline and other indicators continually show bullish signs, especially all at once, forget the covered calls and buy the stock, or speculate in in-the-money calls.

Actually, of all the indicators, the advance/decline is probably the one that carries the most weight with market watchers. This is because it covers a very large sampling of stocks and cannot be tilted by sudden jumps in the price of any one stock or industry group, as can happen with any of the averages or other indicators dealing with dollar amounts.

Many of the indicators that investors devise for the market in general are carbon copies of those that they have devised for singling out individual stocks. For instance, they will track overall trading volume.

There are some indicators that few independent investors know about. These include the Arms Index, the closing tick indicator, and the put-call ratio. These may be found in *Barron's* every weekend.

The Arms Index is used to locate action. Also known as the short-term trading index, it is derived by dividing the average volume of declining issues by the average volume of advancing issues. The index is computed separately for the New York Stock Exchange, the American Stock Exchange, and NASDAQ.

(NASDAQ is the computerized trading arm of the National Association of Securities Dealers, which specializes in the trading of over-the-counter stocks. Not all of the OTC stocks are listed on NASDAQ, only those that want the listing and meet certain marketing and financial requirements.) If the index reading is less than 1 (one), then it is clear that most of the market action is in rising stocks. In Table 6-2 you will find an example of the Arms Index. Note that in this particular example, the individual markets are not showing consistent readings. Investors' trading objectives are apparently very different this particular week, for they are heavy into advancing issues on the New York Stock Exchange, but more interested in basement buying in the other markets.

Table 6-2. Short-Term Trading Index (Arms).

Market	Mon.	Tue.	Wed.	Thur.	Fri.
NYSE	.75	1.41	.40	.72	1.25
AMEX	.75	.90	1.00	.64	.64
NASDAQ	.89	1.15	.53	.75	.86

The closing tick indicator gives the relative strength of selected markets near the close of the day. It takes the number of stocks in which the last change in price was upward and subtracts the number of stocks in which the last change in price was downward. If the closing tick figures are positive, then the market is showing strength at the close. If it is negative, then the market is showing weakness. This is a rather important indicator, despite the fact that few investors seem to know about it. The stock market rises and falls each day. A day is only a contrived break in activity, however, much as the second quarter break is in a football game. Just as a team losing 21-14 may have scored two touchdowns to their opponent's one in the second quarter, thereby signalling new strength, so can the market. It can actually be down for the day and up at the closing tick, signalling the possibility of a bull phase, no matter how short. Table 6-3 shows a typical closing tick indicator.

Table 6-3. Closing Tick Indicator.

Market	Mon.	Tue.	Wed.	Thur.	Fri.
NYSE	− 320	− 216	+ 316	+ 156	+ 361
AMEX	− 24	− 85	+ 34	− 22	+ 81
DJIA	− 6	− 6	+ 18	− 2	+ 18

The Chicago Board Options Exchange (CBOE) put-call ratio looks at put-call activity on the stocks that make up Standard & Poor's 100 Index, and the

CBOE equity ratio. Theory has it that if the ratio is 70 puts to 100 calls written on Standard & Poor's 100 and 65 puts to 100 calls on the CBOE equity ratio, then the signal is bullish. On the other hand, a ratio of 40 puts to 100 calls on either index is bearish. (See Table 6-4).

Table 6-4. CBOE Put-Call Ratio.

	Trades		
	Puts	Calls	Ratio
S & P 100	621,441	665,162	93/100
CBOE Equity	261,963	834,921	31/100

Some investors who have been in the market for decades have developed their own favorite indicators. These indicators might simply be a dozen or so stocks or some combination of selected stock averages and index values. In a few instances, investors have been watching and playing the same 15 or 20 blue chip stocks for so long that they can forecast overall market trends simply by their price or volume movements. A few advisors recommend making up your own indexes, arguing that the popular indicators are wrong too often to be dependable. Somehow, they are often right when you decide to ignore them, and often wrong when you decide to believe them.

You will find that the more professional writers, analysts, and brokers are often very candid about the contradictory and unscientific nature of the stock market, and the dependability of stock and economic indicators. As Jay Palmer, a columnist for *Barron's* wrote in ''The Trader'' (*Barron's*: July 25, 1988, p. 62): ''.... Practitioners, applying the same theory to the same data, somehow or another manage to reach entirely different and opposite conclusions.''

In any event, it is important to realize that the indicators are not meant to help anyone call market movements to the dollar or within any specific time frame. The indicators are general pointers. They are simply guides to help serious investors determine general direction over the short-term and the long-term. Short-term and long-term, by the way, are two terms that mean different things to different people. Once they clearly meant less than six months and over six months, or less than a year and over a year. Now it can mean as little as a day (to the speculator) and up to four or five years (to investment counselors).

Just as no one has a crystal ball that can foretell stock prices, no one has devised an indicator that can be depended upon to tell even where the market will be tomorrow. Some stock players, however, do have an uncanny ability to read mass investment sentiment. Few investors, however, are plugged into the stock market as these rare individuals.

The more experienced market watchers understand that relative volume movements in the overall market cannot be interpreted in the same way that they are for individual stocks. Overall market trendlines tell a different story than individual stock trendlines.

Volume is important in helping to identify major market bottoms. Generally, when the market is bottomed out, volume is at its lowest. It's at its lowest because supply has exceeded demand and prices have been on the downswing and will be until investors become excited again about market opportunities. Investors are always interested in getting in low and selling high.

While the lowest volume is at the market bottom, it does not stand that the highest volume is at the market peak. Although it is not true in every case, generally the most consistent peaks in trading activity will come when the market is about 60% to 70% of its way to peaking. If it is not true in every case, how does one know what period of market advance is indicated by current relative volume? The answer is to be as conservative as possible when interpreting the signals. If there is a relatively marked increase in volume for a two- or three-week period, assume you are at least half-way to the market peak and prepare to bail out when the price advances another 30%. This rule will certainly be challenged by those who like to squeeze out every dollar, but it's a rule for those who want safety first.

The more astute investors are just as interested in overall market fundamentals as they are in volume and price movements. For instance, they will track the average P/E ratios for stocks that make up the major indexes. If they take a look at Standard and Poor's 500 Stock Index and see that the P/E ratio is currently at 14.9 when a year ago it was at 20.6, they understand that stocks are certainly at better bargain prices today.

In addition to the P/E ratios, smart investors will look at other fundamentals such as total earnings and average dividend payouts for the index stocks. If earnings are up, the market is on a very solid base and the downside risks are reduced. If yields are far higher than the previous year and competitive with interest rates, then the market is that much stronger and smart money will begin taking long positions.

DAILY FLUCTUATIONS

The market is not as predictable over the short term as it is over the long term. It is true that forecasts are on target every once in awhile. There is always some investment counselor who can prove he predicted a crash or market bottom, but there are so many forecasts made each and every day that some of them are bound to be on target and someone is going to come out a hero. Besides, if you wait long enough, whatever you predict about the general direction of the market will probably come true. The market swings up and down in anticipation of business cycles or special news. If you claim it's going down, you'll eventually be right. If you claim it is going up, you'll also be right eventually.

Daily fluctuations can frustrate or terrorize not only the individual investor, but also the big-money investors. Trying to predict daily market swings is about the same as trying to predict the fears, frustrations, gambling instincts, and general character strengths and weaknesses of tens of thousands of people. There is no telling what might trigger overselling, which brings the market down, or overbuying, which brings the market up.

There are many economic and market forces, and related statistics, that can drive the market up today and down tomorrow, or leave it drifting helplessly.

You will find some of the news that will keep both big and small money on edge by reading the financial columns in the big city dailies or papers like the *Wall Street Journal* and *Investor's Daily* (see Fig. 6-2). For instance, trade and inflation numbers are always awaited eagerly. The market can get very dull prior to the release of this information. When the trade deficit comes in low, that's usually good news for the value of the American dollar and might put a torch under the investment community. If the inflation figures come in high, however, it can counter the good news about the dollar.

When expiration dates for stock options and index options approach, there is generally a flurry of activity on the market and prices can be sent either direction in reaction. Generally, trading the day after the contracts expire is volatile, as the expiration effect wears off and the market strives to balance itself. The market, as a matter of fact, behaves a little bit like Mother Nature. Mother Nature always tries to make up for excesses—dry spells after too much rain, rain after too many dry spells. The market has this same tendency. Make-up time is highly unpredictable in both the natural world and the unnatural world of finance and banking.

If talk of inflation hits the news, then there will be a lot of shuffling in the marketplace, particularly with the types of stocks that can benefit from a depreciating dollar, if any actually do in the long run. A lot of money moves out of most of the technology stocks and into the stocks of companies that provide the public with necessary staples, or it goes into the bank.

Strong indications that interest rates might climb can often send finicky professionals to their computers and independents to their telephones to bail out, instantly changing market direction and forcing 5 to 10% price drops in the indexes. Then, as the contrarians move in to take advantage of the unexpected drop, the market may start swinging the other way, make up for losses, or actually set new highs.

If you think the market may have stabilized or begun to move in a clearly defined direction, you will be surprised to hear that investors have once again bailed out and/or retreated to the sidelines because of weakness in the bond markets, in anticipation of the latest consumer price report from the government, or because some market leaders, like IBM or GM, have begun to show weakness.

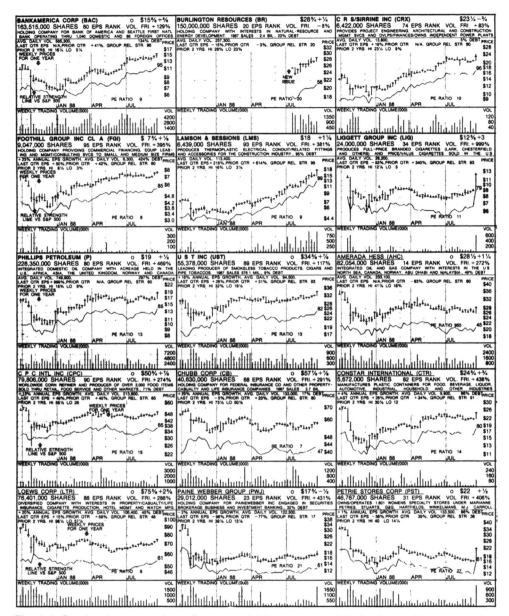

Fig. 6-2. Stock prices sometimes fluctuate widely even on a daily basis, as these examples from *Investor's Daily* clearly illustrate. *Investor's Daily* provides these volume and price statistics for stocks that reach new highs or show impressive volume gains. When stocks that serve as the underlying interests for puts and calls show even modest percentage gains, the owners of the related options can realize impressive returns. (Reprinted by permission of *Investor's Daily, America's Business Newspaper*), © Investor's Daily Inc. 1989.

The market rises, falls, or goes to sleep in anticipation of the same news events each week or month. The experienced investor learns to live with the short-term swings. Anyone who goes into the market and clearly expects that his capital will immediately begin to appreciate, is soon in for disappointment and possibly a room at a local asylum.

The market will bounce. Covered call writers need not worry too much about the bounces as long as they have done their homework and written options against stocks showing strong fundamentals. Stock buyers who are riding only the shares are always in for some frustrating periods. They cannot take advantage of minor pullbacks. The covered call writer can, however, provided he or she is alert enough to know when to let the contracts' expire and when to buy back the calls, and has been smart enough to stick with out-of-the-monies. You would think out-of-the-money is a rather negative connotation, and it is for most people and in most situations. For the covered call writer, however, being out-of-the-money actually means quite the opposite. He or she is squeezing the most out of the current stock while remaining insured against downside risk. Few investors or speculators in the stock market sleep quite as well as the covered call writer.

7

Wrestling the Bear

IN EVERY BULL MARKET THERE ARE BEAR PHASES, AND IN EVERY BEAR MARKET there are bull phases. Few market watchers actually know whether they are in a bear or a bull market until long after the fact. Nevertheless, investors usually hedge their positions so they can change their investment mix with each turn of the market. As a covered call writer, you can do a little hedging yourself. The game of covered call writing, however, is played somewhat differently in sliding markets than it is in rising markets.

Sometimes the market doesn't just slide, every stock drops as though a trap door was thrown open by some sadistic force. This is why some traders prefer to make their money selling short. While the risks are greater in selling short because a stock can rise to a greater extent than it can fall, the short seller feels that picking losers or downside swings is easier than picking winners or upside moves.

CRASHES

There is always the danger of a market crash (see Table 7-1). This has happened on occasion, most recently in October of 1987. In this particular case, however, the entire fall was due more to a series of technical inefficiencies than to any economic debacle. When crashes occur, it is very hard to keep one's head. The major danger is being heavily indebted to your broker through margin buying.

As the stock falls, margin traders are required to put up more and more money to cover equity requirements, and losses can easily triple or quadruple.

Table 7-1. Even the Blue Chips Can Go Down.
(Point Drops in the Dow Jones Industrials
from Friday, October 16, Close to Monday, October 19, Close, 1987)

Stock & Previous Close	Change	Stock & Previous Close	Change
Alcoa (56.00)	−13.50	Kodak (90.125)	−27.25
Allied Signal (39.125)	−11.50	McDonald's (43.625)	− 7.50
American Exp. (31.125)	−21.50	Merck (184.00)	−24.00
AT & T (30.00)	− 6.375	Minn. Mining (70.250)	−14.25
Bethlehem Steel (16.50)	− 5.125	Navistar (6.00)	− 1.125
Boeing (43.625)	− 5.125	Philip Morr. (102.75)	−14.625
Chevron (49.50)	− 8.25	Primerica (44.375)	−10.25
Coca Cola (40.50)	−10.00	Proctor & G. (85.00)	−23.625
Dupont (98.50)	−18.00	Sears (41.50)	−10.50
Exxon (43.75)	−10.25	Texaco (36.50)	− 4.50
General El. (50.75)	− 8.875	Union Carbide (27.375)	− 2.375
General Motors (66.00)	− 6.00	United Tech. (48.625)	− 7.625
Goodyear (59.50)	−17.00	USX (34.00)	−12.50
Inter. Paper (46.375)	−12.50	Westinghouse (60.50)	−20.25
IBM (135.00)	−31.75	Woolworth (42.25)	− 6.00

The margin trader usually bails out in a hurry, thereby putting additional downside pressure on a given stock or the market in general. The second danger is being in the market in the first place unless you happen to be a short seller or a covered call writer. A covered call writer is, in fact, a short seller.

It is clearly advantageous to be reminded of stock market crashes. They happen so infrequently that new generations of stock pickers forget the ever present threat and continue to ride the bull market. Writing in *Barron's* a few months before the October 1987 crash, financial wizard and wit, Allan Abelson, reminded us of this tendency for the young to forget or let history be. ''The geriatric portfolio manager,'' he wrote, ''suffering from incurable caution, will inevitably miss the last 10% move in any stock. By contrast, the healthy 27-year-old MBA can be counted on never to quarrel with the tape or the price of a stock. His rallying cry is 'fully committed,' and that, as it happens, is how many of his customers end up.''

Abelson penned this penetrating observation shortly before the Dow Jones Industrial average peaked just above 2700 in August of 1987. The market had been on an impressive bull run; prices climbed, sometimes regardless of negative news. To top things off, some highly positive Wall Street analysts were predicting a march to 3000 for the Dow Jones Industrials. One very bullish analyst, looking at all the foreign interest in U. S. stocks, and the money on the sidelines waiting to take a position, thought that 5000 would be a possible peak for the DJ Industrials by 1990. A few wise contrarians started betting their money on a downslide. It was an ideal situation for them. The investment community, known as The Street, was bullish by a wide margin, the market had been advancing despite negative economic news, and too many people were making a lot of money.

As it turned out, the farsighted and patient contrarians saw their strategy start to pay off on Friday, October 16. The market suddenly took a dip. On a volume of 338,480,000 shares, which represented record turnover, almost every stock fell. There were some winners, of course, but these were mainly gold stocks and motel stocks. The Dow Jones Industrials dropped 108.35 points, and the Dow Jones transportation stocks and utility stocks also plummeted. According to some estimates, the market drop meant more than a $300 billion loss in the value of publicly held companies in the United States. (Fig. 7-1 charts the Dow Jones Industrial averages for 1987.)

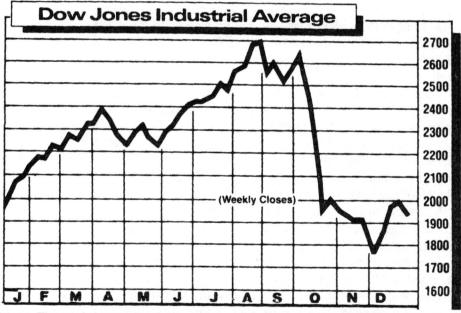

Fig. 7-1. The market is unpredictable. Stocks are only worth what someone is willing to pay for them. Here we see the peaks and valleys for the Dow Jones Industrial averages for the year 1987, the year of the October crash. Notice how the averages climbed from the 1900s to about 2700 before plummeting to below 2000 that October. Put buyers and short sellers made a fortune during the crash. Covered call writers at least eliminated some of their downside risk. (Reprinted by permission—*The Wall Street Journal*, ©Dow Jones & Co., Inc. 1987)

Investors who were running naked with only long positions, who had not hedged themselves with puts or covered calls, were hurt. They were surprised, too, because generally speaking the American economy was healthy. More astute economic forecasters and market predictors, however, guessed that the market had peaked around 2700 (DJ Industrials average) and a correction of about 20% was in order.

For the most part, everyone's optimism was not seriously diminished. Over the weekend following the 16th, the big money met at roundtables or over dinner to plot their strategy for the coming Monday. Stay in or pull out? Well, how far can the market really go down when the economic future looks more positive than negative? These were the questions on their minds.

Everyone waited anxiously for the opening bell the next Monday. The bears and bulls were facing off. As it turned out, claw and fang prevailed over hoof and horn. The Dow Jones Industrial average fell 508 points, 26% of that drop coming in the last half-hour of trading. The great crash of October 28, 1929 was nowhere near as impressive. On that fateful day, the market fell only about 13%. By comparison, the 1987 debacle chalked up almost a 23% decline.

The investment community was stunned. The Dow Jones Industrials were now resting at 1738.74. There was no warning; it just seemed to happen, but how? Average P/Es were high, but not so high as to force a drop of almost 744 points in the industrials in just two days. The economy was weakening, but there were no signs of a coming depression or even a hard recession. What went wrong?

Some argue that portfolio insurance and index arbitrage may have started the downturn, but it is highly unlikely that they kept it going. Other forces were at play. According to Richard Roll, in a book titled *Black Monday and the Future of Financial Markets* (Dow Jones-Irwin), the stock market fall was similar to what was happening worldwide. To countries like the U. S. that were engaged in computerized market-playing, the fall was not quite as bad as in less technologically adept markets. His conclusion is that the real culprit was the very volatility of the stock markets in general, this volatility caused by highly leveraged accounts that require quick and extensive selling to cover money that is lost with each point or two drop in stock price.

Investors were extremely nervous during this phase of the record bull market, anyway. The market was high, seemingly advancing for no good reason, and there were a number of investment counselors screaming, "get out!" When Friday's prices plunged, there were a lot of investors showing impressive profits and they did not want to see them washed away.

Why not? There were bargains almost from the start of the trading day. Merck was down 22 points at opening; Westinghouse $9^1/_2$; IBM 13; General Electric $8^3/_4$. Openings were delayed and so were trades. There was a 30-minute trading gap for Merck stock even after an opening delay of more than an hour. Exxon did not begin trading until almost 11:30 and suffered more than 5 minutes of trading gaps. Trading delays like these can create havoc with the index arbitragers. To take advantage of opportunity spreads, they need to act fast and furiously. This was impossible on October 19. On occasion, investors had to wait an hour or more to buy or sell stocks. The index arbitragers were literally shooting in the dark.

The result was that the market closed with a record drop on October 19. A lot of money was lost. The sad part of it all was that an exchange ruling, designed in response to trading activity that sped the fall of the market in 1929, prevented short sellers from becoming as rich as the long positioners were becoming poor, and thus handicapped the marketplace in the long run. New York Exchange rules will not allow anyone to sell short a stock if the previous price change was downward.

It is true that in October of 1929, short selling drove prices further down. At that time, however, there was an entirely different market than we have today. The stock market of the 1980s is a stock and index futures gamble. On October 19, 1987, short selling might have driven stock prices down, but it would have increased futures prices—the futures that actually led the 1987 market crash.

SELECTING THE UNDERLYING STOCK

If the previous section successfully emphasized the fact that the stock market can go down at any time and that the investor must always be prepared for such a downturn, it has been successful. Now let's look at how the covered call writer can automatically hedge his stock bets in the case of downturns, and how he might survive a bear market.

Let's assume that you have been anxious to increase your income. CDs, savings bonds, or savings accounts are not paying you enough interest. You have roughly $10,000 to invest and the stock market has been climbing. You do not have $10,000 to lose, however, so you are not about to gamble on the market.

You have been reading about the stock market extensively, trying to keep up on all the contradictory reports. You decide the market is relatively high, but do not anticipate much of a downturn over the short term. You decide to pick a stock with good, sound fundamentals, so that even if the market does plummet and take your stock with it, the issuing corporation's balance sheet and projected earnings will eventually bring your investment back into the black.

You have been around long enough, however, to know that a man or woman of your means cannot make it big in the stock market. Big money takes big money. You might be able to make a million in the stock market, but only if you have $5 million or more to invest in the first place. With $10,000, you would need to find a stock that will double in price almost seven times to make a million. It's possible that a stock will do this—that's the great attraction of the stock market—but it will hardly do so in a year or two or three. It could take 30 or 40 years, and then only your heirs will benefit from your selection. It could happen in 30 or 40 years if you pick the right stock at the right time, and if the stock can ride its own fundamentals and market trendlines to great heights. You may also pick a loser. The stock may halve in price six times. Stocks do seem to go down in price much quicker than they advance.

Your goal, then, is very practical. You will use your capital as a means of increasing your income. Let's assume it is October 1987. First, you talk to brokers and scan the papers and investment news to find the stocks paying the highest dividends. You know that stocks paying the highest dividends usually depreciate in price if interest rates go up. You'd like the high dividend income, but not if it means you'll see your capital depreciate. At this time interest rates have little way to go except up. Of the stocks that appeal to you, Warner Communications seems the most attractive. You like the stock for a number of reasons, though it has its good points and bad.

- It is an optionable stock, which means you can write covered calls against it. Additionally, it seems to have a clearly defined range over the maximum length of time for option contracts with strong upside potential. You feel you can, therefore, better gauge when to write your calls.

- The dividend is relatively unimpressive—less than 2%. You are more interested in the income you can generate with calls rather than the dividends the stock will yield. The opportunities for capital appreciation in the long run far outweigh the disadvantage of a low dividend.

- The profit margin for the company is around 6% and return on common equity is about 16%. These are relatively impressive statistics. They tell you that Warner is a relatively strong stock that is worth at least its current price.

- The debt to equity ratio is about 30%. This means that Warner is clearly able to handle its liabilities and protect itself from future losses, should they occur.

- There are 126 million shares outstanding. You feel that this is not very much for a strong company like Warner. Companies that have a lot of outstanding shares need to make a great deal of money to put upside pressure on the price of each share. Too small a float of shares outstanding not only means the possibility of great advances, but also of great retreats in the value of the shares.

- Average daily volume is in the hundreds of thousands of shares. This tells you that the investment community is watching the stock and is also interested in it. You are, by no means, planning to take a position in a stock nobody wants.

- Institutional holdings are about 60%. This tells you there's some big money in the stock. There are takeover possibilities, but with 126 million shares outstanding and the price per share around $30, a buy out would cost well over $3 billion. Besides, the investment community is advertising that Warner stock is worth $50 per share, so any buy out would be costly.

- The trendline is bullish. You note that stock has dropped from its peak two months earlier, but that its direction since 1984 is clearly upward.
- Earnings have been increasing and appearing as though they will be going up again next year. There are projections of $2.50 per share for next year.
- Book value is about $7 per share, yet you have read reports that the private value is actually worth three to five times that number. You are getting mixed signals here. If it is indeed $7 per share, the stock has a lot of downside risk. You decide, for safety's sake, to believe the lower figure, which confirms your decision to make the stock a covered call candidate.

Having read and reread the financial statements and reports that collaborate the figures listed above, you feel you have found a stock with which you are comfortable. Given your current goals you decide that this is the best investment you can make in the stock market. Other stocks that may be of interest are too highly priced, not optionable, do not pay dividends, or have too much of a downside risk over the long term.

You are ready to commit some money, now that you've found your target, but the market has been strong and you would rather wait for the next dip in prices before you take your position. You have a little bit of the contrarian in you. The market downturn comes on October 16. Little do you know that this is just the beginning of a crash. You feel it is a momentary bear phase in an extended bull market.

You need to decide whether or not you should immediately write a call or wait to see what the stock does. As you know from experience, you rarely buy a stock at the beginning of the next upswing, so you plan to write the calls immediately. You ask your broker for the available calls and the going prices and expiration dates. You already know most of this information from checking the newspaper, but your broker can give you the latest quotes.

WRITING THE CALLS

You are told the stock is at $30 per share. The options you are considering are the 25 through 40s, October, November, and February. You buy 300 shares and now consider the calls.

For the October 30s, the calls are at-the-money. As the day is not over, there is always a chance that a jump in price can result in the option owner exercising his rights because this is the expiration week for the October contracts and it is already Friday. You decide to just sell the October 35s for $37^1/_2$ cents. Your premiums for writing the three calls total $112.50. The calls expire the

Share Price: $30

Strike Price	Call Premiums		
	October	November	February
25	r	s	6
30	2	s	$3^1/4$
35	$3/8$	s	$1^1/2$
40	$1/8$	s	r

NOTE: In the above listings r = no trade, s = no option. Additionally, in these and future examples, premiums or stock prices have been slightly changed to simplify the arithmetic.

next day. You still have your stock plus $112.50. (Commissions on the call premiums would probably come to $35 at a discount broker.) The call premiums are sent to you immediately.

The following Monday you hear the market is crashing. You try and call your broker, but like tens of thousands of other investors you cannot get through. You have no idea what is happening to your stock. It is afternoon by the time you do get through to your broker.

"Warner Communications," he tells you, "is at $21 per share."

What do you do now? The market is crashing; in one day you have lost $9 per share or $2,700 before commissions. Should you get out while the going is still good—or will the market rebound? "I'm not selling," you say, "this stock has strong fundamentals. It's going back up sometime. I'm holding on." You look again at the calls. The Octobers have expired, but options for February calls are available.

Share Price: $21

Strike Price	Call Premiums		
	November	December	February
25	$2^3/4$	s	$3^1/2$
30	1	s	$1^1/2$
35	$3/8$	s	1
40	$1/4$	s	$1/4$

All the calls you are considering are out-of-the-money. The February 25s seem enticing. That's a $3^1/2$ premium. If you sell three of these calls, you will receive $1,050 in premiums before commissions are subtracted. If the stock is called, however, it will be called at $25. That means a $1,500 loss on the stock, which offsets completely any premium income you would receive and leaves you in the red.

Another possibility is to write the February $1^1/_2$s and make an additional $1^1/_2$, but there's too great a chance the stock will make it to the strike zone by February. Besides the total return for holding the stock from October to February will not be very much at all. You would receive $562.50 in premiums on a $9,000 investment. That's a mere 6% return over four months.

Finally, you decide to write the November 30s for $1 because you don't think the stock will move up 9 points in 30 days. You will break even on the stock, plus get $300 in premiums. It will not be much of a gain for holding the stock for one month, but it looks like the safest play. If the stock is not called, then you'll have a total of $412.50 in premiums and the chance to write new calls.

You write the November 30s and receive $300 in premium income (see Table 7-2). The next day the stock rises to $22^1/_2$. It is beginning to rebound after the crash. You check on the call premiums and try to decide if you should change your position.

Share Price: $22^1/_2$

Strike Price	Call Premiums		
	November	December	February
25	2	3	$4^1/_4$
30	1	1	$1^1/_2$
35	$^3/_8$	$^3/_4$	1
40	$^1/_4$	s	$^{11}/_{16}$

The price has gone up, but the November calls you wrote are still at the same price. The February 25s have risen, however, and now you wish that you had waited another day before buying the November 30s. At $4^1/_4$, the February calls look even more attractive. You know it is impossible to do exactly the right thing when playing stocks or options, however. There is always something better. There is always another day with better opportunities. There is always much more money to be made, but most of the time you never know it until after the fact. Settle down and play your own game as well as you can and you will come out all right.

The market continues to gyrate after the crash. No one can tell if the losses incurred on October 16 and 19 will be made up in coming months. Everyone is watching nervously. Investors are going in and out of the market. It is easy to tell that everyone is scared. Many people have been hit hard, but that is not what has them scared. They do not know what caused the investment disaster. Why did the market plummet the way it did?

_____Table 7-2. Profit and Loss Summary._____

Security	Purchase Date	Purchase Price	Sale Date	Sale Price	Gain	Loss
300 WC stock	10/16	$9,000	3/15	8,700.00		$300.00
3 WC calls Oct. 30s	(Expired)		10/16	112.50	$112.50	
3 WC calls Nov. 30s	10/21	337.50	10/19	300.00		37.50
3 WC calls Feb. 25s	10/26	900	10/21	1650.00	750.00	
3 WC calls Dec. 30s	(Expired)		10/26	300.00	300.00	
3 WC calls Feb. 35s	(Expired)		12/14	150.00	150.00	
				Totals	$1,350.00	$337.50

Percent return on original investment of $9,000: 11%.

It is October 21. The marketplace figures Warner Communications stock is at bargain prices. The investment community jumps in and forces the price up to $26⁷/₈ per share. The option markets respond in kind, but the November 30 calls do not move much. The strike zone is still too far away and the expiration date too close.

The February 25s have increased considerably, however. The premium for a February 25 is $5¹/₂. If you sold three of these and your stock was called, it would be much the same as selling the underlying stock for $30¹/₂. You could come out ahead overall, actually receiving, before commissions, $1,762.50 on premiums. If the stock were called and you had to sell it at the break-even price of $30 per share, you would still realize a 20% return from writing the calls.

Right now you want to kick yourself for having written the November 30s for $1. There is no need to punish yourself, however. How could you anticipate the jump in prices in such a short time? You could only make your decision based on the way things looked at the time. Nevertheless, you check the call listings again. Not to gloat, but to decide whether or not you should change positions.

The problem with the 25s is that they are in-the-money. The general rule of thumb is not to write in-the-money calls. Buy in-the-monies and sell at- or out-of-the-monies, preferably the latter! These are general rules, however, and sometimes exceptions must be made.

Share Price: $26^7/_8$

Strike Price	November	Call Premiums December	February
25	$3^1/_4$	$3^3/_4$	$5^1/_2$
30	$1^1/_8$	2	$2^7/_8$
35	$^5/_8$	1	$1^1/_2$
40	$^1/_4$	s	$^3/_4$

You decide this is time for one of those exceptions. You buy back the 25s and then sell the February 25s for $5^1/_2$. You lose $^1/_8$ of a point on the transaction because the premiums are now $1^1/_8$ instead of $1.

Now, you wait anxiously to see what happens the following day. If the stock takes off, you will be very disappointed. It will have meant that you should have avoided writing calls and just played the stock. Only time will tell if you are playing the game in the best way possible.

The next day, the stock tumbles by almost two points. The premiums on the calls also tumble. You check the call premiums once more to determine what to do. Generally, when you write calls you need not watch them quite as closely as this. In a crazy market that is trying to rebound from an historic crash, however, price movements that usually take months may happen over a period of days.

Share Price: $25

Strike Price	November	Call Premiums December	February
25	$2^3/_4$	3	$4^1/_4$
30	$^7/_8$	$1^3/_4$	$2^1/_4$
35	$^3/_8$	$^7/_8$	$1^1/_4$
40	$^3/_{16}$	s	$^1/_2$

The calls you wrote are at-the-money, and the premiums are now $1.25 less than yesterday. If you buy them back, you would receive a $450 profit and then could write the December or February 30s. You decide to wait another day. The market is gyrating too much and you are afraid of overreacting by going in and out of these options on a daily basis. The calls are at-the-money so you take a time out.

Patience often pays. The stock continues to move slightly up and down. Then on October 26, five days after you wrote the new calls, the stock plunges to $21^1/_2$ per share. Again, you run a check on call premiums.

| Strike | Call Premiums | | |
Price	November	December	February
25	$1^1/_2$	$2^1/_4$	$3^1/_2$
30	$^1/_2$	$1^1/_2$	$1^1/_4$
35	$^1/_4$	$^1/_2$	$^3/_4$
40	$^1/_8$	s	$^3/_8$

Share Price: $21^1/_4$

The stock market has you completely baffled. You wonder if it is a new marketplace because it is very different from the one to which you are accustomed. Perhaps these wild swings in prices are to be expected on a daily basis. You are caught in the market storm and still trying to squeeze a profit out of your investments. The stock is down to $21^1/_4$ and the premiums on your calls have been reduced.

You study the trendlines and fundamentals of the stock again. The short-term swings tell you nothing. The marketplace is trying to find its balance after the crash. The fundamentals of the stock tell you a lot, however. Nothing has changed for Warner Communications in the last week. All the ratios are good. As before, the $7 book value is the only thing that really has you worried.

You consider taking a profit on the February calls and selling safer calls that may not be called. You also consider selling the February calls and just riding the stock. The shares seems to be swinging up and down, but you think the stock is due for another rebound in price.

You decide to close out the February calls, and buy them back at $3. Because you sold them for $5^1/_2$, you make a $250 profit from each call for a total profit of $750. (See Table 7-2 for your P&L statement to date.)

Now you have to decide whether or not you should just ride the stock or write another call. Since your game plan has been primarily to increase income through dividends and options, with capital gains a secondary objective, you choose to stick to your plan. You consider other calls that are attractive under current market conditions. No matter how sure you are about any upswings, if the market can find a reason to go down it will. Another call will help you if there is a downslide.

Now that you have made your decision, you encounter one major problem. As you scan the call listings, you realize that because the market has been bouncing around you are only interested in writing calls with near-term expiration dates. Being fundamentally bullish, you expect that Warner will be in-the-money by February.

You cancel out the November calls because you have only 300 shares of stock and the total amount of premiums you could receive would be $300 for the

October 25s or $150 for the October 30s. The 35s and 40s are not worth considering because the premiums are too low. You decide the December 30s look like your best bet and phone your broker with instructions to write three of those calls. You then receive $300 in premiums.

The following day the stock jumps $1^3/_8$ points, but the effect on out-of-the-money calls is relatively minor. This is not an unusual situation. Out-of-the-monies usually do not change much on a daily or even weekly basis when their expiration dates are far into the future and the underlying stock has not moved significantly. This is why it is particularly important to study the option listings for consecutive and lengthy periods. By studying the options you can become familiar with the relationships between price movements in the underlying stocks, expiration dates, striking prices, and call premiums. Option buyers or writers are operating under a false premise when they assume each movement one way or another in a stock's price will change the value of all available calls (or puts) on that stock.

Sometimes the premiums available from calls (or puts for that matter) seem to move in unpredictable ways. Depending upon demand, they may even move down in price as the underlying stock moves up. You will notice this when you compare the listings below with previous ones. Look at the February 25s for Warner. On October 26, when the stock was at $21^1/_4$, the February 25 calls were at $3. On October 27, with the stock up to $22^5/_8$, the calls are at $2^3/_4$. In this case, the stock increased $3/_8$ of a point, but the calls decreased $1/_4$ of a point. This is due to something called non-synchronous trading, rather than any underlying rule related to call premiums. The last calls were traded when the stock was at a lower price and no calls were traded while the stock was moving toward its high for the day.

Share Price: 22^5/_8$

Strike Price	Call Premiums		
	November	December	February
25	$1^1/_2$	$1^7/_{16}$	$2^3/_4$
30	$^1/_2$	$1^1/_{26}$	$1^3/_8$
35	$^1/_4$	r$^1/_{26}$	$^3/_4$
40	r	s	$^1/_2$

The December calls you wrote are still at $1. There has been no change. Likewise, there has been no change in any of the November calls or the February 35s. November and December 25s have dropped a bit, but the February 30s have shown a slight increase. As you scan these listings, you realize that there is no great advantage to changing your current position. You decide to stay with the December 30s.

On October 28, the stock climbs another $3/8$ of a point. Like most long-term investors, you like to see slow upward movements in the price of a stock. This usually means that the stock will hold close to its current price. Large jumps forward or backward usually result in corrections that send investors to their psychiatrists.

Scanning the listings for Warner calls, you note that the premiums for the December and February calls have declined again, except for the 35s and 40s. The calls you have written have also declined, but not enough to encourage you to change your position.

Share Price: $23

Strike Price	Call Premiums		
	November	December	February
25	$1^1/2$	$1^1/2$	$2^1/2$
30	$1/2$	$3/4$	$1^3/8$
35	$5/16$	$r^1/2$	$7/8$
40	$1/8$	s	$1/2$

You might be tempted to buy back the December 30s and write February 25s, but you are still bullish on Warner. You purchased the stock because you liked the fundamentals. Since these fundamentals have not changed except for the relative depreciation in Warner holdings due to the crash, you still feel bullish and expect that the February 25s will make the strike zone much too attainable. You would still like to keep the stock, however, particularly because the calls are so attractive.

Still bouncing after the October 19 crash, the market continues to swing wildly. The investment community looks at Warner Communications again and decides it is relatively undervalued and due to climb back up to its annual highs. In one day the stock climbs to 24, then 25, then 26, then to 27, and finally to $27^3/8$. The climb is sufficient enough to put upward pressure on the call premiums. It is now decision making time again. You check the option listings in your daily newspaper to find out how the calls are faring.

Share Price: $27^3/8$

Strike Price	Call Premiums		
	November	December	February
25	$3^1/8$	$3^7/8$	$5^1/4$
30	$1^1/8$	$1^1/2$	$2^1/2$
35	$3/8$	$r^1/2$	$1^1/2$
40	$1/8$	s	$9/16$

Your December 30s have moved up in price. It is clear that if you did buy them back, you would lose $150 plus commissions. You are a bit worried that the stock, showing some new strength, might reach the striking price before December, in which case it would probably be called. However, if the stock is called at $30, you will still break even and have received $1162.50 in premiums over the period. The stock will have literally not moved for the two months you held it, but you will have enjoyed a 13% return on your original $9,000 investment because you wrote the series of calls.

You decide that the arithmetic dictates that you simply hold your position and wait out the December expiration. After all, your situation is not as desperate as it was earlier when the stock plummeted right after you purchased it. The calls you have written to date have enabled you to cover yourself through a four point decline in the stock and assured a 13% return (again, before commissions) if you were called. That's 13% over a two-month period.

The stock, meanwhile, continues to fluctuate a bit, but stays relatively close to the October 29 close. You have not even been checking the option listings, though you have been checking to see if the stock has reached $30 per share. After about three weeks, you check the listings again. It is November 19. You are checking the November 18 close, which is two trading days away from the November expiration date for option contracts. The November out-of-the-monies will be selling for very low premiums and the December out-of-the-monies will have dropped in price or will be generating little or no interest.

Share Price: $26^1/8$

Strike Price	Call Premiums		
	November	December	February
25	$1^1/8$	$2^1/8$	$3^1/8$
30	$1/16$	$1/2$	$1^1/4$
35	$1/16$	$r^1/2$	$5/8$
40	$1/16$	s	$3/8$

Your December 30s are now at $1/2$. With the stock currently just above $26 per share, you consider for a moment buying back the calls. You know, however, that with only a month until expiration, there will be continued downside pressure on the calls, even if the stock advances slightly. You decide to wait the market out.

The November calls expire and now the option listings record those available for December, January, and February. The stock continues to hover around the $27 per share price.

On December 14, five trading days before the December expiration, you double-check the option premiums and the price of the stock to see if you should go to the expiration date with the calls you have written or buy them back and play it safe. As they are still out-of-the-money and this is the week of expiration, they would necessarily be at very low premiums.

Share Price: $27³/₄

Strike Price	Call Premiums		
	December	January	February
25	3¹/₂	3¹/₂	4¹/₄
30	¹/₈	1⁵/₁₆	1³/₈
35	r	s	¹/₂
40	s	s	³/₁₆

Your December 30s are now commanding a premium of 12¹/₂ cents. You can buy them back for $36 before commissions and ensure that your stock is never called. That is probably the smartest thing for you to do, but you decide to take a minor gamble that the shares will not jump 2¹/₂ or more points in less than a week and don't sell.

As it turns out, you are correct. The shares never climb to the striking price, so after two months of holding the stock and writing calls (somewhat feverishly due to a highly erratic market), you show a $2¹/₄ paper loss on the stock and $1162.50 in call premiums for the period.

Now what? Do you sell the stock and subtract the loss from the premium income? In this case, you would realize a $675 loss on the 300 shares that would have to be subtracted from the premium income of $1162.50. That leaves you with a mere profit of $457.50, or 5% for the two months. It is, of course, nothing to be ashamed of because if you can continue the same rate you will see a 130% return on principal over a one-year period.

You decide to keep the stock and write new calls. Neither the January nor the February calls have attractive premiums for the out-of-the-monies. The in-the-monies are not quite as attractive as they were earlier when you wrote the February 5¹/₂s, and then closed them out at $3. In case of another downturn, you decide not to run naked with the stock. You sell the February 35s, which gives you another $150 in premium income.

The contracts expire worthless, as you had hoped. Then (and only for the sake of wrapping up these examples), you sell the stock for $29 per share. This results in a $1 loss on the price of each share for a total loss of $300 on the stock trade. If you look at Table 7-2, you will see the results of your wrestling match with the bear using a weapon called the covered call. In this example, you have lost money on the stock, but the calls covered your losses and put you in the black.

MANY WAYS TO PLAY

In the previous examples, you have probably noted that there were a number of possible ways to play each and every situation.

Now, with a great deal of hindsight, you could say that you would have been better off writing this call or that. You might even realize that in some cases you could have done very well by writing in-the-money calls. The objective of the examples has been to try and proceed on the basis of how you might react if you did not know what would happen to prices over the period discussed.

Nonetheless, you may have reacted differently each and every drop or increase in the price of the stock. You may have been satisfied with lower premiums and the lower associated risk of the stock being called. On the other hand, you might have opted for the highest possible premium in each and every case. There is no one correct way to play covered calls. You have many options, so to speak. You must be sure, however, that the premiums you are receiving will keep you ahead of the game in case your stock is called. You must also be ready to reverse your position whenever the opportunity warrants it.

We saw you get caught in a bear market. The stock plummeted immediately after you purchased it and never went back up to the purchase price during your time of ownership. Too often, investors get caught in very similar circumstances.

As it turns out, Warner Communications climbed well above the $30 striking price the following year. There was no way for you to anticipate that happening. Like many small but knowledgeable investors, you usually do not lose money because you pick the wrong stocks, but because your timing is bad and you cannot hold on for extended periods. Writing covered calls helps to make up for those very typical shortcomings. As you can see from these examples, despite the fact that you finally decided to unload the stock, you still showed an 11% return on your total investment.

What about those commissions? How much would they have reduced your profits? With current brokerage rates, you should assume that the amount of trading these examples required will result in buy and sell commissions on both the underlying stock and the options that will reduce your true rate of return to about 7%. In all cases, it is well to realize your return will be greater if your trading activity is kept to a minimum. Still, 7% for the period is nothing to sneeze at.

REMATCH

Your first match with the bear was over a stock that eventually climbed back to one point away from the original purchase price. So what you were wrestling was a bear trespassing in a bull market. What would happen to the covered call writer who got caught with a stock that did not march upward during the time it is held?

The worse case scenario is always a stock that goes out of business. Even in this case, however, any premium income earned before the stock disappeared from the market would soothe any investment wounds incurred. Generally, however, you should be skilled enough not to jump into a stock that has the potential of disappearing. That does not mean you will not make bad picks, only that you should not make totally disastrous ones, if you have any idea at all of what you are doing. The exception would be a conscious decision on your part to take a gamble on a long shot. Bad picks are inevitable and, except for the highly weathered speculators, most investors are unwilling to admit or recognize their mistakes until they've held on much too long.

If technical or fundamental analysis indicates you have picked a southern star instead of a northern one, the best bet is always to get out as quickly as you can. Take your losses and look elsewhere to make them up. Stocks rarely climb back up as quickly as they have fallen. You can always stay in the game, however, and try to cover the losses from the stock with winnings from calls. If a recently purchased stock suddenly drops, most investors have a tendency to hold on in dire hope that there will be a rebound. It's hard for them to admit they could have been so wrong, and harder still for them to swallow their losses.

In the first example of selling covered calls during market decline, Warner Communications was the underlying stock. It had strong fundamentals and the trendlines for a strong rebound.

What if you had decided to purchase Digital Equipment instead of Warner Communications? This stock had been attracting wide investor interest and was showing a great deal of strength, but had become greatly overbought by the time of the crash. Let us suppose that you had purchased 100 shares of it, either because you did not do your homework or did not do it well enough. In this case, the stock will not rebound during the time you hold it, as did Warner Communications.

Turning back the calendar to October 16, we find you once more weighing available options, but this time they are on Digital Equipment instead of Warner Communications. You have just purchased 100 shares of the stock at $172 per share and decide you would like to write a call immediately.

Share Price: $172

Strike Price	Call Premiums		
	October	November	January
170	$1/2$	s	$13^{1}/4$
175	$1^{3}/8$	s	$10^{1}/2$
180	$4^{3}/8$	s	$8^{1}/4$
185	$3^{1}/2$	s	$6^{1}/8$
190	$2^{1}/8$	s	$5^{1}/2$

If you write a January 170 (a $1,325 premium) and your stock is called, you will be assured a 7.79% return on your investment for the three-month period. That is a rather tempting call and because you are the type of individual who likes to play a sure thing, you phone your broker with the necessary instructions. The next morning you wake up with a smile because you know there's a check for close to $1300 (never forget commissions) in the mail to you.

The smile disappears when you call your broker later in the day to find out how Digital is doing. He tells you it is dropping like it has a one way ticket to the poor house, and that the whole market is going down. Digital is at $130 per share, he tells you, and you are frantic. You ask about the January 170 calls and are told they are at $2.

It is time for you to make a decision. The stock has dropped 40 points and the call 11½ points. You have lost $4,000 on the stock; so far the call you wrote has covered the loss. Whether or not you decide to sell the stock, you know you want to buy back the call, so you enter a closing order.

You check the option listing for Digital over the weekend and find the following premiums for available calls. The calls for October have now expired.

Share Price: $130

Strike Price	Call Premiums		
	November	December	January
140	s	s	10
145	s	s	7½
150	s	s	4¾
155	s	s	4¾
160	s	s	4
165	s	s	2½
170	2½	s	2
175	1½	s	3
180	1¼	s	2½
185	⅝	s	1¼
190	¾	s	1¼

Like most investors who experienced that wicked Friday in October of 1987, it is hard for you to believe that after all your research, the stock you selected dropped 24% in one day. You are now in a panic as you look for a strategy that will turn red ink into black. Your survival instincts tell you to sell the January 140s, but your greed takes over and you decide to wait for a rebound before writing another call. On October 19 you wait patiently to see what happens to your stock, but the news over the radio has you in a panic. The Dow Jones Industrials are taking another dive. It looks like record losses on the exchanges. You try your best to get through to your broker but, like almost every other investor that day, the lines are continually busy, and you cannot stay by the phone forever. When you do get through to your broker, you learn the news is bad for the market in general, but a little better for you—Digital is up 3 points.

You wait anxiously for the morning paper to check call premiums. As it turns out, you were probably lucky you could not get through to your broker the day before because the call premiums have risen nicely, making it that much more attractive for you to be a writer again. As you scan the call listings, you note that while the stock has only gone up 3 points in price, the January 140s have risen 8 points, the January 145s have risen 7¹/₂ points, and the January 150s almost 5 points. It appears that the option writers are expecting the stock market to bounce back. That is the only way you can account for these high premiums. You study the option listings with renewed interest.

Share Price: $133

Strike Price	Call Premiums November	December	January
140	s	s	18
145	s	s	15
150	s	s	10
155	s	s	6¹/₂
160	s	s	8
165	s	s	4¹/₈
170	3	5	5¹/₂
175	2¹/₄	3	5
180	1¹/₂	r	5¹/₄
185	1¹/₂	s	3¹/₂
190	1¹/₄	s	3

The question you must contemplate is whether or not a 3-point jump after a 40-point decline is a sign that Digital can regain lost ground. It isn't and you decide it is time to face facts.

You study the January 140s. The $18 premium means that if you sold it and your stock was called, it would be almost the same as selling the stock at $158. That would still leave you about $1200 in the red, but remember that the first call you wrote on Digital brought in a premium of $1,125. That means that even if the stock is called, you will break even with the help of the covered calls.

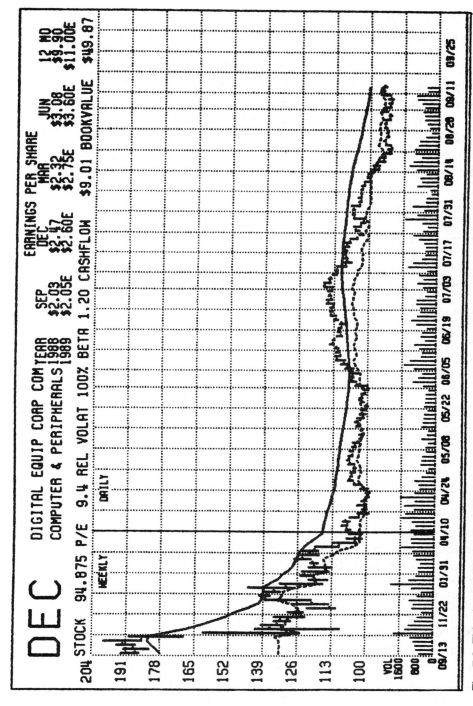

Fig. 7-2. This chart of Digital Equipment shows price and volume changes. The tracks Digital for the year from September 1987. Notice the dip during the crash and the stock's difficult time recovering. The solid line represents the 30-day moving average, the dotted line the relative price. Vertical lines at the bottom of the chart represent volume statistics. The other vertical lines represent price fluctuations. (Copyright © 1988 by Value Line, Inc.; used by permission.)

So you write the January 140s. On the next day, October 20, the market increases as though in a hurry to escape the heat of the deep south. Digital rides the heat wave and closes at $144^1/$_2$ for the day. In one hard push, investors have driven the stock past the striking price. The call you wrote is now in-the-money. Once again you would have been better off waiting at least another day before writing a call, but how could you know? Taking everything into consideration, your decision to write the January 140s the day before was the best you could have made. No one has a crystal ball or future copies of the *Wall Street Journal*. Besides, it was actually the January 150s and January 155s that saw the greatest percent change.

Now let's scan the option listings for October 20 and see how the different calls responded to the increase in Digital's per share price.

Share Price: $144^1/$_2$

Strike Price	Call Premiums November	December	January
140	s	s	19
145	s	s	15
150	s	s	15
155	s	s	12
160	s	s	10
165	s	s	9^1/$_2$
170	3^3/$_4$	6	9
175	2^1/$_2$	4^1/$_8$	6^1/$_2$
180	2^1/$_{16}$	4	6
185	1^1/$_4$	s	5
190	1^1/$_4$	s	4

As in all the previous examples, note that the share price represents the price at which the last option was traded and not the actual closing price on the New York Stock Exchange. This is typical of option listings, and not peculiar to the examples in this book. Nevertheless, for our purposes it is not necessary to distinguish last share price for an option contract and the last price at which the stock actually traded. All you need to know now is that having waited an additional day to write the January 140s would have brought you only an additional premium of $1.

With your call currently in-the-money, you wonder if it might be best to buy it back and unload the stock altogether. The loss would be $100, but you would have gained more than that by the $11^1/$_2$ jump in the stock price. This might not be a bad strategy at this time, but it is still your hope that Digital might take another price jump.

You decide to consider some of the other options. The 150s are suddenly looking good to you. If you write them and the stock is called, you would come out ahead of the game, wouldn't you? You would have to sell the stock at a $2,000 loss, but you will receive a total of $2,825 from this call premium and $1,325 from the first one that you wrote, less your loss from buying back the January 140s.

You see the light. You buy back the January 140s and take the $100 loss. Then you sell the January 150s and pocket the $1,500 premium. You now have an out-of-the-money call. The next day the stock drops to $132 and continues its downhill slide the day after when it trades at $127 per share. The drop requires you to reconsider your current positions.

You study the option listings and decide whether you should buy back the old and write a new, or buy back the old call and sell the stock, thereby taking yourself out of the market in two easy steps. All the pain and frustration will be behind you. These are two questions speculators often ask themselves.

Share Price: $127

Strike Price	Call Premiums November	December	January
140	s	s	$10^1/2$
145	s	s	7
150	s	s	7
155	s	s	6
160	s	s	5
165	s	s	$3^1/2$
170	$1^1/4$	$2^3/4$	$3^1/2$
175	$3/4$	r	$3^1/2$
180	$3/4$	$1^1/2$	$2^1/2$
185	$7/8$	s	$2^3/8$
190	$1/2$	s	$1^1/2$

You remind yourself that you are a covered call writer. That is how you play the market. So the answer to the question of whether or not you stay in for the battle is answered. You are going to work those calls until you've made up the loss you've incurred from the stock, or at least come close to making up that loss.

The stock continues to swing wildly in price. You watch with great anticipation as it drops 10, 15, then 20 more points, before it gains again. On October 26 it is at $116^3/4$ and you feel it is time to revise your strategy.

Share Price: $116³/₄

Strike Price	November	Call Premiums December	January
135	s	s	s
140	s	s	7
145	s	s	5¹/₂
150	s	s	4¹/₂
155	s	s	4
160	s	s	3⁷/₈
165	s	s	3³/₈

If you decide to sell the stock, you must close out the open call, unless you have the required equity in your account to maintain a naked position in the option. From a practical standpoint, however, you do not want to be short on a naked call because of the losses you can incur if it moves up in price. You would have to purchase the underlying security at the current market price, then sell it at the lower striking price. The striking price would be lower if the stock were called.

You decide to buy back the January 150s at $4¹/₂. That gives you a $1,050 gain on the call. Checking your record book, you note the following gains and losses from playing the covered calls on Digital.

October 18:	+$1,125			
October 20:		−$100		
October 26:	+1,050			
	$2,175	−$100	=	+$2,075

If you sold the stock now, you would incur a loss of $5,325 ($17,000 − 11,675). Therefore, you are still in the red so you go back to writing covered calls. There are no options selling at high enough premiums to attract you, however. You decide to wait. You are so far behind now that you need very high premiums to continue your game plan.

The next day the option premiums move up, along with the price of the underlying stock ($129). The December 135s climb to $7. These appear to be a worthwhile gamble, so you write the call. Your total premium is $700.

This write brings the total amount of premiums you have received to $2,875. As it turns out, you keep the contract until its expiration date. The stock is never called so you have the twofold benefit of being able to keep the premium and the stock. You are still in the red, however.

The stock, meanwhile, is at $128. Recent reports indicate that Digital is hurt financially. Wall Street's crystal-ball gazers, fundamentalists, and technicians do not anticipate a rebound for a long time. You decide it is time to get out. You can continue to play covered calls for the next couple of years until you get your money back, but it is clear to you that there are better opportunities in the market that will help you recover what you lost on Digital.

With a deep breath and the air of a good loser, you phone your broker and tell him to sell the stock at market. He reports back that he has unloaded it for $128 per share, or a loss to you of $42 per share.

If you had not dealt in covered calls, your total loss would have been $4,200. Writing the calls brought you $2,875 in premiums. Your true loss—before commissions—is $1,325. A $1,325 loss is a lot easier on the pocketbook than a $4,200 loss. You may not always come out a winner as a result of your stock and covered call combinations, but in a sliding market you will never lose as much as you would have if you did not write the covered call.

You begin now to think about writing naked calls that would let you benefit from a declining market without having that benefit offset by the declining stock. The truth of the matter is that many investors make an impressive income by writing naked calls. They have to be extremely careful, however, because one upward price swing that results in the underlying stock being called will require a great deal of money.

This will become more obvious to you after you are shown how to ''ride the bull.'' Before the writing of covered calls in a climbing market is discussed, the convenience of a margin account for covered call writers needs to be addressed.

8

The Necessity and Convenience of Margin

STOCK OPTIONS ARE TRADED IN MARGIN ACCOUNTS, THOUGH YOU WILL quickly learn that the margin requirements for a covered call writer are very different from those for an option buyer or a writer of naked options. Margin requirements for covered call writers are always fulfilled as long as the underlying stock is on deposit with the broker.

MARGIN ACCOUNTS

You must complete an application to open a margin account with your broker, whether it is a full-service or discount firm. This is because you are opening a line of credit with your broker when you apply for a margin account. He wants to know that your personal balance sheet qualifies you for the credit you want. The margin agreement will also give the broker some other entitlements, including among other things, the right to use the stock purchased as collateral for the loan, the right to sell securities in the account without notice to assure the money due him, and the right to charge interest on all money borrowed from the broker.

A brief overview of margin was presented in chapter 3 in relation to its necessity for selling short. Let's take a look at it now from the point of view of buying long because as a covered call writer you may at times be tempted to purchase the underlying stock on margin. (Figure 8-1 shows that the amount of money borrowed to purchase stocks is considerable.)

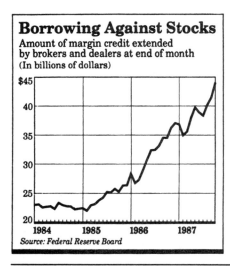

Borrowing Against Stocks
Amount of margin credit extended
by brokers and dealers at end of month
(In billions of dollars)

Source: Federal Reserve Board

Fig. 8-1. As this chart shows, the amount of money borrowed to purchase stocks is considerable. Margin is one of the ways in which investors get the kind of leverage they need to make a little money do the work of a lot of money. Margin easily puts the investor in harm's way, however, because while he can make much more, he can also lose much more. (Reprinted by permission—*The Wall Street Journal*, © Dow Jones & Co., Inc. 1987)

Before you do remember this: buying stock on margin is highly risky. It is not recommended for most investors except in the circumstance described below. It is not recommended because for each penny a stock declines, you can lose up to two pennies. The risk of loss, in the final analysis, is far greater than what you would realize by buying on a cash basis, as you will soon see.

So why do investors buy stock on margin? They buy on margin because they can make two pennies for each one penny a stock advances.

What types of investors are best suited for a margin account? There are probably a few different answers to this question, but in this author's opinion:

- experienced speculators who fully understand the risks involved and know what kind of stocks are worth the gamble.

- short sellers who have no choice but to open a margin account. Without a margin account, brokers will not allow an account to sell short.

- investors who want to buy in round lots (shares of 100 stocks or more), but lack the few extra dollars to get the last few shares. Because of the premium charged investors on odd-lot purchases, it is sometimes more economical to borrow a small percent of the money required and round out a purchase.

- investors who want to take a position quickly, but do not expect to have enough funds to pay for their stock until a few days after the settlement date.

- covered call writers who need the advantage of margin when they decide to buy back their options.

- option traders in general, as options are traded in margin accounts.

As of this writing, brokers require a minimum of $2,000 in any margin account before purchases may be charged to it. This means that if you were to buy $2,100 worth of stock, and this purchase represents the first margin purchase for you, you must put up $2,000. If you were to buy $4,000 worth of stock, you would still only have to put up $2,000. The remainder of the money due would be provided by the broker, who will use your stock as collateral for the money he has put up. When you sell the stock, he will take whatever part of the proceeds he needs to cover the amount due on the loan.

Some novice investors are under the impression that because the broker has put up some of the money for the purchase, he also shares in whatever loss is incurred. It is funny how people new to the market come up with such highly implausible ideas. Say you purchase $4,000 worth of stock on margin, using a $2,000 loan from your broker. The stock declines by 50% and you sell. You still must pay the broker back the full $2,000, plus interest that you owe him. No matter what happens to the stock—whether it doubles in price or goes down by 50%—you must pay the broker the full amount of the money he loaned you for the purchase, plus interest.

Buying stock on margin is very easy once you have opened an account. You simply inform your account executive that you are making a margin purchase and you are billed for a minimum of $2,000 or half the cost of the stock, whichever amount is higher.

FEDERAL RESERVE SYSTEM REQUIREMENTS

Actually, the broker may or may not put up half the amount of the purchase. It depends upon the current Federal Reserve System regulations. Federal Reserve margin requirements tie in with numerous other economic controls. Margin requirements in the past have been as low as zero dollars. During the crash of 1929, they were 10%; at this writing they are 50%.

Not to be confused with the Securities and Exchange Commission (SEC), the Federal Reserve is a nationwide system made up of a board of governors, the Federal Open Market Committee, twelve Federal Reserve banks and their twenty-four branches, a Federal Advisory Committee, and numerous member banks. Its primary function is to contribute to the management of the U. S. economy by controlling the flow of money, stabilizing the U. S. dollar, and maintaining a balance in international payments. The board of governors has the power to approve discount rates that Reserve banks may charge other member banks in the system, vary the percentage of the deposits that member banks must maintain as reserves, determine maximum interest rates for time and savings deposits, and, finally, to set the margin requirements for credit on securities transactions.

The SEC, on the other hand, is an independent government agency commissioned to administer federal securities laws. These laws are designed to protect the investment public. The SEC requires that public corporations adhere to certain rules and laws. Companies that are listed on any of the exchanges or over-the-counter markets are legally obligated to make numerous disclosures to the investment public, including all pertinent organizational and financial information that is required for realistic evaluation of their shares or other securities. The SEC is the public policeman. It enforces laws that are designed to prohibit fraud, manipulation, or any other abusive procedures that may result in the loss of credibility for the financial markets or unfair personal loss to the investment community.

BROKER AND EXCHANGE REQUIREMENTS

Brokers and exchanges sometimes may put additional margin requirements on investors. The Federal Reserve's initial margin requirement is 50% at this writing. This means that you only have to put up half of the cost of your stock. Brokers, and sometimes exchanges, however, require another type of margin called equity margin. Equity margin requirements vary from broker to broker to the extent competitive pricing allows. Some exchanges do not have any such requirement. Generally, however, the equity margin requirements of brokers surveyed for this chapter are 35% for accounts having at least two stocks of equal value in the portfolios, and 50% for one position accounts. Table 8-1 provides a definition of equity margin and initial margin.

―――――――――――――Table 8-1. Important Definitions.―――――――――――――

Equity Margin	The amount of cash or marketable securities brokers require for maintaining an account. If an investor fails to meet the equity margin requirements, the broker has the right to sell the necessary amount of securities in the account to make up the difference.
Initial Margin	For those who purchase stock on credit, the amount of money they must put up on the initial transaction.

This means that if you purchase $4,000 worth of AT&T on 50% margin, each time the stock drops in price you must put up additional money so that your equity in the stock remains equal to what the broker had to put up. If, however, you had equal dollar amounts of AT&T and Quantum Chemical (or some other stock) in your account, then their average depreciation can be considerable before you are required to put up additional dollars, even after the 50% margin purchase.

Equity margin requirements are computed in the following way.

$$\frac{\text{Market Value of Shares} - \text{Debit Balance of Margin Account}}{\text{Market Value of Shares}} = \text{Equity}$$

If the equity is less than the minimum required by the broker, you are required to put up additional money.

Rarely do brokers allow you to purchase stocks on margin if those stocks are under $5 per share. This is because lower-priced stocks are by nature very volatile and risky investments. Take, for instance, a stock that is selling at $5 per share. A drop of one full point represents a 20% loss for the shareholder. While the point movements may not be great for low-priced stocks, they represent nonetheless, large percentage swings in terms of the investor's position. If these low-priced stocks are purchased on margin, the investor has little cushion with which to maintain his position without putting up additional equity or having to sell the stock to meet his obligations to the broker. The investor does not have the equity cushion in the lower-priced stocks that he has in the higher-priced.

MARGIN ACCOUNTS FOR COVERED CALL WRITERS

Now that you know what margin means for stock traders, let's look at what it means for writers of covered calls. Margin has a very different meaning for the covered call writer than it has for the stock trader.

Margin for covered call writers means having a sufficient number of shares in the underlying security to cover the options that you are writing. It means nothing more than that.

Consider that each call represents 100 shares of stock. That means that if you write one call on a stock, you must have on account with your broker 100 shares of the underlying stock. If you write two calls, then you must have on account 200 shares of the underlying stock. If you write three calls, then you must have on account 300 hundred shares of the underlying stock.

Owning the required number of underlying shares gives you immediate protection if your stock is called. For example, suppose you own 500 shares of IBM and have written 5 calls on the stock. On the day before the contract expires (the expiration date, if you remember, is the Saturday after the third Friday of the month of expiration), the value of the stock moves well beyond the striking price and is called. You owe someone 500 shares of IBM stock.

Your broker has nothing to worry about. He knows you can cover your obligations. Why? Because the stock you otherwise would have had to purchase to cover yourself is already in your account.

It also puts you at ease as a call writer. You do not have to worry about getting the money to buy the stock to cover your position. It's already there in your account. You'll sleep a lot easier than buyers of stock on margin, as well as much better than naked (uncovered) stock option writers (discussed in the next subsection). This is because your margin requirements are immediately satisfied since you own the underlying stock and have it on deposit with your broker—providing, of course, that the number of shares you have on deposit covers the number of calls that you wrote.

Should the covered call writer buy stock on margin? The answer to this question is, of course, yes, but not carelessly. For example, there will be times when you find a particular call option on some stock highly attractive, but you do not own round lots (100 share lots). Let's say you only own 290 shares. It might very well be to your advantage to buy the remaining 10 shares on margin so you can write 3 calls at a very attractive premium. You will have to decide if the premium, less commissions on both the stock and option transactions, justifies paying the interest to the broker for the shares bought on credit. If the numbers are right, buy on margin—but do not overdo it.

MARGIN REQUIREMENTS
FOR NAKED OPTION TRADING

Now, that you understand something about margin accounts and buying stock on margin, bear in mind that margin requirements for buyers and sellers of naked options are based on different formulas than those governing stock purchases on margins.

To buy a call or a put, of course, traders must pay the full amount due, including commissions. Sellers of naked equity options must put up an amount that is equivalent to current premiums plus 5 to 15% of the market price of the underlying shares, depending upon how far out-of-the-money the options are. Your broker will supply you with the sliding scale he uses for determining margin requirements for naked writing. (See Table 8-2.)

_____Table 8-2. Margin Requirements for Option Traders._____

Investors	*Requirement*
Put & Call Buyers	Full payment for options trade.
Naked Stock Option Writers	Payment cannot be less than the premium for the option plus 5% of the value of the stock. But this minimum is for far out-of-the-monies, and investors can expect to post up to 15% of the stock's value. There may be initial minimum margin requirements just to open an account.
Covered Call Writers	All margin requirements are satisfied through ownership of the underlying stock, if that stock is on deposit with the broker, and the number of shares is equivalent to or more than represented by the options.

9

Riding the Bull

WHEN THE MARKET IS GOING UP, OR MORE SPECIFICALLY, WHEN THE UNDERLY-
ing stock is going up, the writer of covered calls wants to write options that will
expire or that can be bought back, depending on the circumstances.

The game is still the same—squeeze as much income as possible from the
underlying stock. The dilemma for the covered call writer in a bull market is not
how much his premiums will be offset by a decrease in the value of the underlying shares, but how much more he will make if he unloads his calls.

The basic fundamental and technical considerations for selecting the underlying stock described earlier apply now also. The underlying stock is purchased
because of its strength and future prospects, even if these future prospects are
expected to be somewhat limited to a value just below the striking price.

If the covered call writer assumes his position because he anticipates a
declining market, he is in the right stadium but playing the wrong game. If there
is good reason for him to assume that the underlying security is going to decline
in price, then buying puts or short selling stocks is usually the smarter way of
playing the market.

INVESTMENT KNOWLEDGE AND INSTINCT

Fundamental analysis, as explained in chapter 7, requires disciplined research
into a company's past and present performance, as well as estimated guesses at
what both the corporation and the stock might do. This approach to determining
buy or sell recommendations for a particular stock is concerned mainly with the
financial, marketing, and management affairs of the corporation that has issued

the underlying stock. Everything that can be catalogued from the accounting data is weighed: accounts receivable and accounts payable, current ratios and quick ratios, revenues and assets, operating ratios and equity ratios.

Technical analysis looks at volume and price movement in the underlying stock. In addition to monitoring the daily trading volume, technical analysis continually monitors the trading range for the price of the stock. It also necessitates the development of highly complex formulas that include this data with moving averages, certain ratios, and other statistics. The variables that make up the formulas used by technical analysts will vary depending on what they feel is most significant.

The astute investor knows that neither the fundamentals nor the volume and price movements, nor the formulas used for technical analysis, can be depended on each and every time. This is where investor instinct comes in. Just as the tennis coach may show you all the offensive and defensive moves and all the backhand and forehand strokes, he can never make you a winner unless you have the instincts necessary to command the court and respond to your opponent. In the same way, an investor cannot depend solely on fundamental and technical data to come out a winner. He must also know when to make his moves and how to respond to an ever-changing and fickle marketplace.

Even in a strong bull market all the ratios can point to financial stability and all the technical indicators to topside performance, yet the shareholder can lose money. This is because there is always a definite distinction between a corporation's financial performance and a stock's price and volume movement. The value of the corporation is determined by hard and fast accounting data subject to the interpretation of auditors, which leaves true value a somewhat subjective thing. The value of the corporation's stock, however, is determined by one of the fundamental laws of economics—the law of supply and demand. Interest in stock at any given price is influenced only by what people believe the stock may be worth tomorrow, an investment rule that cannot be repeated enough.

Why do investors take a chance on stock investments then, if the fundamental and technical analyses guarantee absolutely nothing? The answer to this question is probably hope. They hope that they can do better than they would if they put their money in interest-paying investments. They hope that this time the fundamentals or the trendlines will be accurate indicators. They hope that nothing happens to drastically change expected future developments—they hope the odds will remain in their favor.

The covered call writer can at least change the odds.

WRITING THE CALLS

So that direct comparisons can be made, and to give the examples here and in chapter 7 more meaning, we return to the events of October 1987 and once again use Warner Communications as the underlying stock.

In chapter 7, Warner was purchased at $30 per share and immediately thereafter started to depreciate in value. It was caught in a bear market, a bear phase of a bull market, or, in any event, a bear slide during the period of your investment. You purchased it and watched your capital depreciate like someone had set it afire. When you finally bailed out, the stock was still below the price at which you purchased it (see Fig. 9-1). The movement of the stock had relatively little negative impact on your personal P&L statement because the covered calls you wrote not only covered your losses on the stock trade, but brought you additional premiums.

Now, you will ride the bull. Interested in Warner Communications, you do some research. Everything you read and study tells you to buy. Knowing that it takes a great deal of money to make a great deal of money by buying and selling stocks, you take a practical approach. You will write calls against the underlying stock you own and play the market for the dividends and premiums you can command.

When you first consider the stock, it is at $30 per share. The call premiums are indicated below.

Share Price: $30

Strike Price	Call Premiums October	November	February
25	r	s	6
30	2	s	$3^1/_4$
35	$^3/_8$	s	$1^1/_2$
40	$^1/_8$	s	r

NOTE: In the above listings r = no trade, s = no option. Additionally, in these and future examples, premiums or future stock prices have been slightly changed to simplify the arithmetic.

Because you are somewhat bullish on the stock and expect its price to swing between $30 and $35 per share for the next six months or so, you are not particularly anxious to sell the at-the-monies. That leaves out the October and February 30s. As the rule of thumb that always guides you states never to sell in-the-monies except under unusual circumstances, the 25s are out of the question. As you continue to size up the available options, you decide there is nothing far enough out of the money and paying a high enough premium to make writing a call attractive. You decide to wait.

The following Monday the market takes a dive, and along with it goes Warner Communications. The stock drops to $21 per share. Pleased that you were smart enough to stand by the sidelines until the right opportunity pre-

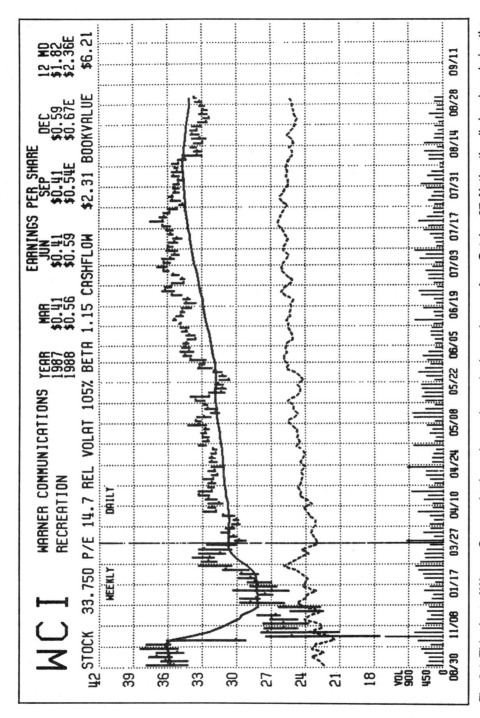

Fig. 9-1. This chart of Warner Communications share price and volume changes from October 87. Notice the dip in prices during the crash of 87 and the stock's successful recovery by the following August. Vertical lines at the bottom of the chart represent volume statistics. The other vertical lines represent price fluctuations. (Copyright © 1988 by Value Line, Inc.; used by permission)

sented itself, you now purchase 300 shares of Warner Communications. After such an extensive drop in price, you expect a rebound. Whereas in the earlier examples you fell with the bear market and had to take the defensive immediately, you can now be somewhat aggressive. You consider the available options.

Share Price: $21

Strike Price	November	Call Premiums December	February
25	$2^3/4$	s	$3^1/2$
30	1	s	$1^1/2$
35	$3/8$	s	1
40	$1/4$	s	$1/4$

October contracts have expired. November, December and January options are now being offered. There are a number of premiums that look good to you now. You decide on the November 30s. If the stock is called at $30, you will receive a $9 per share capital gain, plus a $1 per share premium. That means that in just about one month you could receive a total of $2,700 in profit on the underlying stock and a $300 premium from the calls. In one month, you would have realized a $3,000 return on a $6,300 investment. That is almost 50% on your money in one month.

On the other hand, if the stock is not called you at least have $300 in premiums to ease your losses or to add to whatever gain you may realize. It is quite conceivable that Warner Communications may advance to $28 a share by the expiration date, in which case, even if the stock is not called you can realize a profit of $7 per share by selling the stock, or, of course, write another call.

The next day, the stock climbs to $22^1/2$, fully a point and one-half above what you paid for it. Nevertheless, the November 30 call premium remains at $1. Because the call has not gone up in price, you could enter a closing order to purchase back the three November 30s and suffer only the loss necessitated by the cost of commissions. Then you could sell your Warner stock for the $1^1/2$ point profit. You decide you are playing for higher stakes and stay with your current positions.

What strikes you as particularly unnerving is the fact that the November 25s have actually gone down in price, despite the advance in the stock. What scares you is the unpredictability of the marketplace. Investors seem to be panicking, unsure of whether to take advantage of price dips. As you check on the current available premiums, you note that the February 25s have increased in price, giving some hint that the marketplace sees the three-month potential for Warner as being rather good.

Share Price: 22^1/_2$

Strike Price	Call Premiums		
	November	December	February
25	2	3	4$^1/_4$
30	1	1	1$^1/_2$
35	$^3/_8$	$^3/_4$	1
40	$^1/_4$	s	$^{11}/_{16}$

As the market now stands, it appears your decision to sell the November 30s and stay with them is very wise. In the previous chapter, during which you lost $9 per share in one day, you could not be quite as cool and patient in your approach to playing the covered calls on Warner. This is because you needed to make up for lost ground. Now, with your stock moving up and the striking price still out of range, you are playing a winning game. Of course, you want to win as big as you can.

As the expiration date nears for the November options, Warner Communications jumps to 26^7/_8$, giving you almost a $6 per share profit on the stock. Meanwhile, the November 30s have climbed only $^1/_8$ of a point. You decide you want to sell the stock. You can't take a chance on losing a total profit of $1,752.50 in one week.

You call your broker and ask him to buy back your three November 30 calls on Warner Communications and then sell the 300 shares of stock at market. Your broker checks the market prices of the calls and stock, then varifies your desire to buy and sell at those prices. He then puts in the orders.

There is always the chance that the broker might not buy back the options at the market price quoted when you phoned in the order—a major disadvantage of placing market orders. There is also the chance that he may not sell the stock at the original market price because stocks, like options, will fluctuate in price during the day. For purposes of this example, however, we will assume that the broker is able to execute the orders at the expected prices. The result is a $1,762.50 gain on the stock transaction and a $37.50 loss on the covered calls.

That is a total profit of $1,725 on a $6,300 investment in Warner stock, or a 27% return on your money in less than a week. Not bad at all! Imagine what would be your annual return if you could continue making money at this rate.

We know now, for it is long after the fact, that you could have held the stock through the November expiration date without fear of being called because the stock price never reached the $30 striking price. Nonetheless, it is to your advantage to take profits as soon as possible. A bird in the hand is worth two in the bush is as true a statement today as it was in the past. When a stock jumps

29% in a week, take your profits. Chances are it will retreat after such a move and you can always go back into it, or look for another opportunity. On the other hand, if a stock moves 29% over a six-month period, there probably will not be a serious correction in its price, and you may want to hold on to it. The prevailing theory is that when a stock takes large percentage jumps or slips in a short period of time, expect a major correction, providing a takeover, bankruptcy filing, or some other unusual circumstance is not in the making.

WRITING AGAIN

On October 26, Warner Communications stock takes another plunge in price. It retreats to $21¹/₄ and now you have new interest in it. Checking the call premiums, you find the following listings.

	Share Price: $21¹/₄		
Strike Price	November	Call Premiums December	February
25	1	2¹/₄	3
30	¹/₂	1	1¹/₄
35	¹/₄	¹/₂	³/₄
40	¹/₈	s	³/₈

The temptation to buy back in is too great. You are familiar with the latest financial data about Warner Communications and, as far as you are concerned, nothing has happened in or about the company to markedly change its bottom line or future projections. It is just rolling along with the market in general, so you purchase 300 shares of the stock.

Now you must decide whether to write calls or just play the stock. The stock has recently dropped almost six points and if it can do it once, it can do it again. Stocks can always find a reason to go down, regardless of the rate of their previous plunge. If you doubt at all this little bit of stock market wisdom, consider how many times you have purchased a stock and watched it drop below the purchase price before taking off, if it ever did take off. By all stock market logic such a quick drop should unleash a correction, but who knows if that correction will take place now or after the next six point drop?

The February 25s give you protection to $18. If the stock drops to $18, you are just about breaking even because of the premium income. On the other hand, if the stock is called before the February expiration, which is roughly three weeks away, you will realize a 3⁷/₈ point gain on the sale of the stock and a $1 per share premium from the calls. Translated, that means a return of $1,162.50 from the sale of the stock plus $300 in premiums. That's a profit picture of $1,462.50 in roughly three weeks on a $6,300 investment in the underlying security or a 23% return.

You decide to look for greater capital gains, so you prefer the November calls with the close expiration date. They offer a better chance of being able to hold on to the stock and ride it to higher prices. You write the November 25s for $1. You feel the striking price is at a safe distance from the stock price.

Before long, however, the stock reaches $25 and the calls you are following have the premiums listed below.

Share Price: $25

Strike Price	Call Premiums		
	November	December	February
25	$2^1/4$	3	$4^1/4$
30	1	$1^3/4$	$2^1/4$
35	$3/8$	$7/8$	$1^1/4$
40	$3/16$	s	$1/2$

As the listings above indicate, you could easily buy back the November 25s, which have not changed in price, and sell the underlying stock for almost a $2 profit. The winnings are small in such a play, however, so you decide to maintain your current position until better opportunities present themselves.

The stock climbs into the striking zone before the expiration date, making the November 25s in-the-monies, and very costly to buy back.

Share Price: $27^3/8$

Strike Price	Call Premiums		
	November	December	February
25	$3^1/8$	$3^7/8$	$5^1/4$
30	$1^1/8$	$1^1/2$	$2^1/2$
35	$3/8$	r	$1^1/2$
40	$1/8$	s	$9/16$

As you fear, the stock is called and you must sell it not at the market price of $27^3/8$, but at the striking price of $25 per share. Still, you come out ahead earning $1,162.50 from the sale of the stock and $300 in premiums. Add this income and gain to the $1,725 you made from the first transaction and, in just a couple of weeks, you have realized a total profit of $2,887.50 on a $6,300 investment. This represents a 46% return on your money in about two weeks.

This is an unusual return on your investment and not one to be expected under normal circumstances. In this example, however, we are dealing with the very erratic market that prevailed in late 1987, just after the crash. The volatility of underlying stocks during this time allowed some unusual situations. At best, this example represented what can possibly happen. Short-term profits such as this can never be counted on and are rare occurrences at best.

In the example, the $2,887.50 return is not actually a result of covered call writing. In the first part of the example, the call was closed out at a loss and the stock sold for a profit. This tactic is part of covered call writing. It is part of the flexibility inherent in this type of trading program. When playing covered calls there is always the option of buying back the calls in order to profit from the stock, or buying back the calls to profit from the calls. The covered call writer has a great deal of flexibility and many ways to make a dollar, unlike the average investor who simply buys stocks long in each and every transaction.

PERSPECTIVES

As you may have realized, the terms bull and bear are relative to what you invest in and when you make your investment. To better understand this, consider the following.

1. In every bear market there are bull phases and in every bull market there are bear phases. If you go in and out of the market during an upswing phase, and your friend goes in and out during a downturn phase, you have both taken advantage of bull and bear markets, regardless of how reports eventually define the market. Because of possible daily price swings, you and your friend may well have benefited from or lost in the bull and bear phases that took place on the same day.

2. As all stocks do not move in the same direction at the same time, you may invest in a stock that is rising while a friend of yours is involved in a declining stock. As far as you are concerned, your stock (regardless of whether or not you are bullish about it) is enjoying a bull market, while your friend's selection is suffering a bear market, again regardless of how economists may finally define the type of market in which you have been dealing.

The terms bear and bull not only define a market trend, but also an investment attitude. Therefore, you may be bullish though the market is declining, and you may be bearish though the market is advancing. The relativity of the terms bear and bull was emphasized in the two separate examples of how to play covered calls on Warner Communications. Because you purchased the stock at $30 in the first set of examples, and it never climbed back to that price before you unloaded it, we considered this a bear market. In the second set of examples presented in this chapter, you were able to purchase the stock at $21 and ride it upward, so we considered the same investment period as a bull market. Though you were playing the same stock in roughly the same period in each set of examples, the way the stock moved after initial purchase necessitated a different game plan.

In the first example, when you purchased Warner Communications at $30, you were satisfied to sell the October 35s for $37^{1}/_{2}$ cents. After all, you were only a couple of days from the expiration date and you doubted Warner would shoot to $35 per share in that time. You were right, of course, but you never expected the drop in price that soon followed. When the stock plummeted and the stock price and call premiums were as follows, you decided to write the November 30s for $1. Your reaction naturally included panic, despite belief in the stock's fundamentals, and a "get my money back" attitude. You were hoping for some type of rebound. If Warner did not reach $30 by November, the 300 shares you owned would bring in at least $300 as a result of the covered call premiums.

Share Price: $21

Strike Price	November	Call Premiums December	February
25	$2^{3}/_{4}$	s	$3^{1}/_{2}$
30	1	s	$1^{1}/_{2}$
35	$^{3}/_{8}$	s	1
40	$^{1}/_{4}$	s	$^{1}/_{4}$

The November 25s would bring in higher premiums and limit your losses if you were not called, but you had no way of knowing that Warner would eventually climb back and you did not want to be forced into selling at a loss if your stock was called at $25.

In the second set of examples described in this chapter, even though you took a position in Warner Communications when it declined to $21, you still decided to sell the November 30s. You have now turned your bullish attitude from potentiality to actuality. This time you were interested in the November 30s because you felt the calls would either protect you from a further three point decline or increase your profit from holding the stock, whether or not it advanced beyond the striking price. You were not playing the game just to get your money back, instead you were playing for profit.

If the stock declined a couple of points, you could still buy back the calls and sell your stock or just maintain your position. If the stock advanced at a higher rate than the calls because of the approaching expiration date, the calls could be bought back and the stock sold, in which case the loss on the calls would be less than the profit on the stock. Either way, profit would be ensured. If the stock was called at $30, you would realize a $9 per share profit on the stock and the $300 in premium income. What an easy game!

The difference in strategy necessitated by the bear and bull market conditions became more apparent in the secondary transactions. In chapter 7, when you were losing badly and the stock advanced to $26$7/8$ while the November 30s advanced only $1/8$ of a point, you decided to change positions and purchase back the calls at a slight loss. Selling the February 25s for the premiums, indicated in the following listings, at least represented the equivalent of selling your stock for $30$1/2$, even though it appeared you were absolutely sure of being called.

Share Price: $26$7/8$

Strike Price	Call Premiums		
	November	December	February
25	3$1/4$	3$3/4$	5$1/2$
30	1$1/8$	2	2$7/8$
35	$5/8$	1	1$1/2$
40	$1/4$	s	$3/4$

In this chapter, when your cup runneth over, the jump in stock price and minor movement in the November 30s assured you a tidy profit. Once again, you decided to change positions, not to take advantage of the February 25s, but to reap the profits from selling the stock for a 5$7/8$ point gain.

This transaction took you out of the market until the stock dropped again to near $21 and you took a new position, writing covered calls as before. When you were in the bear market you were hanging on for dear life, watching for every opportunity to write and rewrite calls until your premiums made up for the corresponding loss in the price of Warner shares. You had little choice but to continue desperate, and in this case successful, attempts to bring in new and higher call premiums until you could unload the stock safely. The examples used the same stock during the same time period, but created entirely different ball games.

AFTERMATH

Warner Communications actually rebounded very nicely, as did many other stocks, after the October 1987 crash. In the summer of 1987, it was fluctuating between $36 and $40. Despite the beating it took during and shortly after the panic, nine months later it was testing its summer 1987 prices.

Digital did not fare near as well. Up around $200 per share during the summer of 1987, it never rebounded to test those highs. Nine months after the crash the stock fell to below $100 per share. An active covered call writer who decided to hold on, however, would have been able to greatly reduce the amount of losses realized from stock depreciation. A writer who plans to hold onto the stock for the next couple of years may possibly realize a profit from his stock and covered call combinations, even if Digital only advances half as far as it fell.

It is important to realize that knowing when to unload a stock is as necessary for the covered call writer as it is for the naked investor, although the necessity of unloading is never as great for the covered call writer.

RISK/REWARD ADVANTAGES

As you can see by now, writing covered calls offers any investor the potential for relatively handsome rewards in return for extremely low risks. There are few opportunities in the investment community that compare with covered call writing from this perspective, though there are indeed many other investment strategies that can bring in far greater reward.

The covered call writer takes a very practical approach to the stock market. She realizes that in order to make big money in the stock market, two important things are required beyond general investment smarts. The first is big money because a 30% profit on a million dollars represents far more discretionary income than 30% on $5,000. The second is leverage. An investor tries to increase her returns by buying low-priced stocks, borrowing heavily to invest, playing naked options, or increasing her trading activity. Each of these leveraged strategies have dangerous pitfalls. Low-priced stocks leave a trail of extensive percentage losses with each $1/32$ of a point that they drop. Borrowing heavily means that if the investments do not meet their promise, the investor may lose more than she put up. Increased trading activity means extensive commissions and a greater possibility of taking a position in the kind of losing situation that can wipe out all the gains of the last five years.

Her strategy is not to go after the large profits that carry the kind of risk that can wipe out every cent she has for investment, and maybe more. Rather, her goal is to find the very safest way to play the stock market and to play it for its maximum possible return on investment. Her rule of thumb is safety first.

Safety first is also the rule of thumb for many big money investors who find it very practical to use only covered call writing as their market strategy. Covered calls are not strictly for the little guy.

10

Playing the
Possum Market

DECLINING MARKETS ARE BEAR MARKETS AND ADVANCING MARKETS ARE BULL markets. Markets with no apparent direction do not have a special name. To make up for this oversight, we shall call a market moving within a very tight range a possum market. If we have interest in a stock that will be moving up and down less than 10% over semi-annual periods, we will consider this a possum play.

Possum plays generally involve stocks that pay high dividends and have strong fundamentals. Investors are mainly interested in these stocks for dividend income, with premium income considered a secondary play. Possum plays generally involve buying the stock, selling far out-of-the-money covered calls, and letting expiration dates and dividend declarations do the rest.

DIVIDEND MATH

Dividends on common stock do not change with the price of the stock. If a particular stock pays a $1 dividend when it is selling for $10 per share, the 10% return is not maintained when the stock advances or declines. An investor's true dividend yield must be figured on the basis of the dividend available at the time of purchase. A good number of stocks, for which options are listed, pay attractive dividends. Companies have no legal obligation to continue their dividends, of course, but dividend cuts or cancellations are generally rare. If they do occur, they are generally well announced.

Anytime the board of directors deems it in the company's benefit to cancel or reduce (or raise) dividends, it will do so. Only when dividends are actually declared must they be paid by settlement date. Investors looking for stocks that are ideal candidates for covered call writing during quiet markets must be sure that the stock in which they are interested has a good dividend history and future, this last generally identifiable by a study of the stock's fundamentals.

One of the most popular stocks is AT&T, even since the breakup. Investors like to purchase this stock, tuck it away in their portfolios, and enjoy the dividends until they are forced to sell for some reason. They expect that when they do sell, AT&T will be at a higher price than they had paid for it. Of course, this is not always true of AT&T or any other stock. There are no guaranteed stock investments. Few AT&T shareholders actually trade the stock over the short or intermediate term. The chart below shows the dividend yield at varying AT&T stock prices. The dividend in effect at this writing is used. (AT&T often changes the dividend annually.) As you can see, if a passbook savings account is paying 5.6%, the dividend is to your advantage if you pay $20 for the stock. If the stock costs you $30, however, your money would earn a greater return in the savings account.

AT&T Common	Current Dividend	Dividend Yield
$20	$1.20	6.0%
$21	$1.20	5.7%
$22	$1.20	5.5%
$23	$1.20	5.2%
$24	$1.20	5.0%
$25	$1.20	4.8%
$26	$1.20	4.6%
$27	$1.20	4.4%
$28	$1.20	4.3%
$29	$1.20	4.1%
$30	$1.20	4.0%

It is important to note that AT&T, like other stocks used in the examples throughout this book, has not been singled out as a recommended stock for purchase, although it may very well be a sound investment that fits into your investment goals. It was simply selected because it is a popular optionable stock that makes a good example for the subject at hand.

Suppose that you purchased AT&T at $20 when it was paying a 6% dividend. You saw no dividend increases when the stock reached $30 per share, at which time the dividend rate was actually 4%. As an income player, you would be wise to take advantage of the 50% increase in the price of the stock and sell your holdings. You would receive a $10 per share profit on top of whatever dividend you received. This allows you to look for and buy another stock with strong fundamentals (and an attractive trendline) that is paying a relatively high yield.

Many shareholders will not part with their blue chip stocks, though this attitude in the long run is usually unwise for naked holders because of the opportunity costs involved. For investors who are very attached to their portfolio, writing covered calls gives you the best of both worlds—the additional income that can be achieved from more frequent trading and the possibility of holding on to those blue chip stocks.

PREMIUMS AND DIVIDENDS

If you took a position in AT&T for the dividend income and expected the upside potential for the stock to never be more than 20% in a six-month period, then you would be wise to consider out-of-the-money covered calls to supplement your income. Let's look at calls on AT&T when the price is at a hypothetical $25. (All prices are hypothetical.)

Share Price: $25

Strike Price	Call Premiums		
	August	September	January
25	$3/4$	1	$1^7/8$
30	$1/8$	$1/2$	$3/4$

Considering your long-term holding plans, you would want to avoid the at-the-money calls. A slight advance in the stock would put them in-the-money and leave the stock subject to call. The $30 September and January options, however, fit your program. The January expiration is four months beyond the September, yet the premium is only $1/4$ point more. It is hardly worth putting your stock at risk for a four-month period for a mere $1/4$ point advantage. Therefore, the September 30s appear to be your best bet. Selling the September 30s would bring you a premium of 50 cents per share.

Assuming that you can continually bring in 50 cents per share from premiums on calls that are out-of-the-money by more than 20% and, on the average, two months from expiration, your annualized income from premiums would be $2 per share. Since AT&T is paying a dividend of $1.20 per share, your premium income brings your return to $3.20 per year, which is a total yield from dividends and premiums of 12.8%. That is certainly not a lot of money, but it does allow you the advantage of continuing to ride the price of the stock as it moves upward, while increasing your income from the holdings.

PRICE MOVEMENTS

How do you decide on a safety range for a call's striking price especially in a stagnant market? The answer depends upon how attached you are to your stock. In our example, it was assumed you did not want to unload your blue chip "piece of America" unless absolutely necessary. While a 20% move in AT&T over a six-month period would be quite unusual, so would the chances of your stock being called.

You would be surprised at how much stocks actually fluctuate over short periods, even during stagnant markets—or what I have taken the liberty of calling possum markets. If you are unlucky in your timing and purchase the stock at the trailing edge of an upswing, you are going to be surprised by the short-term loss you may experience. If you have just purchased a stock at the trailing edge of a short-term downward trend, then you will soon experience a relatively nice capital gain.

Further clarification is necessary here. It is indeed true that statistics indicate that after a six-month period the price of a stock will probably be at its original price. This is why many astute investors are willing to sell puts and calls instead of writing them, and why most option buyers continually lose money when they don't hedge by using put and call combinations. A stock moving only 15% one way or another, however, can bring greater returns or losses to investors who go in and out of it within that period of time because of the rate of change in the high to low price swings.

If you have a pet stock that is paying a high dividend and trading narrowly, sell out-of-the-money calls with relatively close expiration dates and striking prices that are about 25% away. As you know from previous chapters, if the value of the stock increases, the price of the calls may decrease as the expiration date nears. Then you can always buy back the option at a profit and continue to hold the stock.

If you have taken your positions in the stock and calls only because of the total dividend and premium income available, then whether or not you eventually have to sell the underlying stock is of no special consequence. Providing the call you write is far enough out-of-the-money you will realize a capital gain on top of the premium income if your stock is called. If the stock retreats, the call premiums will help cushion your loss or prevent it.

11

Caveats

IN MOST OF THE PRECEDING CHAPTERS, THE ADVANTAGES OF COVERED CALL writing have been emphasized. In chapter 2, however, you were briefly introduced to some of the disadvantages of writing covered calls. These disadvantages, which directly relate to option selection and commissions, are further clarified in this chapter. Descriptions of some very special risks inherent in option trading, which can vastly change the safety of covered call writing, are also discussed. These special risks have less to do with the type of money call you write, or the underlying stock you select, than with the way in which the equity option markets work.

The trading disadvantages are:
- high brokerage fees
- price fluctuations
- income tax

The special risks are:
- secondary market cancellation
- market disruptions in the underlying stock
- exercise restrictions
- broker insolvency
- time considerations

BROKERAGE FEES

To begin with, brokerage fees are generally very high for writing and buying stock options. Covered call writers must weigh the cost of these commissions in order to determine their true return on investment. At many full service brokerage houses, the pricing structure does not differentiate between small and large transactions. If someone wrote 2 calls on IBM for $18 each, the brokerage fees would be the same as trading 200 shares of stock at $18 per share.

Discount houses, however, not only have reduced rates but also special incentive rates. For instance, at one brokerage house in New York an option trader can buy or sell up to seven puts or calls, each having premiums under $1, for about $35.

Brokerage fees should be among the last of the criteria an investor uses to select options for covered call writing. The priorities should be to find those stocks that will probably perform as well as or better than the market and then to find over-priced calls on those stocks. There are investment newsletters and services available that will help you find these ideal candidates. Just remember that even a stock selected by a pro does not always perform as expected.

The effect of brokerage fees on a covered call writer's true rate of return must be calculated along with the buy and sell commissions on the underlying stock. For instance, if you purchase 1,000 shares of Harcourt Brace at $10 and sell 10 calls on the stock, you will be burdened with roughly $100 in commissions for the shares and $75 in commissions for the calls. This $175 will be subtracted from the call premiums and stock proceeds whenever you finally account for your positions in the stock and calls.

Sooner or later, you will sell Harcourt. If the stock reaches the striking price before the expiration of the call contract, you will be selling it much earlier than expected. The calls, too, may have to be purchased, if you decide that it is to your advantage to close out your position before the stock makes it into the strike zone. In the examples in previous chapters, there were a number of times when it was advantageous to close out a call and purchase another one, or to close out the call and continue to maintain a position in only the underlying stock.

The high cost of doing business in both the stock and option markets is a sad fact of life for the average, independent investor. Large investors, with either lots of money to invest and/or a great deal of repeat business to offer, can negotiate with brokers for special commission discounts. The small-money trader who buys and sells stocks or options frequently does not have the financial muscle to negotiate with the full-service brokerage firms. He or she generally turns to the widely advertised discount houses whose lower fees can help stretch profits or reduce losses.

PRICE FLUCTUATIONS

Stock movements are highly unpredictable, although the general trends of individual stocks over selected periods may be easily charted. There are always surprises. The stock that seemed to lie stagnant for three years may suddenly plunge or rise in price for reasons that are not immediately apparent to you. Some stocks are highly volatile with wide swings in price. Despite all the formulas that stock watchers devise, the stock on which you have just written a call may suddenly surge. If it surges past the striking price, there is a very good chance it may be called from you. You will have to sell the underlying security to cover your contract obligations. In such cases as this, it is important to find a premium and striking price that, should your stock be called, offer a rate of return that makes the gamble worthwhile. This is not to hint that every time a stock advances past the striking price it is called. Many times a stock will move higher than the striking price, but retreat before the corresponding call is exercised. When this happens near the termination of the contract, however, the stock is almost guaranteed to be called.

Special situations also arise that put sudden upward pressure on the price of the underlying stock. Takeovers or stock buy backs are some examples of news that can make a stock much more attractive to the investment public. One of the most agonizing positions to be in is that of the covered call writer who went after $5 premiums that, in the final result, cost him the opportunity to make a $25 profit on the underlying security.

The point of the discussion is that once your call is in-the-money, you must be aware that at anytime you may be assigned an exercise.

What about these exercise assignments and the necessary settlements that take place frequently on the option exchanges? How do they work?

To begin an explanation of exercise assignments, it is necessary to first underscore the fact that the major exchanges, through which you will do your option trading, are owner/members of the Options Clearing Corporation (OCC). The purpose of the OCC is to provide the means for clearing and settling all option transactions. The OCC is not obligated to any transaction not reported to it by the market in which the trading activity has taken place. It is also free of any obligation if the member market is unable to meet contractual obligations (total net premiums), although its general policy is to do so regardless of whether or not the member market has indeed met its obligations.

Whenever the OCC issues a call or any type of option, it is required to either purchase or sell the underlying stock for whatever happens to be the exercise price. What actually happens, however, is that the OCC passes the responsibility of making account assignments on to your broker, if you are one of the writers of the subject options.

There is always the rare possibility that you will not receive notice of exercise until one or more days after the date when the exercise has taken place. In those cases, when the assignment has taken place on the Friday just before the expiration date, you may have to wait until the following Monday or Tuesday for a report of the assignment. (Remember that options expire on the Saturday after the third Friday of the month of expiration.) It is rare when an option writer receives notice of exercise during market hours the same day that the exercise occurs.

There are two distinct procedures by which your broker may assign exercises to accounts. It is probably a good idea to learn the method your broker uses. The first method is simply a random assignment. The second is a FIFO procedure—first in, first out. Brokers depend on a stock clearing corporation to handle the actual settlements. The clearing corporation does not get directly involved with any broker accounts, however, and it is the broker who handles settlements with the customer.

INCOME TAX

As soon as you receive an option premium, you have taxable income. When you have a paper loss on the stock but premium income, there is no way to reduce the dollars that should be taxed. If you repeatedly write calls on an underlying security that continues to decline, it is very possible that you may have a $5,000 loss on the stock, but a corresponding gain from writing calls. The sad result is that you have to pay taxes on the full amount of the call premiums, despite the fact that the decline in the price of the stock has offset any premium income.

SECONDARY MARKET CANCELLATION

The option markets are specifically structured to assure as much liquidity as possible. This liquidity is important to the success of these markets, for without it investors will lose interest and do their trading in more dependable environments. It is absolutely necessary for option traders to know that they can close out their positions prior to expiration time if they feel it is in their best interest to do so. It is not possible to expect a 100% score in reaching liquidity objectives, however. There just can't be any guarantees.

Too many variables can affect the option markets and result in the cancellation of certain options. These variables include the lack of a market in a particular option or series of options, the decision of one of the exchanges or other markets to discontinue a particular option or series of options or to impose severe restrictions, and the occurrence of over-active markets that make efficient control and administration impossible.

In the first of these variables, liquidity cannot be maintained because investor interest is not present. Like the stock exchanges, the option markets are auction markets. There must be buyers and sellers to keep the markets operative.

In the second, the governing body of the particular option market may deem it in the market's best interest to temporarily postpone or completely cancel options, if for any reason the underlying security's finances become suspect by the OCC, an exchange, or other market. You will find, however, that when any of the option markets find it necessary to discontinue trading in a selected option, they will most likely refrain from doing so until that option has expired.

In the case of over-active markets, the chaos that results from investor enthusiasm or other unexpected events, such as data inaccessibility because of computer network or mainframe breakdowns, necessitates trading halts. The option markets, you will find, are vulnerable to many of the same back room problems that the major stock exchanges face.

While market cancellations in an option or series of options is particularly hazardous to the game plan of naked traders, it also presents a problem to the covered call writer. Whenever a market in a particular option fails, the writer must necessarily wait out expiration or assignment. He or she has no opportunity to change position by entering a closing transaction. This is, of course, an extremely rare situation. If it does occur, however, there is a way out of the dilemma, though it requires a substantial cash investment. The covered call writer who would like to unload the option and just ride the stock, but cannot because of the unavailability of a market, can purchase an equal number of shares in the underlying stock. Then, if the underlying stock does increase markedly in price, the investor is not required to sell the second group of shares at the striking price, as he is for those shares on which the call contract was written.

Market postponement or cancellation of a call can be a very real setback for call writers whose game plan includes a long-term covered call play on the underlying stock, during which they expect to write, buy back, or ride to expiration, then write new calls on the underlying stock. If the availability of the call is cancelled before or after the next expiration date and the underlying stock is well below the original purchase price, the long-term income strategy certainly cannot work. There are no calls for rewriting and the covered call writer is stuck with a paper loss that may have to be turned into a cash loss. Imagine the frenzy covered call writers and other option traders were in when, during the crash of 1987, trading in many stocks was seriously delayed and any option trades had to be done blindly. In one day, put holders tripled and quadrupled their money and naked call writers made hefty short-term income if they closed out their open-positions, while covered call writers, as in the case of those writing calls on Digital, found themselves with badly depreciating stocks that far offset any premium income.

MARKET DISRUPTIONS IN THE UNDERLYING STOCK

Option traders are playing two games at once—the stock market and the option market. This is because stock options are necessarily based on the publicly traded stock of some major corporation. If for any reason trading must be halted in that corporation's stock, the related market for options must also be halted. Trading in a particular stock can be discontinued for any number of reasons, including unusual activity, announcement of a takeover attempt, an actual tender offer, news of liquidation procedures, or filing for reorganization under Chapter 11.

If there is a trading halt in an underlying stock, there is no way of telling what will be the reopening price. When tender offers or bankruptcy filings are the cause of trading halts, the reopening price of the underlying stock often varies by 50% or more. This can create substantial winnings or losses for option holders and writers. If the reopening price is just the beginning of a continued surge in the price of the underlying stock, even more money can be made, lost, or missed. Imagine having 10 in-the-money calls, for which you paid $1.75 each, on Macmillan when it received takeover bids in 1988. You would have quite easily made $25 on each call, thereby turning a $1,750 investment into $25,000 in a period of a few months. Now, think of the opportunity missed by the covered call writer who sold 10 calls out-of-the-money (by $1.75) on Macmillan for 75 cents. The covered call writer would have fared much better, however, than the naked call writer who could quite possibly have lost all his hard-earned cash and maybe a piece of his house when he had to buy the underlying stock at a much, much higher price to cover his obligations to the buyer of his calls.

EXERCISE RESTRICTIONS

There is another time when option traders face the risk of being locked into their positions. This is when the OCC or one of the option markets intervene in normal clearing operations and disallow the exercising of a certain option or series of options in which trading has been halted. When this occurs, both put and call writers and buyers are locked into a kind of financial gordian knot. The knot does not become untied until either the options are once again trading or the exercise restrictions are lifted.

BROKER INSOLVENCY

Brokers do go out of business, but fortunately, customer accounts are protected by the SIPC and most often by additional insurance. Of course, broker insolvency is indeed rare, but it happens. Always know with whom you are dealing. It is important to take a good, hard look at the financial statements for the brokerage firm with which you plan to do business. For your convenience, Table 11-1 gives a partial list of major brokerage houses with which you can easily set up stock and option trading accounts—after you have double-checked their financial health. Remember that sometimes a separate application is required for option trading. Setting up an account with these brokers will not necessarily entitle you to deal in calls.

_____Table 11-1. Some Full-Service and Discount Brokers._____

Brokerage Firm	Discount	Full-Service
Advest		X
Bear Stearns		X
Brown & Co.	X	
Dean Witter		X
Drexel Burnham		X
A.G. Edwards		X
Fidelity Brokerage	X	
Gruntal		X
Edward D. Jones		X
Kidder Peabody		X
Merrill Lynch		X
Thomas McKinnan		X
Norstar Brokerage	X	
Oppenheimer		X
Paine Webber		X
Piper Jaffray		X
Prudential Bache		X
Quick & Reilly	X	
Rose & Co.	X	
Charles Schwab	X	
Shearson Lehman		X
Smith Barney		X

Financial stability should not be the only prerequisite for selecting a broker. There are two other considerations that this author considers necessary. Some brokerage houses require customers to sign a "mandatory arbitration" clause, which simply means you cannot sue your broker if he or she fouls up your account by misinterpreting your instructions or by deliberately making independent transactions in your account. Try to avoid these brokers.

You should also use a brokerage firm that makes it easy to select or change the account representative with whom you want to deal. As reputable as a brokerage firm may be, there are always account executives that overstep the bounds of respectable behavior, treat your orders as though they were simply numerical transactions rather than real money transactions, are constantly trying to sell you on sure things, or want you to set up a discretionary account that allows them to churn your account and rack up commission dollars.

Once a broker gets into financial trouble, the trader may find each and every one of her open positions closed out without warning. There are safeguards that the OCC imposes in such instances to protect investors. Mainly, these have to do with financial requirements for the OCC's member firms. Member firms are required to have a minimum net capital, special margin deposits with the clearing corporation, and a certain amount of their assets as pledged collateral. They are also required to make contributions to the clearing fund. All payments to the clearing fund must be made in cash or with U. S. government-backed securities that meet specific maturity requirements.

12

Correcting Investor Misconceptions

THE OPTION MARKETS WORK VERY DIFFERENTLY FROM OTHER MARKETS, although in some cases there are indeed similarities. By the time an investor is ready to consider option trading, even if it is of a type as safe as covered calls, she often needs to be shaken free of certain misconceptions before there can be any hope of long-term success. We all try to relate new information to our academic or practical experiences. Even an avid student who has plowed through the first 11 chapters of this book will probably arrive at this one with some ideas that are not found in the text. Let's consider some of the misconceptions that often get in the way when someone tries to understand covered calls specifically, and the option markets in general.

COVERED CALL WRITING DOES NOT GUARANTEE PROFIT

A first misconception is that covered call writing guarantees profit. Profit is a tricky word in the investment community. Let's say you invest an equal amount of money in two stocks. You then sell one because it has doubled in price, while the other stock has depreciated by 50%. Have you profited? By all measures, you have only come out even because what you gained on the one stock you lost on the other. From a tax standpoint, however, you have a definite gain on which you must pay income taxes.

With this in mind, consider a covered call writer who earns $1,000 in premiums on, say, ITT stock. If the underlying stock then drops in price by an equal amount, has the writer really profited? What he earned in cash, he lost on paper.

From a tax standpoint, he actually came out a loser. Although he earned $1,000 in premiums, he probably had to pay $280 in income taxes. That means his true return was $720 on the premiums, less $1,000 on the stock. Except in the view of the IRS, that is clearly a $280 loss. Of course, the underlying security may advance in price and the investor may eventually sell at a profit, but the time span may be considerable. With the time value of money being what it is, he is still a loser even if he later sells at a profit.

There is another catch to the idea that covered calls guarantee a profit. Remember that there are in-the-money, at-the-money, and out-of-the-money calls. From the examples presented in earlier chapters, you already realize that even premium income can be wiped out if the relationship between the size of a premium and the striking price is not advantageous. Premium income is usually only safe from eradication when out-of-the-money calls are written. Even writing out-of-the-money calls, however, does not guarantee the elusive thing called profit. The depreciation in the underlying stock can make up for any gains realized from premiums received.

In the final analysis, all that covered call writing guarantees is income—not profit. You must look at the income from premiums in much the same way that you look at dividends from stock ownership. Those dividends are no more than income. They may or may not contribute to your profit, depending on the proceeds received when the stock is sold.

CALL WRITERS ARE NOT PUT BUYERS

A second misconception is that writing a call is the same as buying a put. This is a very common misconception. The confusion is somewhat understandable, based on the fact that call writers make money when a stock goes down and so, too, do put buyers. However, call writers can also make money if a stock goes up, as long as it does not go beyond the striking price. Covered call writers can also make money if a stock stands still. Put buyers, however, do not have these advantages.

Puts and calls are not an easy game to grasp. The best way to enter the put and call market is to start with an understanding of covered calls. Once you have done a half-dozen or so trades, you might want to venture into buying calls, then buying puts. Quite possibly, when you have a great deal of money and a great deal of experience in stock and option trading, you may want to write naked calls and puts. For the short and intermediate term, the very best way to get your investment feet wet is to write covered calls.

The important difference between puts and calls is that a call gives its owner the right to buy 100 shares of a common stock within a clearly defined time period. You already know the basics of this game from reading this text. Additionally, you now realize that what makes call options so attractive is that you do not necessarily have to exercise them to make a profit or cut your losses. You can simply resell them. The other item that makes calls so attractive is the premium income.

The put, on the other hand, gives its owner the right to sell 100 shares of stock within a clearly defined time frame. You would use a put in the following manner. If you feel that Digital is about to drop significantly, you would purchase a put. As the stock depreciates in price, the put will increase in price, particularly if it is an in-the-money put (the striking price is higher than the price of the stock). (See Table 12-1 for further clarification of money positions for puts and calls.)

As the option game goes, you may either buy or sell options. You are never limited to one position or the other. This holds true for both puts and calls.

_____Table 12-1. Comparative Money Positions for Puts and Calls._____

Stock	Current Price	Striking Price	Put Position	Call Position
Harcourt	$17	$20	In-the-money	Out-of-the-money
Harcourt	$17	$15	Out-of-the-money	In-the-money
Litton	$90	$95	In-the-money	Out-of-the-money
Litton	$95	$92$1/2$	Out-of-the-money	In-the-money
Subaru	$20	$25	In-the-money	Out-of-the-money
Subaru	$25	$20	Out-of-the-money	In-the-money
TCBY	$20	$20	At-the-money	At-the-money

Because a put buyer is betting a stock will go down, he's in-the-money when the striking price is higher than the stock price. Because a call buyer is betting a stock will go up, she's in-the-money when the stock price is higher than the striking price.

WRITING COVERED CALLS IS NOT ALWAYS BETTER THAN BUYING THEM

A third misconception is that writing covered calls is always the smartest way to play the market. If this were true, there would never be any buyers for the options you want to write. The great advantage to covered call writing is the guaranteed income and the chance for minimal capital gains up to the striking price.

The advantage to buying a call is that the owner may possibly make unheard of returns on the investment. It is not unusual for call buyers to see their investments quadruple over a period of weeks, and sometimes to increase as much as ten- or twenty-fold during the life of the option. If the stock does not move within the contract period, however, the buyer could lose his entire investment. Thus the reason for writing covered calls rather than buying calls. There is a lot less risk involved, although the profit potential is severely diminished.

The important thing to remember about calls (and puts as well) is that the longer the life of the call contract, the greater the value of the related call. If the underlying stock has not changed in price as the expiration date approaches, there will be downside pressure on the premiums. This is clearly to the writer's advantage because he can always buy back the calls at the lower price and make a profit in much the same way as he would from any short sale. This is clearly a disadvantage to the the owner of the call, who must not only hope that the underlying security advances in price, but also advances enough to make up for the downside pressure resulting from the diminishing lifetime of the contract.

COVERED CALL WRITING IS NOT BETTING AGAINST YOURSELF

A fourth misconception is that when an investor writes a covered call he is saying that he does not expect his stock investment to pay off. This is hardly the case. The covered call writer is actually covering his bases, but this is not the same as betting against himself.

The returns that smart money can realize from writing covered calls are, over the long term, usually much better than those that naked investors of either stocks or options realize over the same period. There are some exceptions, of course, because the nature of the stock and option markets assure unusual opportunities for those who are in long or short positions at the right time.

An average annual gain of approximately 15% is often realized by professional investors who use covered call strategies. In some cases, annual gains for this same smart money group approach the 25% mark, although in unusual years like 1987, the gains could be single digit. Value Line, Inc., which provides investment advice to its subscribers, has recorded statistics that show that from 1978 to 1982 its covered option writing recommendations averaged about a 36% gain. For the period from 1983 to 1987 they averaged about 24%. It must be remembered, however, that buyers of calls during those periods sometimes saw their entire investments wiped out. At other times they saw their investments multiply.

Covered call writing is not betting against yourself. Rather it is a strategy used by the astute investor who wants to keep the underlying security for one reason or another while increasing the return on his investment.

PREMIUMS VARY IN RELATION TO STOCK PRICES

A fifth misconception is that premium values for different stocks are determined using the same ratio. This is rarely true. Premiums for individual equity options, regardless of their money positions, are always affected by a number of variables that seem to weigh differently for different stocks. A simple check of the option listings in your favorite financial paper or the financial section of a daily newspaper will indicate how much the stock price/option premium ratios differ for equity options with the same expiration dates.

Among the factors that determine an option's premium are, of course, the relationship between the striking price and the market price of the underlying stock, the time remaining until contract expiration, current interest rates, and the price movement and volatility of the underlying stock.

STOCK SPLITS DO NOT MEAN HIGHER OPTION COVERAGE

A sixth misconception is that a stock split means that the option holder has a contract on a greater number of shares. If a stock were to be split in a 2 for 1 ratio, many option holders expect that each option they have will represent twice as many shares.

To begin with, it is important to understand that a stock split is basically a marketing gimmick. It does not change the shareholder's proportion of ownership in the corporation. The main reason for a corporation to split its stock is to reduce the price to a level that will attract a greater number of investors. It's a play on the supply and demand seesaw. The lower price is expected to create a greater level of demand. As demand increases, then the price should also increase. What usually happens over the short term is that the price of the stock rises after the split is declared, then falls after the split takes place. What happens over the long term depends on how the stock continues to hold up under investor scrutiny.

From an accounting standpoint, the stock split is simply a numbers game that does not actually change the value of the shareholder's equity in the corporation. The par value of each share is reduced in the same proportion as the split. A two for one split means a one to two change in the par value of the stock. If you have 100 shares of a $10 stock before the split, you have 200 shares of a $5 stock afterwards.

A little math tells you that you have no more or less than you had before. However, if the dividends per share are increased, you will suddenly receive additional income from your holding. Should the shares increase in price, the rewards are even greater because you now have twice as many shares that will benefit from each improvement in price. If the stock decreases, however, then you are losing money on twice as many shares.

When the stock on which you have written a call splits, do not expect the option to represent a greater number of shares. Rather expect that the exercise price and the number of options will be adjusted accordingly.

OPTIONABLE STOCKS ARE AVAILABLE OVER THE COUNTER

A seventh misconception is that optionable stocks are only available for stocks on the major exchanges. This is clearly not true because there are a number of frequently listed, optionable stocks also available in the over-the-counter (OTC) market. Theoretically, you should be able to trade options on almost any stock. It is far more convenient, however, to find buyers and sellers in the major market places.

Should you consider stocks that are not listed on the major exchanges as underlying issues for your writing efforts? The answer to this question is both yes and no. The governing rule for beginners should be to stay clear of options on foreign stocks that are traded on the foreign exchanges and to remain clear of OTC options. Some stocks that are listed on the OTC market, however, have their options listed on the U. S. option exchanges. These last stocks are clearly worthy of consideration.

"MOST ACTIVE" DOES NOT MEAN "BEST"

An eighth misconception is that options that appear on the most active lists are the best investment because big money always knows which options are the winners. Don't bank on this philosophy.

One of the really nice things about playing either the stock, option, commodity, or any of the other financial markets is that you do not have to put up your money to test a theory. Whatever game you want to play, whether it is writing calls or buying stock, you can always play on paper. Tomorrow or the next trading day, you can test out this misconception. Look at the option listings and note the boxed sections indicating the most active options (see Fig. 12-1). Then track these until the contracts expire and take a count of those that increase and decrease in price. You will find that most active does not mean best buy all the time. Remember, too, that most of the more advanced investment strategies involving volatile stocks require the purchase of both puts and calls at the same time. If the stock falls, the investor makes money on the puts. If it climbs, the investor makes money on the calls.

STOCKS CAN ALWAYS GO LOWER

A ninth misconception is that optionable stocks that are at new lows are the best gamble for covered call writing. When a stock reaches a new low, the only things you can be sure of are that:

- most of the people who had been buying the stock long are now losing—or have actually lost—a great deal of money;
- put buyers, naked call writers, and short sellers have been making money;

MOST ACTIVE EQUITY OPTIONS

CBOE

CALLS

Name	Sales	Last	Chg.	N.Y. Close
I B M Aug115	22040	9⅛	− 2⅛	123¾
I B M Aug125	20257	1 9-16	−15-16	123¾
I B M Aug130	13724	⅜	− 7-16	123¾
I B M Aug120	13029	4¾	− 1¼	123¾
Polar Aug45	7801	½	− ½	41¼
Polar Aug40	7406	2¼	− 1⅛	41¼
M C I Oct17½	6544	1	− ¼	16⅝
Zayre Aug22½	6273	½	− 3-16	21¾
I B M Sep130	5690	1⅝	− 9-16	123¾
Ford Aug50	5009	4	+ ½	53¾
I B M Sep120	4779	6½	− 1	123¾
Boeing Aug50	4718	12⅜	+ 1⅞	62¼
Boeing Aug45	4698	17¼	+ 1⅝	62¼
Ford Sep50	4499	4¾	+ ½	53¾
RJR Nb Aug45	4450	6½	+ ⅝	51⅜

PUTS

Name	Sales	Last	Chg.	N.Y. Close
I B M Aug125	11275	2 5-16	+ 1-16	123¾
I B M Aug120	9297	⅝	− 3-16	123¾
A E P Aug30	8322	3	+ ¼	27⅜
I B M Aug115	3445	3-16	− 1-16	123¾
Mobil Aug50	2610	5¾	− ½	45
I B M Sep120	2421	1¾	+ 1-16	123¾
Polar Aug40	1912	13-16	....	41¼
Chryslr Aug22½	1824	3-16	− ⅛	23⅜
Walmrt Sep30	1783	⅜	− ⅛	32⅛
I B M Aug130	1777	6⅜	+ ¾	123¾
I B M Sep125	1529	3¾	+ ⅜	123¾
Ford Aug50	1510	3-16	− 3-16	53¾
I B M Oct110	1455	¾	+ 1-16	123¾
Hewlet Aug50	1438	1½	+ 7-16	49¼
I B M Oct120	1344	2 9-16	+ ⅛	123¾

NYSE

CALLS

Name	Sales	Last	Chg.	N.Y. Close
VF Cp Sep30	2667	2¾	+ 1⅞	31¾
Maytag Aug25	2476	⅝	+ ¼	23⅝
VF Cp Nov30	2434	3⅜	+ 2	31¾
Trnsco Nov22½	2200	11¾	+ 7⅞	34⅛
VF Cp Aug30	2142	2	+ 1⅝	31¾
Trnsco Nov30	1884	5¼	+ 2¼	34⅛
Trnsco Sep35	1629	1	+ ½	34⅛
Maytag Sep25	1584	1⅛	+ ⅜	23⅝
Trnsco Aug30	1107	4	+ 2¼	34⅛
Maytag Aug22½	799	1⅞	+ ½	23⅝
Nynex Aug65	733	1¼	+ ⅛	65½
Maytag Oct25	713	1⅝	+ 7-16	23⅝
VF Cp Sep35	704	¾	....	31¾
VF Cp Aug35	703	⅜	+ 5-16	31¾
ConFrt Sep30	614	3⅝	− ¼	33⅛

PUTS

Name	Sales	Last	Chg.	N.Y. Close
VF Cp Aug30	750	½	− 2	31¾
ConFrt Sep30	200	5-16	− 9-16	33⅛
Shearsn Dec20	200	½	− ½	24¼
Maytag Sep22½	198	⅞	− 3-16	23⅝
Mellon Sep30	125	1⅜	+ ⅛	28⅞
Mellon Dec25	100	7-16	− 1-16	28⅞
Trnsco Nov30	100	⅞	− ⅝	34⅛
CSoup Aug25	93	⅛	− ⅜	27⅛
Maytag Aug25	85	1½	− ⅞	23⅝
Maytag Oct22½	84	1¼	− ½	23⅝
Maytag Aug22½	83	⅜	− 3-16	23⅝
IrvBk Aug65	78	½	+ ⅛	67
JRiver Sep25	65	1⅛	− ⅛	24⅜
IrvBk Oct65	56	3⅜	+ ⅛	67
CSoup Sep30	53	3	....	27⅛

AMEX

CALLS

Name	Sales	Last	Chg.	N.Y. Close
Tennco Aug45	9778	3½	+ ⅜	48½
Gillet Aug40	8594	1-16	−15-16	35⅞
Tennco Aug40	7487	8½	....	48½
Bally Aug20	7189	3¼	+ 1⅜	23
G T E Aug40	6616	1⅛	+ ⅝	41
Bally Aug22½	6598	1⅛	+ 9-16	23
Pillsby Aug40	6266	5-16	− 1-16	37⅛
Gillet Sep40	6214	7-16	−1 11-16	35⅞
Am Exp Aug30	5835	¼	+ 1-16	28⅞
Gillet Sep35	5141	1 15-16	−3 13-16	35⅞
G T E Sep40	4966	1¼	+ 5-16	41
Am Exp Oct30	4421	1⅛	+ ¼	28⅞
Pillsby Sep40	4231	1⅛	....	37⅛
Pillsby Aug35	4197	2¼	+ ¼	37⅛
Texaco Sep50	3931	13-16	− 3-16	47⅛

PUTS

Name	Sales	Last	Chg.	N.Y. Close
Dig Eq Aug105	3027	2⅞	+ ⅝	103⅜
Gillet Aug40	2777	4¼	+ 3¼	35⅞
Gillet Sep35	2316	1¼	+13-16	35⅞
Dig Eq Aug100	2295	⅞	+ 1-16	103⅜
Gillet Sep40	2266	4¾	+ 3⅛	35⅞
Chevrn Aug55	2042	7⅛	....	47
Zenith Aug22½	1735	1	+ ⅛	22
Kroger Aug35	1505	⅞	− ⅝	33¾
Gillet Aug35	1330	½	+ 5-16	35⅞
Texaco Oct55	1291	7½	− 1¼	47⅛
Bally Aug22½	1272	9-16	− 7-16	23
Dig Eq Oct105	1215	5⅝	+ 1⅛	103⅜
Pillsby Aug35	1171	⅛	− 7-16	37⅛
Texaco Aug45	1072	⅛	− ⅜	47⅛
PhilPt Aug17½	1055	3-16	− 3-16	17⅞

PHIL

CALLS

Name	Sales	Last	Chg.	N.Y. Close
FtHowP Aug55	29923	¼	− 1⅛	53⅛
FarmGp Aug55	14072	2⅜	− ⅛	54
FtHowP Sep55	12979	¼	− 1½	53⅛
McGHll Aug70	12329	1⅞	+ ⅜	67¼
McGHll Aug65	9739	4½	+ 1½	67¼
FtHowP Dec55	7298	5-16	−1 11-16	53⅛
QkrOat Sep55	7092	1 7-16	....	51¼
F N M Aug50	6367	⅝	+ ¼	48¾
A Hess Aug25	5100	2⅝	− ½	27⅜
FarmGp Aug60	4955	⅞	− ⅛	54
QkrOat Sep50	4834	3⅜	+ 2⅜	51¼
A Hess Nov25	4656	3⅜	− 1⅜	27⅜
QkrOat Aug50	4299	2 1-16	+ 1½	51¼
McGHll Sep70	4067	3⅞	+ 1⅜	67¼
FtHowP Mar55	3870	5-16	....	53⅛

PUTS

Name	Sales	Last	Chg.	N.Y. Close
QkrOat Aug50	2858	1	− 6⅛	51¼
LomNF Sep22½	2750	4½	− ½	19
McGHll Aug65	2674	1¾	− 1	67¼
FarmGp Aug55	2545	3⅞	+ ½	54
FarmGp Aug50	2194	1⅝	+ ⅝	54
Abbt L Nov45	1621	1 3-16	− 7-16	46⅜
Abbt L Aug45	1199	5-16	− 7-16	46⅜
McGHll Aug70	1035	4½	− 1	67¼
Duk Pw Aug50	1000	5¼	....	45⅝
SupVal Oct22½	1000	1 9-16	−15-16	21¾
QkrOat Sep50	990	1⅝	....	51¼
FtHowP Aug50	967	⅛	....	53⅛
McGHll Aug60	911	5-16	−11-16	67¼
Anheus Sep30	868	1	− ½	29⅞
A Hess Aug25	808	1-16	− 1-16	27⅜

PACIFIC

CALLS

Name	Sales	Last	Chg.	N.Y. Close
AmPres Aug35	10165	9-16	− 3-16	31¼
AmPres Oct35	7611	1¾	− ¼	31¼
AmPres Sep35	6298	1¼	− 1-16	31¼
AmPres Aug30	4404	2	− ½	31¼
AmPres Oct40	4174	9-16	− 3-16	31¼
SmkB Aug50	3888	1 1-16	+13-16	49¾
SmkB Sep50	3255	1⅞	+1 5-16	49¾
Compaq Aug60	2998	1 1-16	− 3-16	58¾
DataGn Sep20	2451	15-16	− 3-16	18⅞
AmPres Oct30	2108	3⅞	+ ⅛	31¼
GMills Sep50	2096	1½	+ ¾	49½
GMills Aug50	1993	⅝	+ ⅜	49½
SmkB Aug45	1962	4¾	+ 3	49¾
PerkEl Dec25	1885	1¾	+ ⅝	24⅜
AmPres Sep30	1801	3	− ¼	31¼

PUTS

Name	Sales	Last	Chg.	N.Y. Close
Micrsft Aug55	1961	2⅝	+2 1-16	53½
Compaq Aug60	1899	2¼	− ⅝	58¾
Micrsft Aug60	1549	6½	+ 4½	53½
Compaq Aug55	1392	⅜	− ½	58¾
AmPres Aug30	1100	11-16	− 1-16	31¼
SunMic Aug35	952	3-16	−11-16	38⅜
Micrsft Aug75	921	21½	+ 6	53½
AmPres Sep30	871	1⅜	+ ⅛	31¼
Gentch Aug25	861	1⅜	− ⅛	24
SmkB Aug45	812	3-16	− ⅜	49¾
Cray Sep75	757	1	....	81
AmPres Oct30	726	2	+ ½	31¼
Micrsft Aug70	724	16½	+ 6⅛	53½
AmPres Aug35	669	4¾	....	31¼
JiffyL Oct10	664	1⅜	+13-16	9⅝

Fig. 12-1. Comparative money positions for puts and calls.

- put writers have been losing money drastically; and
- covered call writers may or may not be losing money overall, even though premium income has been steady.

As for the future direction of the stock, there is nothing on which to base any assumptions unless you have just had an expert look at the technical basis and fundamentals that are directing investor influence. Stocks can always go lower. In fact, they may go lower much faster than they go higher. Rolling down the hill is always easier than climbing back up even in terms of stock movement. And if you have purchased stock on margin, you may not be in a position to benefit from any turnaround.

PUTS AND CALLS ARE NOT ON A SEESAW

A tenth misconception is that calls may be expected to move in the opposite direction of puts because puts increase with depreciating prices and calls increase with appreciating prices. The option investor who counts on this philosophy during any time in his investment career is going to be sadly disappointed. Calls and puts on stocks moving in a very narrow range may each depreciate at the same time.

With each and every option, the forces of supply and demand affect premiums. The expiration date also increases the decay of both calls and puts. There might very well be a predictability between in-the-money puts and in-the-money calls, but there is not usually a correlation between at- or out-of-the-money options.

Take for instance an underlying stock that is remaining within a fraction-of-a-point trading range. Puts and calls will each be declining in price because the biggest influence on the options are the approaching expiration dates.

STOCKS ARE NOT ALWAYS CALLED IMMEDIATELY

An eleventh misconception is that the underlying stock is always called as soon as it moves far enough beyond the striking price to make exercise profitable. The truth of the matter is that very often a stock will move into and then retreat out of the strike zone without ever having been called. As a matter of fact, it is relatively rare for a stock to be called before expiration time. From an option pricing standpoint, the only time it is really advantageous to exercise an option is on dividend or expiration dates. So the chance of your stock being called before *the expiration date* is very slim.

OPTIONS HOLDERS HAVE NO RIGHTS TO DIVIDENDS DECLARED

A twelfth misconception is that investors should not sell covered calls because once they do so, any dividends declared are paid to the option holder instead of the stock holder. This is never the case. Option buyers do not have any legal right to declared dividends. Dividends always go to the shareholder. Remember that option holders only have a right to buy or sell a stock at an agreed upon price.

COVERED CALL PORTFOLIOS ARE
EASILY MANAGED AS WELL AS EASILY STARTED

A thirteenth misconception is that covered call writing requires a great deal of portfolio management, as well as being difficult to set up. The truth is really quite the opposite. By consistent attention to stock and option movement, it is possible to extract extra income dollars from option premiums. Covered call writing in its most elementary application, however, requires simply selling a call on the stock you own and maintaining both positions—owner of the stock and seller of the call—until the contracts expire or the stock is called.

Covered call portfolios are also relatively easy to set up. The first way is to begin writing calls against stocks that you already own. The second way is to find stocks that lend themselves to a covered call strategy and to purchase them when their calls offer above average returns. There are a number of investment services or brokerage firms that offer advice on option trading that can be of special service to you. When you establish a covered call portfolio following this procedure, you sell the options immediately upon buying the underlying stock.

NAKED WRITING CAN BE DANGEROUS AS WELL AS PROFITABLE

A fourteenth misconception is that naked writing is the smarter way to go because covered call writing requires too much of a cash outlay. In fact, while the investor who writes naked calls more often than not finds winners, losers easily make up for any previous gains.

Consider for a moment two investors, one a covered call writer by the name of Pamela Lynn and the other a naked call writer by the name of Judd Palladin. Pamela purchases 1,000 shares of Harcourt Brace at $10,000 and sells 10 out-of-the-money calls available at a $2 premium. Her income is $2,000. Suppose that Harcourt jumps to $20 per share and the calls increase in value to $20. Now in-the-money, the options are exercised and Pamela has to cover her position by delivering 1,000 shares of the underlying stock. There is no problem because she already owns the shares. She cannot take advantage of the jump in the price of the stock, but she does not lose any money except for what she might have to pay in commissions. Meanwhile, she has made $2,000 on the calls.

Assume Judd wrote 10 at-the-money naked calls on Harcourt when the stock was at $10, and that he too, received $2,000 in premiums. When the options and the stock each rose to $20, the stock was called. Judd had to purchase 1,000 shares of Harcourt at $20 and sell it at $10, for a loss of $10,000.

The naked put writer runs into a similar hazard, only she is taking a gamble that the underlying stock will move upward. For instance, if Pamela writes a $1 put on Harcourt that has a striking price of $10, she is betting that Harcourt will stay at $10 or above. If Harcourt shares fall below $10—say to $5—the put may be exercised and she will have to sell the stock at $10 and buy it back at $5, for a $5 per share loss.

In both call and put writing, margin requirements would probably necessitate that both Pamela and Judd deposit additional money in their accounts long before the exercise date arrived. Otherwise the broker would sell the losing puts or calls to prevent continued losses that might not be covered by the writer.

As a front-page story in the December 2, 1987 *Wall Street Journal* (by staff reporters Scott McMurray and Jeff Baily) reported, some investors during the October debacle lost every penny they had. The story was about naked put trading and tells of one investor who lost $360,000. When options go the wrong way, naked writers can lose their money very fast. As the article reports, however, the independent investor was not the only one to suffer. The larger brokerage houses also were hit hard, particularly Charles Schwab, when the company could not move in time to cover a $15 million dollar loss in one account. Schwab was lucky, however. Some brokerage firms were lost forever during the October crash. Professional traders were hit hard, also. The same *Wall Street Journal* story tells of a pro who moved too late to cover his put positions, thereby losing more than $50 million.

OPTION LISTINGS ARE NO MORE THAN HISTORICAL RECORDS

A fifteenth misconception that many investors harbor is that option listings contain all the data one needs to make a decision whether to buy or write. Option tables that list striking prices, exercise dates, and premiums are simply score sheets of the previous day's trading activities. The information contained in these fact sheets can certainly help the watchful investor spot certain options that offer unusual returns, but there is certainly not enough data in the listings to encourage anyone to place an order without doing some detailed research into the fundamentals and trendlines of the underlying stock. Covered call writers want to write calls on stocks that will do as good as or slightly better than the market in general. If they write calls on stocks that plummet, they have made a poor decision on the underlying stock. If they write calls on stocks that skyrocket, they have also made a poor decision. Thus, they must know something about the stock market's prospects in general, as well as specifics on the underlying stock.

13

10 Basic Rules for Call Option Writers

EVERY AUTHOR AND FINANCIAL ADVISOR PROBABLY HAS HIS OWN SPECIAL ADVICE for those considering writing calls, whether naked or covered. While some may want to see the list of recommendations below expanded, few would probably want to delete any of them.

1. Be sure you understand the goals of writers as well as buyers of calls. To begin with, every option speculator who includes covered calls in her strategy has at least one of the following goals in mind. She is eager to squeeze a fairly high income from her portfolio, whether it consists of one stock or many. She wants to diversify her portfolio in a way that will ensure possible gain even in possum or slightly bearish markets. She wants to ensure her positions by eliminating some of the downside risk.

    The call buyer, on the other hand, wants to get an unusually high return from a relatively small investment. She wants to be able to take positions in highly promising stocks that she could not otherwise afford. For the cost of $2 or $3 options, she can gamble on stocks that sell for $200, $300, or more per share. She wants to be sure that her losses will be no more than what she had to put up to purchase the calls in the first place.

2. Understand the basic terminology used in option trading. There are nine basic terms to master. They are, admittedly, confusing at times. The first and second, of course, are put and call options. A put option is one that gives the owner the right to sell the underlying security at a

fixed price. The call option gives the owner the right to buy the under-lying security at a fixed price. The third word—writer—refers to the seller of an option.

The fourth term refers to the date on which the option expires and is the expiration date. The striking price is the fifth term. It refers to the price at which the owner may buy or sell the underlying stock according to the option agreement. It is also sometimes called the exercise price. The sixth is the date on which the option contract expires. It is the expiration date. The seventh is the price at which the option is selling or the premium. The eighth term refers to the seller of a call who also owns the underlying stock. This term is covered writer. The ninth refers to a seller who does not own the underlying stock. The term is naked writer, or uncovered writer.

3. Understand that it is the premiums at which options are available that drive the option markets. If premiums are high relative to the striking price, exercise date, interest rates, and the difference between stock and striking price, then the option markets will be stagnant. When those premiums are high enough to attract writers, yet low enough to excite buyers, then the option markets are in full swing.

Option buyers are looking for outstanding returns on their invest-ments. They buy and sell options with the same strategy that stock investors buy shares in what they believe will be top performing stocks. They want to make money on the difference between the purchase and selling prices.

In some cases, though certainly not many, buyers of options are not as interested in trading options as they are in eventually acquiring the underlying security. For instance, an investor may be very inter-ested in owning a few thousand shares of Aetna Insurance, but she does not have the money to make the purchase and will not have it for, per-haps, six months. She could probably borrow the money and then buy on margin, but that's a dangerous situation. It provides a great deal of leverage because it is borrowed money on top of borrowed money, but whenever an investor is highly leveraged, she is also in harm's way. Instead of borrowing, she purchases calls, preferably in-the-money calls if she can afford them, or out-of-the-money calls if she's going for a big win.

4. Be sure you have a basic understanding of economics so you can evalu-ate whether or not it is the correct time for you to invest. You will also need to understand what stocks may do better than the market in gen-eral. Necessary to this basic understanding of economics is knowledge of the business cycle and its periods of expansion and contraction, knowledge of how interest rates effect common stock prices, knowl-

edge of inflationary signs, and how inflation can defeat many investment strategies. There are clearly times when you will want to hoard cash, as well as times when you may want to be more than 50% invested. A lot has to do with the opportunity cost of money and what opportunities will present themselves in the near future.

For instance, if six-month certificates of deposit are paying 10% per annum, you may be very wise to go after that kind of return. You will not be considered wise, however, if you go after that interest rate if it is anticipated that one month down the line certificates will be paying 12%. The same logic applies to the stock market. If stocks are going to be even cheaper six months down the line, then do not invest now. Sell short, if you must do something. That means also consider puts.

5. Know the underlying stock. Every stock that is listed on the option exchange is worth investigating. The problem is, just how should you play your investment. Some stocks are fine long-term candidates because they are going to out perform the market even when the market looks as though it is going to go up. Others are short-term candidates because they will not perform as well as the market. Historically these fall far faster than the indexes. Still others are put or call candidates because they move over short periods of time, and therefore move within the contract periods of longer-term options. Bear in mind, however, that buying puts or calls and selling short are still highly risky investment strategies.

A basic understanding of economics means knowing how to read financial reports, particularly balance sheets and profit and loss (P&L) statements. It also means knowing something about technical analysis, although it is generally much easier to subscribe to a service that charts stocks for you. Keep the trendlines for stocks whose fundamentals you like handy. This makes it much easier to decide whether to purchase or sell at any given time.

6. Never select the underlying stock on which you wish to trade options by yourself. Always subscribe to at least two newsletters, one of which may be published by your broker. As a matter of fact, all of the larger brokerage houses publish investment guides and newsletters and make them available free or for relatively low subscription rates. These are not only ideal for spotting worthwhile investments, but the publications are also an education in stock investing. Very often, each of the newsletters you subscribe to will have a different buy or sell recommendation for the particular stock or stocks in which you are interested. The more an astute investor reads the contradictory information, the more likely he or she will receive it as a signal to stay away, unless he or she knows which source to trust.

7. Know your goals. Remember that an option buyer or writer has many choices to make. There are always different options available on the same underlying stock, each with different striking prices, premiums, and expiration dates. You may use any one of three strategies when trading options, or mix them throughout your portfolio. You may simply hedge your bet and look for enough in premiums to protect your account from price depreciation in the underlying security or securities. You may only be interested in achieving the highest possible income. Or you may be primarily interested in seeing price appreciation in the underlying security, with the additional income from writing calls simply an income supplement. For each of these strategies, you will be interested in writing different types of calls (see Table 13-1).

8. Keep tabs on your calls. It is true that one of the nice features of covered call writing is that you do not have to be constantly checking the papers to see if you are showing a gain or loss. You do not even have to pay special attention to expiration dates. From a very practical standpoint, however, a constant check on the prices of your written calls will help you increase your annual rate of return. Paying attention to major price fluctuations enables you to buy back and write again whenever it is profitable for you to do so.

9. Diversify, even if you are only interested in covered call strategies. If your financial position makes it possible, have at least three stocks on which you write covered calls. This way you can try to time your writing so that you receive additional premium income each month. Portfolio diversification also reduces your risks on the underlying stock. If Harcourt goes down, and it is your only stock, then your portfolio goes down. If you hold both Harcourt Brace and another stock in another industry, however, then you reduce your risk. Then if Harcourt goes down in price, it may or may not affect your overall portfolio.

   Do not diversify to the extent that you reduce the kind of volatility in your portfolio that makes being in the market worthwhile. If you spread your holdings too thin, you will not be able to sell calls in quantities that make your strategy advantageous. Adequate diversification can usually be achieved with 10 or 15 stocks from a number of industry groups, but generally the small investor does not have the money to spread over even this number of stocks.

10. Read the financial papers and listen to the financial news on radio and television. Keep your eyes and ears open. Stay tuned to the world. Everything of national or international consequence will affect your portfolio in one way or another. As an investor, you are tied into the national or international scene.

Table 13-1. Covered Call Strategies.

Primary Goal	Money Position	Reason
Increase Income	Write at-or near the-money calls	Premiums are high and stock may not be called.
Price Appreciation	Write out-of-the-money calls	Premiums offer some income and the striking price is high enough tha you will not lose out on a major upswing.
Downside Protection	Write far in-the-money calls	High premiums offer protection for more significant drops.

14

The Option Markets

THE OPTIONS CLEARING CORPORATION (OCC) TO WHICH YOU WERE BRIEFLY introduced in an earlier chapter, is regulated by the Securities and Exchange Commission (SEC). The OCC is an incorporated business whose stock is owned by the stock exchanges that create the secondary markets for options.

THE OPTIONS CLEARING CORPORATION

Founded in 1973, the OCC was specifically designed to facilitate the needs of the Chicago Board Options Exchange (CBOE). As it turned out, the listed option markets began to take off. Investors became aware of the way in which options could help them diversify their portfolios, give them the opportunity for the kind of returns that stocks do not generally offer, and give them additional income. As a result, the stock exchanges began to enter the option marketplace. As would be expected, these stock exchanges saw the need for an organization that would serve as a risk manager, as well as an information management service. The OCC seemed to be the perfect answer to their needs.

As a risk manager in a highly volatile investment game, the OCC functions as the guarantor of all listed option contracts in the United States and, through associate members, as a guarantor of certain options traded in foreign markets. When you write or buy options, you are not actually writing or selling to another trader or even to a broker. You are actually writing for the OCC or buying from the OCC. The clearing corporation has the responsibility for assuring that there are matching positions, and that there are writers and buyers for all options that are traded.

As an information management and premium-settlement service, the OCC serves as the central nervous system for the option markets. It uses the most advanced technology for the purpose of processing and directing incredible volumes of financial data in a short period of time. The OCC distributes hard and soft (computer generated copy transmitted by data or telecommunications processes) copy reports on the previous day's trading activity and price movements, as well as all margin requirements. The OCC manages premium settlements by collecting the necessary money from its membership and using the money to pay the premiums due writers within one hour.

The financial obligations that the OCC amasses each and every day are handled with the utmost efficiency not only because of the internal and affiliate organizations of the OCC, but also because the corporation has set up a unique network of clearing banks to assure liquidity. This banking network consists of more than 200 banks worldwide, with many of these in the United States.

The OCC is governed by a 16-member board of directors. Each of the six participating exchanges and the nine clearing member firms are represented. The sixteenth director is the board chairman and chief executive officer.

MAINTAINING MARKET INTEGRITY

Writer obligations total enormous sums of money. The OCC itself is not directly able to guarantee that the contractual obligations of these writers will be met. This responsibility is left to the many brokerage firms that function as clearing members.

As you learned earlier, clearing members are required to meet stringent financial requirements and must provide the OCC with whatever collateral is necessary to cover a writer's obligations. They are required to contribute to the funds that protect the OCC from a clearing member's inability to cover its positions. Additionally, the clearing members must pay $7^{1}/_{2}$ cents per contract, though they may expect refunds whenever OCC revenues are in excess of that actually needed to meet operational needs and required reserves. These regulations are strictly enforced in order to protect the integrity of the option markets, which in a single day can generate close to 3 million contracts.

The minimum requirement for membership is $150,000 in net capital. On top of this, a member firm must also be a registered broker-dealer under the Securities and Exchange Act of 1934, and must be organized and staffed in a manner sufficient for the orderly and successful execution of trades.

Because the stock and option markets have grown to such an extent that they are no longer primarily national marketplaces, the OCC now allows foreign firms as members. These foreign members are divided into two separate groups: exempt and nonexempt.

Nonexempt members are subject to the same stringent financial rules and reporting requirements as the U. S. members. The exempt members, however, are subject to a qualified set of financial rules and reporting requirements that vary depending upon the country of origin. No one is accepted for membership without on-site financial assessment by the OCC's staff, and without the approval of at least 9 of the 16 members of the board of directors.

Because of the rare combination of speed and precision with which the option markets must function, the OCC has developed a series of special services to further increase the speed of operation and add to the precision. Through these special services, described in following paragraphs, the membership is able to respond with lightening speed and economy to the demands of the marketplace. Through its wholly owned subsidiary, the Intermarket Clearing Corporation, the OCC is able to offer the same programs and services to the futures industry.

The OCC has a service that it calls C/MACS. This is the Clearing Management and Control System, which enables post-trade and expiration activity to be directly received by OCC. What C/MACS does is provide a check on the back office operations of the clearing membership. Through C/MACS, the OCC can perform auditing functions, send inquiries and acknowledge data, and change, delete, or add information to records as required.

Through its DVP service (Delivery Versus Payment Authorization), the OCC simplifies the transfer and delivery of foreign funds. The procedure works in the following manner. Certain banks are given the authorization to join the OCC network and function as a guarantor that all payment of U. S. or foreign funds will be completed on the same day that delivery is made by the OCC's agent bank. This means that all settlement payments can be handled during the normal banking day, thereby preventing the chaos that may result because of short-term liquidity problems on the part of the clearing membership.

Other services designed by the OCC provide its membership with the ability to take advantage of all types of option products and markets. These other option products include foreign currency options, index options, and the U. S. government security options. (See Table 14-1.)

Index options are basically option contracts based on popular stock indexes that are compiled and published by the exchanges and other sources. Debt options are contracts on U. S. Treasury securities that have delivery requirements on the underlying securities, much as do the equity options discussed in this book.

THE MARKETS

The six member-owners of the OCC at this writing are:

- American Stock Exchange (New York),
- Chicago Board Options Exchange (Chicago),
- National Association of Securities Dealers (D.C.),

- New York Stock Exchange (New York),
- Pacific Stock Exchange (San Francisco),
- Philadelphia Stock Exchange (Philadelphia).

Table 14-1. OCC Option Products.

Name	Type	Exchange
American Style Foreign	Foreign Currency	Philadelphia
Computer Technology	Index	American
Equity	Stock	All
European Style Foreign	Foreign Currency	Philadelphia
Financial News Composite	Index	Pacific
Gold/Silver	Index	Philadelphia
Institutional (European Style)	Index	American
Major Market	Index	American
National Over The Counter	Index	Philadelphia
NYSE Beta	Index	New York
NYSE Composite	Index	New York
Oil	Index	American
PSE Technology	Index	Pacific
S&P 100	Index	Chicago
S&P 500	Index	Chicago
U.S. Treasury Bill ($1 million, 13-week)	Debt	American
U.S. Treasury Bond	Debt	Chicago
U.S. Treasury Note (5 year)	Debt	Chicago
U.S. Treasury Note ($100 thousand, 10-year)	Debt	American
Value Line Composite	Index	Philadelphia

The American Stock Exchange was the first to participate with the Chicago Board Options Exchange in the OCC. This was back in 1975. This venture into part-ownership of an option clearing organization represented another major milestone in the history of this important exchange, which has usually taken a backseat to the New York Stock Exchange in terms of stocks listed and traded.

The American Stock Exchange had its humble beginnings back in 1849 when its floor brokers were really trading outside and on the sidewalk. That is where their trading continued, for the most part, until the exchange officially moved indoors in 1921. The original name of the exchange was the New York Curb Exchange. Old-timers in the investment community still sometimes refer to it as The Curb. In option trading, however, it is at the forefront of activity. Table 14-2 lists the options it offers.

Table 14-2. American Stock Exchange Equity Options.

Stock	Symbol	Stock	Symbol	Stock	Symbol
AMR Corp	AMR	Dun & Bradstreet	DNB	Nordstrom	NOQ
ASA Ltd.	ASA	Emerson Electric	EMR	Novo Industrial	NVO
Aetna	AET	Fleetwood Enterprises	FLE	Olin Corp.	OLN
Ahmanson	AHM	GTE Corp.	GTE	Pacific Gas & Electric	PCG
Alaska Air Group	ALK	General Re Corp	GRN	Penney, J.C.	JCP
Alcan Aluminum Ltd.	AL	Gerber Products	GEB	Pfizer	PFE
Alexander & Baldwin	ALQ	Gillette	GS	Phelps Dodge	PD
Amax Inc.	AMX	Glenfed	GLN	Philip Morris	MO
American Brands	AMB	Goodyear	GT	Phillips Pete	PHL
American Cyanamid	ACY	Gould Inc.	GLD	Pillsbury	PSY
American Express	AXP	Grace, W.R.	GRA	Pitney Bowes	PBI
American Family	AFL	Greyhound	G	Prime Computer	PRM
American Home	AHP	Harcourt Brace	HBJ	Primerica	PA
Products		Hercules	HPC	Proctor & Gamble	PG
American General	AGC	Hershey Foods	HSY	Quaker State	KSF
Apollo Computer	APQ	Inco, Ltd.	N	Quantum Chemical	CUE
Apple Computer	AAQ	Intel	INQ	Reebok	RBK
Bally Mfg.	BLY	Intergraph	IGQ	Rohm & Haas	ROH
Battle Mountain Gold	BMG	Kellogg	K	Rorer Group	RHR
Bausch & Lomb	BOL	Kimberly Clark	KMB	Royal Dutch	RD
Bell South	BLS	Kraft	KRA	Santa Fe Southern Pacific	SFX
Browning Ferris	BFI	Kroger	KR	Sara Lee	SLE
Caesar's World	CAW	Lilly	LLY	Seagate	SGQ
Caterpillar	CAT	Lotus	LOQ	Snap on Tools	SNA
Cetus	CTQ	Louisiana Pacific	LPX	TRW	TRW
Chase Manhatten	CMB	Lyphomed	LMQ	Tandem Computers	TDM
Chemical Bank	CHL	Macmillan	MLL	Tandy Corp.	TAN
Chemical Waste	CHW	Manufacturers Hanover	MHC	Telecommunications	TCQ
Chevron Corp.	CHV	Masco Corp.	MAS	Tenneco	TGT
Circus Circus	CIR	Mattel	MAT	Texaco	TX
Coastal Corp.	CGP	Merrill Lynch	MER	Union Carbide	UK
Columbia Gas	CG	Mesa Ltd.	MLP	Unisys	UIS
Conagra	CAG	Micron	PMR	USX	X
Con Edison	ED	Microsoft	MSQ	US West	USW
Contel	CTC	Miniscribe	MYQ	Valero	VLO
Cooper Cos	CIC	Motorola	MOT	Walgreen	WAG
Deere & Co.	DE	Mylan Labs	MYL	Warner Lambert	WLA
Digital Equipment	DEC	National Medical	NME	Wells Fargo	WFC
Disney, Walt	DIS	Enterprises		Wyse Tech	WYS
duPont, E.I.	DD	National Semiconductor	NSM	Zenith	ZE

The Chicago Board Options Exchange, however, is the one that deserves the major credit for taking a haphazard option investment market and coordinating it into a sophisticated, efficient, and credible marketplace. Before the CBOE, buying and writing options was a time-consuming and generally undependable enterprise compared with the buying and selling of stocks on the major exchanges. There was not always the readily available buyer or seller. By setting up option trading in much the same way that other exchanges organized stock markets, the CBOE made a major contribution to the investment community. Its listings are given in Table 14-3.

_____Table 14-3. Chicago Board Options Exchange Equity Options._____

Stock	Symbol	Stock	Symbol
Alexander & Alexander	AAL	Control Data	CDA
Alcoa	AA	Corning Glass	GLW
Allen Group	ALN	Delta Air Lines	DAL
Amdahl	AMH	Diebold	DBD
American Electric Power	AEP	Dow Chemical	DOW
American General	AGC	Eastman Kodak	EK
American Telephone & Telegraph	T	Edwards, A.G.	AGE
Amoco	AN	Exxon	XON
AMP	AMP	Federal Express	FDX
Anadarko Pete	APC	First Boston	FBC
Atlantic Richfield	ARC	First Chicago	FNB
Avon	AVP	Fluor	FLR
Bankamerica	BAC	Ford Motor	F
Battle Mountain Gold	BMG	Forest Labs	FRX
Baxter International	BAX	Freeport McMoran	FTX
Bear Stearns	BSC	Gap	GPS
Bell Atlantic	BEL	Gencorp	GY
Bethlehem Steel	BS	General Dynamics	GD
Black & Decker	BDK	General Electric	GE
Boeing	BA	General Motors	GME
Boise Cascade	BCC	Goodrich	GR
Bolar Pharmaceutical	BLR	Great Northern Nekoosa	GNN
Bristol Meyers	BMY	Great Western Financial	GWF
Brunswick	BC	Grumman	GQ
Burlington Northern	BNI	Gulf & Western	GW
CBS	CBS	Halliburton	HAL
Capital Cities	CCB	Harris	HRS
Chrysler Corp.	C	Heinz	HNZ
CIGNA	CI	Hewlett Packard	HWP
Citicorp	CCI	Hitachi, Ltd.	HIT
Coca Cola	KO	Holiday	HIA
Commonwealth Edison	CWE	Homestake Mining	HM

Stock	Symbol	Stock	Symbol
Honeywell	HON	Payless Cashways	PCI
IC Industries	ICX	Pennzoil	PZL
IBM	IBM	Pepsico	PEP
International Minerals	IGL	Polaroid	PRD
International Paper	IP	RJR Nabisco	RJR
ITT	ITT	Ralston Purina	RAL
Johnson & Johnson	JNJ	Raytheon	RTN
K Mart	KM	Rockwell	ROK
Kerr McGee	KMG	Schkumberger	SLB
LSI Logic	LSI	Sears Roebuck	S
Limited	LTD	Sherwin Williams	SHW
Litton	LIT	Southern	SO
Liz Claiborne	LIQ	Southwest Airlines	LUV
Loews	LTR	Squibb	SQB
MCI	MCQ	Syntex	SYN
May Department Stores	MA	Tandy	TAN
McDonald's	MCD	Teledyne	TDY
Mead	MEA	Texas Instruments	TXN
Medtronic	MDT	Toys R Us	TOY
Merck	MRK	UAL	UAL
Micron	PMR	USG	USG
Middle South Utilities	MSU	Union Camp	UCC
Minnesota Mining & Manufacturing	MMM	United Technologies	UTX
Mobil	MOB	Upjohn	UPJ
Monsanto	MTC	Walmart	WMT
NCR	NCR	Warner Communications	WCI
National Semiconductor	NSM	West Point Pepperell	WPM
Norfolk Southern	NSC	Weyerhaeuser	WY
Northern Telecom	NT	Whirlpool	WHR
Norton	NRT	Williams	WMB
Occidental Pete	OXY	Xerox	XRX
Ogden	OG	Zayre	ZY
Paine Webber	PWJ		

The National Association of Securities Dealers (NASD) has done the same for the trading of over-the-counter (OYC) stocks that the CBOE has done for option trading. Now NASD is one of the six participant organizations sharing ownership of the OCC. (NASDAQ assigns four or more alpha characters to designate OTC stocks, but option access symbols require a maximum of three characters. Thus to access stock prices and their respective options, two sets of characters are required. (See Table 14-4.)

The Pacific Stock Exchange, which was born from the merging of exchanges in Los Angeles and San Francisco, is the largest U. S. exchange outside New York City. Its volume and listings are increasing with each passing year. From

_____Table 14-4. NASDAQ Equity Options._____

NOTE: the first character set is the access code for the underlying security and the second set is the access code for the options.

Stock	*Symbols*	*Stock*	*Symbol*
Alexander & Baldwin	ALEX, ALQ	LIN Broadcasting	LINB, LNQ
American Greetings	AGREA, AGQ	LSI Logic	LLSI, LSQ
Amgen	AMGN, AMQ	Liz Claiborne	LIZC, LIQ
Apollo Computer	APCI, APQ	Lotus Development	LOTS, LDQ
Apple Computer	AAPL, AAQ	MCI Communications	MCIC, MCQ
Applied Biosystems	ABIO, ABQ	Mentor	MNTR, MNQ
Ashton-Tate	TATE, TAQ	Microsoft	MSFT, MSQ
Autodesk	ACAD, ADQ	MiniScribe	MINY, MYQ
Avantek	AVAK, AVQ	NIKE	NIKE, NIQ
CVN	CAVN, COQ	Network Systems	NSCO, NSQ
Cetus	CTUS, CTQ	Nordstrom	NOBE, NOQ
Charming Shoppes	CHRS, CSQ	Novell	NOVL, NVQ
Citizens & Souther	CSOU, CUQ	Pic 'N' Save	PICN, PIQ
Comcast	CMCSA, CCQ	SAFECO	SAFC, SAQ
DSC Communications	DIGI, DIQ	Seagate Technology	SGAT, SGQ
Daisy Systems	DAZY, DAQ	Shared Medical Systems	SMED, SDQ
First Executive	FEXC, FEQ	Subaru of America	SBRU, SBQ
Intel	INTC, INQ	Sun Microsystems	SUNW, SUQ
Integraph	INGR, IGQ	TCBY Enterprises	TCBY, YDQ
Jerrico	JERR, JEQ	Telecommunications	TCOMA, T(
Kemper	KEMC, KEQ	U.S. Health Care	USHC, HC(
Kinder-Care	KNDR, KNQ	Yellow Freight Systems	YELL, YLQ

1978 to 1988, its management struggled to help the exchange carve out a leading position in the option markets, and though it trails most of the other exchanges in option trading, its recent foray into index options with something called the Financial News Composite Index, may bring it the additional prestige it seeks. Most of the equity options available on the exchange are listed in Table 14-5.

The Philadelphia Stock Exchange, which was the first truly organized exchange in the United States (1790), is also one of the smaller U. S. exchanges. It currently lists hundreds of stocks, most of which do not trade in enough volume to find daily listings in news and financial papers. Its equity option program suffered some setbacks in 1985, but since then has been on an upward course. Both equity and index option trading on the exchange have been increasing. (See Table 14-6 for listings.)

The New York Stock Exchange has actually been a part of the investment community since the 1700s and got started shortly after the Philadelphia Exchange. Its beginnings were humble. Its members began conducting business in a cafe called the Tontine Coffee House. In the early part of the nineteenth

Table 14-5. Pacific Stock Exchange Equity Options.

Stock	Symbol	Stock	Symbol	Stock	Symbol
Advanced Micro Devices	AMD	Ethyl Corp.	EY	Polaroid Corp.	PRD
		Foster Wheeler Corp.	FWC	Price Co. (The)	PCQ
Alza Corp.	AZA	Gannett Co., Inc.	GCI	Prime Motor Inns	PDQ
American President Co.	APS	Genentech, Inc.	GEQ	Raychem Corp.	RYC
American Medical Int'l.	AMI	General Mills Inc.	GIS	Reebok Int'l.	RBK
Ames Department Stores	ADD	Genuine Parts Company	GPC	Reynolds Metals	RLM
		Hasbro, Inc.	HAS	Rollins Environment	REN
Applied Biosystems	ABQ	HBO & Company	HBQ	Rubbermaid, Inc.	RBD
Ashton Tate	TAQ	Hilton Hotels	HLT	Ryans Family Steak House	RYQ
Autodesk	ADQ	Hospital Corp. of Amer.	HCA		
Avantek, Inc.	AVQ			Ryder Systems	RDR
Baker Hughes, Inc.	BHI	International Technology	ITX	Safecard Services	SFQ
Bankers Trust NY	BT			Schering-Plough	SGP
Beneficial Corp.	BNL	J.P. Stevens	STN	Scientific Atlanta	SFA
Beverly Enterprises	BEV	Jerrico, Inc.	JEQ	Seagram Co., Ltd.	VO
Borden, Inc.	BN	Jiffy Lube	JLQ	Shared Medical Sys.	SDQ
Bowater, Inc.	BOW	Kinder-Care	KNQ	Shoney's, Inc.	SHQ
British Petroleum	BP	King World Production	KWP	Smithkline-Beckman	SKB
Calfed Co.	CAL	Lockheed Corp.	LK	Sony Corp.	SNE
Carter Hawley Hale	CHH	Lucky Stores	LKS	Southern Cal Edison	SCE
Castle & Cooke	CKE	Mapco, Inc.	MDA	Southwestern Bell	SBC
Centerior Energy	CX	Marion Labs	MEC	Stone Container	STO
Charter Medical	CMD	Marsh McLennan	MMC	Sun Microsystems	SUQ
Circuit City Stores	CC	Maxicare Health	MAQ	Stratus Computer	STQ
Circle K Corp.	CKP	Maxtor Corp.	MXQ	TCBY Enterprises	YOQ
Combustion Engineering	CSP	Maxus Energy	MXS	Teledyne, Inc.	TDY
Comdisco, Inc.	CDO	McDonnell Douglas	MD	Teradyne, Inc.	TER
Compaq Computer Corp.	CPQ	Melville Corp.	MES	Texas Utilities	TXU
CPC International	CPC	Minnetonka	MIQ	3COM Corp.	THQ
Convergent Technology	CVQ	Mitchell Energy	MND	Travelers Corp.	TIC
Cray Research	CYR	Mentor Corp.	MNQ	Tyson Foods, Inc.	TYQ
CSX Corporation	CSX	Microsoft Corp.	MSQ	Unocal Corp.	UCL
Daisy Systems Corp.	DAQ	Monotlithic Memories	MZQ	US Air Group	U
Data General Corp.	DGN	Murphy Oil	MUR	Veeco Instruments	VEE
Dataproducts Corp.	DPC	National Patent	NPD	Wang Labs Class B	WAN
Dayton Hudson Corp.	DH	Nike, Inc. Class B	NIQ	Wendy's Int'l.	WEN
Deluxe Check Printers	DLX	N.Y. Times Class A	NYT	Western Digital	WDC
E Systems Inc.	ESY	Pacific Telesis	PAC	Xerox Corp.	XRX
Echlin Corp.	ECH	Perkin-Elmer Corp.	PKN	Xidex Corp.	XIQ
Echo Bay Mines Ltd.	ECO	Pic 'N' Save	PIQ	Zenith Labs	ZEN
Enserch Corp.	ENS	Philadelphia Elec.	PE		

Table 14-6. Philadelphia Stock Exchange Equity Options.

Stock	Symbol	Stock	Symbol
Abbott Laboratories	ABT	First Executive Corporation	FEQ/FEXC
Air Products & Chemicals, Inc.	APD	Fort Howard Paper Company	FHP
Allied-Signal Inc.	ALD	GAF Corporation	GAF
Amerada Hess Corporation	AHC	General Instrument Corporation	GRL
Analog Devices, Inc.	ADI	General Motors Corp. Class E	GME
Anheuser-Busch Companies, Inc.	BUD	Common	
Archer-Daniels-Midland Company	ADM	GenRad Inc.	GEN
Armco Inc.	AS	Georgia Pacific Corporation	GP
Armstrong World Industries, Inc.	ACK	Gerber Scientific, Inc.	GRB
Ashland Oil Inc.	ASH	Golden West Financial Corp.	GDW
Automatic Data Processing Inc.	AUD	Heileman (G.) Brewing	GHB
Bank of Boston Corporation	BKB	Company Inc.	
Bard (C.R.) Inc.	BCR	Home Depot, Inc.	HD
Becton Dickinson and Company	BDX	Honda Motor Co., Ltd.	HMC
Canadian Pacific Limited	CP	Kaufman & Broad, Inc.	KB
Charming Shoppes, Inc.	CSQ/CHRS	Kemper Corporation	KEQ/KEMC
Church's Fried Chicken Inc.	CHU	Knight-Ridder Inc.	KRI
Cincinnati Milacron Inc.	CMZ	Lehman Corporation	LEM
Clorox Company	CLX	LIN Broadcasting Corporation	LNQ/LINB
Coleco Industries, Inc.	CLO	Lomas & Nettleton Financial	LNF
Colt Industries, Inc.	COT	Corp.	
Comcast Corporation	CCQ/CMCSA	Louisiana Land & Exploration	LLX
Commercial Credit Company	CCC	Lowe's Companies, Inc.	LOW
Commodore International Ltd.	CBU	Lubrizol Corporation	LZ
Communications Satellite Corp.	CQ	MCA Inc.	MCA
Community Psychiatric Centers	CMY	Manor Care, Inc.	MNR
Comprehensive Care Corporation	CMQ/CMPH	Marriott Corporation	MHS
Computervision Corporation	CVN	Martin Marietta Corporation	ML
Consolidated Rail Corporation	CRR	McDermott International Inc.	MDR
Continental Corporation	CIC	McGraw Hill, Inc.	MHP
Detroit Edison Company	DTE	Morgan (J.P.) & Co., Inc.	JPM
Dominion Resources, Inc.	D	Morton Thiokol, Inc.	MTI
Dow Jones & Company, Inc.	DJ	Newmont Mining Corporation	NEM
Dresser Industries, Inc.	DI	Owens-Corning Fiberglas Corp.	OCF
Duke Power Company	DUK	PNC Financial Corporation	PNC
EG&G, Inc.	EGG	PPG Industries, Inc.	PPG
Eastern Gas & Fuel Associates	EFU	Panhandle Eastern Corporation	PEL
Emery Air Freight Corporation	EAF	Parker Hannifin Corporation	PH
FPL Group, Inc.	FPL	Penn Central Corporation	PC
Farmers Group, Inc.	FGQ/FGRP	Petrie Stores Corporation	PST
Federated Department Stores Inc.	FDS	Pittston Company	PCO
Financial Corporation of America	FIN	Placer Dome Inc.	PDG

Stock	Symbol	Stock	Symbol
Pulte Home Corporation	PHM	Tesoro Petroleum Corporation	TSO
Quaker Oats Company	OAT	Texas Eastern Corporation	TET
Rite Aid Corporation	RAD	Textron, Inc.	TXT
Rohr Industries, Inc.	RHR	Time, Inc.	TL
Rothschild (L.F.) Holdings, Inc.	R	Transamerica Corporation	TA
Salomon Inc.	SB	Tri-Continental Corporation	TY
Scott Paper Company	SPP	TYCO Laboratories, Inc.	TYC
Security Pacific Corporation	SPC	USF & G Corporation	FG
Service Merchandise Co., Inc.	SMQ/SMCH	Union Pacific Corporation	UNP
Southland Corporation	SLC	United Telecommunications, Inc.	UT
Stop & Shop Companies Inc.	SHP	United States Shoe Corporation	USR
Subaru of America, Inc.	SBQ/SBRU	Waste Management, Inc.	WMX
Sun Company, Inc.	SUN	Woolworth (F.W.) Company	Z
Super Valu Stores Inc.	SVU		

century, the exchange was located at 40 Wall Street. During the Civil War, when an incredibly new interest in the securities markets was created, traders applied for membership in unheard of numbers, and were turned away. Those turned away, reluctant to be excluded from the lucrative business of brokering stocks and other financial instruments, formed their own exchange, which they called the Open Board of Brokers (OBB). The extraordinary competition that resulted eventually brought a merging of the two exchanges into what is known today as The New York Stock Exchange. The exchange is now listing options on a select number of underlying stocks, as well as offering index options. Its equity option listings may be found in Table 14-7.

Each of these option markets have basically the same goal—to provide an orderly market for the trading of stock, index, and debt options. For the most part, they all function similarly, although there are some differences in their

Table 14-7. New York Stock Exchange Equity Options.

Stock	Symbol	Stock	Symbol
Campbell Soup	CPB	Mellon Bank	MEL
Chubb	CB	Nynex	NYN
Consolidated Freightways	CNF	Safeco	SAQ
Helmerich & Payne	HP	Shearson	SLH
Houston Industries	HOU	Tambrands	TMB
Ingersoll Rand	IR	Telerate	TLR
Irving Bank	V	Transco	E
James Rivers	JR	VF	VFC
Maytag	MYG		

organizations, procedures, and requirements. For instance, according to Joseph K. Mimms, managing director of Options and Index Products for the New York Stock Exchange, "The major distinction for NYSE options is that we combine a specialist system, in which a particular trading unit is charged with the responsibility of maintaining a fair and orderly market in an option with the strengths of a system having competitive options traders, who are similar to market makers."

On the Pacific Stock Exchange, members of the option program have the choice of either being market makers, floor brokers, or both. The market maker is a registered member of the exchange whose responsibilities are to not only make transactions as a dealer-specialist, but also to help ensure that the option trading for which he or she is responsible is conducted with the utmost care and according to guidelines that assure a fair and orderly marketplace. The floor broker is also a registered member of the exchange, but his or her responsibilities are primarily to receive option orders from other members of the exchange.

Market makers or floor brokers must meet stringent exchange and SEC requirements. Anyone wishing to participate in option trading on any exchange must be able to prove that they are of exemplary character and have the financial strength and managerial ability to meet their responsibilities. They must also take a qualifying examination.

The criteria used to select the underlying stocks on which options may be traded is fairly uniform for all exchanges. According to Mr. Mimms, "They relate to shares outstanding, the number of public shareholders, net earnings over the recent past, trading volume in the stock, and financial strength, among other things." These other things include permission from the corporation for an exchange to use its stock as an underlying interest (usually only required for OTC stocks), and the standing of the corporation with the SEC.

Occasionally, the criteria that is used to select an underlying issue changes considerably after a stock is selected for option trading. In this case, the exchange will prohibit the introduction of new puts or calls and limit or cancel all opening orders. Corporate mergers are an exception, however. In this case, the exchanges generally prohibit any trading of options in the underlying stock.

Except in the case of OTC stocks, as mentioned above, it is an extremely rare situation when a corporation whose stock is being considered for option trading has any role in the selection process. Selection is entirely up to the discretion of the exchange's board.

While corporations have legal obligations to holders of their stock or debt instruments, they have absolutely none at all to option holders or writers. The corporation that issues the stock selected by an option market is completely out of the trading picture. Holders of the options have no legal ownership in the corporation, have not purchased the options from the corporation, and have no legal right to bring action against the corporation for any reason related to the writing or selling of puts and calls, unless the intended suit is for false reporting of financial data or events that might have effected the decision to take positions in options in the first place.

TYPES OF ORDERS AND TRADING RULES

The option markets have a series of rules that not only assure the efficient handling of customer orders, but also give option traders a great deal of flexibility in specifying the actual conditions under which orders may be placed.

This flexibility in placing orders is extremely important in the volatile option markets in which the premiums of options can fluctuate by 100% or more in one day. This fluctuation is primarily due to the very low price of options. If you sell a call for $1/4$ of a point, a mere $1/8$ of a point change is a 50% loss on the downside and a 50% gain on the upside.

The types of orders accepted on the exchange floor by option makers and floor brokers are listed below, but investors must bear in mind that some brokers will not accept all of these types of orders. In this case, the investor should quickly change his or her broker because time, price, and other contingency orders are important to the success of option trading, whether someone is a writer or a buyer.

- All or None
- Conditional
- Day
- Fill-or-Kill
- Good-Till-Canceled
- Immediate or Cancel
- Limit
- Market

The all-or-none order is also one frequently used in stock trading. It is an order to the broker that the purchase or sale of an option or security must be in the quantity specified or no order is to be placed. To option traders particularly, who are constantly faced with relatively high commission costs, all-or-none orders are always highly recommended. Many times, in the purchase of low-price options, an investor will find that the commissions exceed the cost of the puts or calls. To the writer of covered calls, this means that if a partial order is placed, any income expected from the premiums is immediately eradicated by the broker's fees.

Conditional, or contingency, orders are placed with the understanding that certain prerequisites must be met before the broker is authorized to execute them. Contingency orders are especially important to option traders because they are actually playing two markets at the same time—the market for the underlying stock as well as the market for the related options. A covered call writer might issue the following conditional order to his broker: "Sell 5 November 30 Calls on XYZ stock as long as the stock is under $14.50." If the stock were higher, and therefore closer to the exercise price, the writer would probably want more money for his gamble, so he places the order to write only on the contingency that the underlying security is below a certain price.

Day orders are those that specify that if the order to the broker is not executed the same day that it is placed, it should be canceled. Generally, any order that is placed with a broker is assumed to be a day order unless otherwise specified. If an order is not going to be for the day, it is specified as a good-till-canceled order. In this case, the order to write or sell remains in effect until the order is canceled, executed, or the contract involved expires. Day orders are generally the most sensible for option traders because each day brings new opportunities or changes in strategy.

The good-till-canceled type of order is an ideal way to give the independent investor timeliness. For instance, if you write a call for $1 and way to buy it back at $1/8, you may miss your opportunity during daily or weekly fluctuations in its price because you are not tracking the option on a minute-by-minute basis. How can you? Your broker can set up a program, however, whereby your account makes the purchase automatically, providing no one else is ahead of you on the list of buyers, as soon as the option drops to the price you have specified.

Fill-or-kill orders must be executed as soon as the floor broker receives them. All-or-none is inherent to fill-or-kill orders. If the broker cannot fill the entire order upon its receipt, then the order is canceled. These are especially important to traders who are investing in a combination of securities or are hard-and-fast speculators requiring immediate action to meet special investment goals. Investors will also use this type of order to take advantage of discount commissions on market orders without having to worry that their order won't be placed until after a sharp rise or decrease in stock price.

There is another type of order that is very similar to the fill-or-kill, it is the immediate-or-cancel order. The difference here is that while the order must be executed as soon as it is received on the floor of the exchange, it need not be filled in its entirety. The balance of the order that could not be executed is canceled. Immediate-or-cancel orders also benefit those traders who want to take advantage of discounted commissions on market orders without having to worry about buying or selling at too high or too low a price.

Limit orders establish a specific price that determines whether or not an order will be placed. For instance, if you are interested in purchasing AT&T stock at a maximum price of $30 per share, you simply inform your broker to buy at $30 or less. If you want to sell at no less than $30 to assure a profit goal, then you inform your broker to sell at $30 or better. These are limit orders and they are an indispensable tool to the investor.

It must be noted, however, that sometimes the actual price you pay or receive will be different from your market order. For instance, by the time your order to sell AT&T at $30 reaches the floor, the stock may be at $31, in which case the stock is sold for your account at an additional one dollar per share. If your order to buy AT&T at $30 per share or less reaches the floor when the stock is at $29, the stock is purchased for your account at $1 per share less. Bear in mind that commissions on limit orders are often higher than on market orders.

Market orders are executed as soon as they reach the trading floor. This type of order is best suited for the long-term investor who is not too interested in a stock's short-term price moves. An option trader is not a long-term investor, but rather a speculator. Even the covered call writer is considered a speculator because she must plan for short-term returns. Thus, market orders are rarely ever recommended for option investors.

Every $1/32$ of a point means a lot to option traders who deal in quantities of low-priced options for which that hundredth of a point can mean a doubling or halving of profits. To a covered call writer, $1/32$ of a point can also mean the difference between whether or not the options she has written are exercised. Few option traders chance market orders. Most brokers will advise against them for option traders.

POSITION AND EXERCISE LIMITS

Exchanges limit the number of contracts on a particular underlying interest that may be written on the same side of the market. This is a total limit and not a limit per investor. For example, notice the following options on the Pacific Stock Exchange and their contract limits.

Security	Position Limits
Advanced Micro Devices	8000
Applied Biosystems	5500
Baker Hughes	8000
Borden, Inc.	5500
CPC International	8000
Data Products	3000
Financial News Composite Index	15000
Teledyne, Inc.	3000
Wang Labs, Class B	8000
Western Digital	5500
Zenith Labs	5500

As you can see, the contract limits vary according to the stock and are not uniform. Index options generally have higher limits than equity options. The determining factor is the kind of market that the exchange feels is most appropriate for the option in question.

Just as there are rules limiting the number of contracts on underlying securities, so too are there rules limiting the total number of options on the same underlying interest for a given period of time. Presently, this period of time is five days.

Appendix A
Optionable Stocks

Stock	Ticker	Exchange
3 Com Corporation	THQ	Pacific Stock Exchange
Abbott Labs	ABT	Philadelphia Stock Exchange
Advanced Micro Devices	AMD	Pacific Stock Exchange
Aetna Life & Casualty	AET	American Stock Exchange
Ahmanson, H.F.	AHM	American Stock Exchange
Air Products & Chemicals	APD	Philadelphia Stock Exchange
Alaska Air Group	ALK	American Stock Exchange
Albertson's Inc.	ABS	Philadelphia Stock Exchange
Alcan Aluminum	AL	American Stock Exchange
Alexander & Alexander	AAL	Chicago Board Options Exchange
Alexander & Baldwin	ALQ	American Stock Exchange
Allied Signal Corporation	ALD	Philadelphia Stock Exchange
Aluminum Co. of America	AA	Chicago Board Options Exchange
ALZA Corporation	AZA	Pacific Stock Exchange
Amax, Inc.	AMX	American Stock Exchange
Amerada Hess	AHC	Philadelphia Stock Exchange
American Brands	AMB	American Stock Exchange
American Cyanamid	ACY	American Stock Exchange
American Electric Power	AEP	Chicago Board Options Exchange
American Express Company	AXP	Chicago Board Options Exchange American Stock Exchange
American Family Corporation	AFL	American Stock Exchange
American General	AGC	Chicago Board Options Exchange
American Greetings	AGQ	Chicago Board Options Exchange

Stock	Ticker	Exchange
American Home Products	AHP	American Stock Exchange
American International Group	AIG	Chicago Board Options Exchange
American Medical International	AMI	Pacific Stock Exchange
American President Companies	APS	Pacific Stock Exchange
American Telephone & Telegraph	T	Chicago Board Options Exchange
Ameritech	AIT	Chicago Board Options Exchange
Ames Department Stores	ADD	Pacific Stock Exchange
Amgen	AMQ	American Stock Exchange
Amoco Corporation	AN	Chicago Board Options Exchange
AMP, Inc.	AMP	Chicago Board Options Exchange
AMR Corporation	AMR	American Stock Exchange
Anadarko Petroleum	APC	Chicago Board Options Exchange
Analog Devices, Inc.	ADI	Philadelphia Stock Exchange
Anheuser-Busch Companies	BUD	Philadelphia Stock Exchange
Apollo Computer	APQ	American Stock Exchange
Apple Computer	AAQ	Chicago Board Options Exchange American Stock Exchange
Applied Biosystems	ABQ	Pacific Stock Exchange
Archer Daniels Midland	ADM	Philadelphia Stock Exchange
Arkla, Inc.	ALG	American Stock Exchange
Armco, Inc.	AS	Philadelphia Stock Exchange
Armstrong World Industries	ACK	Philadelphia Stock Exchange
ASA, Ltd.	ASA	American Stock Exchange
ASARCO	AR	American Stock Exchange
Ashland Oil, Inc.	ASH	Philadelphia Stock Exchange
Ashton-Tate	TAQ	Pacific Stock Exchange
Atlantic Richfield Company	ARC	Chicago Board Options Exchange
Autodesk	ADQ	Pacific Stock Exchange
Automatic Data Processing	AUD	Philadelphia Stock Exchange
Avantek, Inc.	AVQ	Pacific Stock Exchange
Avnet, Inc.	AVT	American Stock Exchange
Avon Products	AVP	Chicago Board Options Exchange
Baker Hughes	BHI	Pacific Stock Exchange
Bally Manufacturing	BLY	Chicago Board Options Exchange American Stock Exchange
Bank of Boston Corporation	BKB	Philadelphia Stock Exchange
BankAmerica Corporation	BAC	Chicago Board Options Exchange
Bankers Trust of New York	BT	Pacific Stock Exchange
Bard C.R. Incorporated	BCR	Philadelphia Stock Exchange
Battle Mtn. Gold	BMG	Chicago Board Options Exchange American Stock Exchange
Bausch & Lomb, Inc.	BOL	American Stock Exchange
Baxter International	BAX	Chicago Board Options Exchange
Bear Stearns	BSC	Chicago Board Options Exchange

Stock	Ticker	Exchange
Becton Dickinson & Company	BDX	Philadelphia Stock Exchange
Bell Atlantic	BEL	Chicago Board Options Exchange
BellSouth Corporation	BLS	American Stock Exchange
Beneficial Corporation	BNL	Pacific Stock Exchange
Bethlehem Steel	BS	Chicago Board Options Exchange
Beverly Enterprises	BEV	Pacific Stock Exchange
Black & Decker Mfg. Company	BDK	Chicago Board Options Exchange
Block (H & R)	HRB	American Stock Exchange
Boeing Company	BA	Chicago Board Options Exchange
Boise Cascade	BCC	Chicago Board Options Exchange
Bolar Pharmaceutical	BLR	Chicago Board Options Exchange
Borden, Incorporated	BN	Pacific Stock Exchange
Bowater, Incorporated	BOW	Pacific Stock Exchange
Bristol-Myers Company	BMY	Chicago Board Options Exchange
British Petroleum	BP	Pacific Stock Exchange
Browning Ferris, Inc.	BFI	American Stock Exchange
Brunswick Corporation	BC	Chicago Board Options Exchange
Burlington Northern	BNI	Chicago Board Options Exchange
Caesars World, Incorporated	CAW	American Stock Exchange
CalFed, Incorporated	CAL	Pacific Stock Exchange
Campbell Soup	CPB	New York Stock Exchange
Canadian Pacific, Ltd.	CP	Philadelphia Stock Exchange
Capital Cities/ABC	CCB	Chicago Board Options Exchange
Carter Hawley Hale	CHH	Pacific Stock Exchange
Castle & Cooke	CKE	Pacific Stock Exchange
Caterpillar	CAT	American Stock Exchange
CBS, Incorporated	CBS	Chicago Board Options Exchange
Centerior Energy	CX	Pacific Stock Exchange
Cetus Corporation	CTQ	American Stock Exchange
Champion, International	CHA	Chicago Board Options Exchange
Charming Shoppes	CSQ	Philadelphia Stock Exchange
Chase Manhattan Corporation	CMB	American Stock Exchange
Chemical Banking Corporation	CHL	American Stock Exchange
Chemical Waste Management	CHW	American Stock Exchange
Chevron Corporation	CHV	American Stock Exchange
Chrysler Corporation	C	Chicago Board Options Exchange
Chubb Corporation	CB	New York Stock Exchange
CIGNA Corporation	CI	Chicago Board Options Exchange
Cincinnati Milacron, Inc.	CMZ	Philadelphia Stock Exchange
Circle K	CKP	Pacific Stock Exchange
Circuit City Stores	CC	Pacific Stock Exchange
Circus Circus Enterprises	CIR	American Stock Exchange
Citicorp	CCI	Chicago Board Options Exchange
Citizen's and Southern	CUQ	American Stock Exchange

Stock	Ticker	Exchange
Clorox Company	CLX	Philadelphia Stock Exchange
Coastal Corporation	CGP	Chicago Board Options Exchange
		American Stock Exchange
Coca-Cola Company	KO	Chicago Board Options Exchange
Coca-Cola Enterprises	CCE	Chicago Board Options Exchange
Colgate-Palmolive	CL	Chicago Board Options Exchange
Columbia Gas System	CG	American Stock Exchange
Combustion Engineering	CSP	Pacific Stock Exchange
Comcast Corporation	CCQ	Philadelphia Stock Exchange
Comdisco, Incorporated	CDO	Pacific Stock Exchange
Commercial Credit Company	CCC	Philadelphia Stock Exchange
Commodore International, Ltd.	CBU	Philadelphia Stock Exchange
Commonwealth Edison Company	CWE	Chicago Board Options Exchange
Communications Satellite	CQ	Philadelphia Stock Exchange
Community Psych Centers	CMY	Philadelphia Stock Exchange
Compaq Computer	CPQ	Pacific Stock Exchange
Comprehensive Care	CMP	Philadelphia Stock Exchange
Computer Associates	CA	Chicago Board Options Exchange
Computer Sciences Corporation	CSC	Chicago Board Options Exchange
ConAgra	CAG	American Stock Exchange
Consolidated Edison Company	ED	American Stock Exchange
Consolidated Freightways	CNF	New York Stock Exchange
Consolidated Natural Gas	CNG	American Stock Exchange
Contel Corporation	CTC	American Stock Exchange
Continental Corporation	CIC	Philadelphia Stock Exchange
Control Data Corporation	CDA	Chicago Board Options Exchange
Cooper Companies	COO	American Stock Exchange
Cooper Industries, Inc.	CBE	American Stock Exchange
Corning Glass Works	GLW	Chicago Board Options Exchange
CPC International	CPC	Pacific Stock Exchange
Cray Research, Inc.	CYR	Pacific Stock Exchange
CSX Corporation	CSX	Pacific Stock Exchange
CVN Companies, Incorporated	COQ	American Stock Exchange
Daisy Systems	DAQ	Pacific Stock Exchange
Dana Corporation	DCN	New York Stock Exchange
Data General Corporation	DGN	Pacific Stock Exchange
Dataproducts Corporation	DPC	Pacific Stock Exchange
Dayton Hudson Corporation	DH	Pacific Stock Exchange
Deere & Company	DE	American Stock Exchange
Delta Air Lines	DAL	Chicago Board Options Exchange
Deluxe Corporation	DLX	Pacific Stock Exchange
Detroit Edison	DTE	Philadelphia Stock Exchange
Diebold, Incorporated	DBD	Chicago Board Options Exchange
Digital Equipment Corporation	DEC	Chicago Board Options Exchange
		American Stock Exchange

Stock	Ticker	Exchange
Disney (Walt) Company	DIS	Chicago Board Options Exchange American Stock Exchange
Dominion Resources, Inc.	D	Philadelphia Stock Exchange
Donnelley (R.R.) & Sons	DNY	American Stock Exchange
Dow Chemical Company	DOW	Chicago Board Options Exchange
Dow Jones & Company	DJ	Philadelphia Stock Exchange
Dresser Industries	DI	Philadelphia Stock Exchange
Dreyfus	DRY	Chicago Board Options Exchange
DSC Communications	DIQ	Chicago Board Options Exchange American Stock Exchange
Duke Power Company	DUK	Philadelphia Stock Exchange
Dun & Bradstreet Corporation	DNB	American Stock Exchange
duPont, E.I.	DD	Chicago Board Options Exchange American Stock Exchange
E-Systems, Inc.	ESY	Pacific Stock Exchange
Eastern Gas & Fuel	EFU	Philadelphia Stock Exchange
Eastman Kodak	EK	Chicago Board Options Exchange
Eaton Corporation	ETN	Chicago Board Options Exchange
Echlin, Incorporated	ECH	Pacific Stock Exchange
Echo Bay Mines	ECO	Pacific Stock Exchange
Edwards AG, Incorporated	AGE	Chicago Board Options Exchange
EG&G, Incorporated	EGG	Philadelphia Stock Exchange
Emerson Electric	EMR	American Stock Exchange
Emery Air Freight	EAF	Philadelphia Stock Exchange
Engelhard Corporation	EC	Chicago Board Options Exchange
Enron Corporation	ENE	Chicago Board Options Exchange
ENSERCH Corporation	ENS	Pacific Stock Exchange
Ethyl Corporation	EY	Pacific Stock Exchange
Exxon Corporation	XON	Chicago Board Options Exchange
Federal Express	FDX	Chicago Board Options Exchange
Federal National Mtg. Assn.	FNM	Philadelphia Stock Exchange
Fireman's Fund	FFC	Chicago Board Options Exchange
First Boston, Incorporated	FBC	Chicago Board Options Exchange
First Chicago Corporation	FNB	Chicago Board Options Exchange
First Executive Corporation	FEQ	Philadelphia Stock Exchange
First Interstate Bank	I	Chicago Board Options Exchange
First Union Corporation	FTU	Pacific Stock Exchange
Fleetwood Enterprises	FLE	American Stock Exchange
Fluor Corporation	FLR	Chicago Board Options Exchange
FMC Corporation	FMC	New York Stock Exchange
Ford Motor Company	F	Chicago Board Options Exchange
Forest Labs	FRX	Chicago Board Options Exchange
Foster Wheeler Corporation	FWC	Pacific Stock Exchange
FPL Group	FPL	Philadelphia Stock Exchange
Freeport-McMoRan, Inc.	FTX	Chicago Board Options Exchange

Stock	Ticker	Exchange
GAF Corporation	GAF	Philadelphia Stock Exchange
Gannett, Incorporated	GCI	Pacific Stock Exchange
Gap (The), Incorporated	GPS	Chicago Board Options Exchange
GenCorp	GY	Chicago Board Options Exchange
Genentech, Inc.	GNE	Chicago Board Options Exchange Pacific Stock Exchange
General Cinema	GCN	Chicago Board Options Exchange
General Dynamics Corporation	GD	Chicago Board Options Exchange
General Electric Company	GE	Chicago Board Options Exchange
General Instrument Corporation	GRL	Philadelphia Stock Exchange
General Mills	GIS	Pacific Stock Exchange
General Motors Class E	GME	Philadelphia Stock Exchange
General Motors Corporation	GM	Chicago Board Options Exchange
General Re	GRN	American Stock Exchange
GenRad, Incorporated	GEN	Philadelphia Stock Exchange
Genuine Parts Company	GPC	Pacific Stock Exchange
Georgia-Pacific Corporation	GP	Philadelphia Stock Exchange
Gerber Products	GEB	American Stock Exchange
Gerber Scientific	GRB	Philadelphia Stock Exchange
Gillette Company	GS	American Stock Exchange
Glenfed	GLN	American Stock Exchange
Golden Nugget, Inc.	GNG	American Stock Exchange
Golden West Financial	GDW	Philadelphia Stock Exchange
Goodrich, B.F.	GR	Chicago Board Options Exchange
Goodyear Tire & Rubber	GT	American Stock Exchange
Gould, Incorporated	GLD	American Stock Exchange
Grace, W.R. & Company	GRA	American Stock Exchange
Great North Nekoosa	GNN	Chicago Board Options Exchange
Great Western Financial	GWF	Chicago Board Options Exchange
Greyhound Corporation	G	American Stock Exchange
Grumman Corporation	GQ	Chicago Board Options Exchange
GTE Corporation	GTE	American Stock Exchange
Gulf & Western Industries	GW	Chicago Board Options Exchange
Halliburton Company	HAL	Chicago Board Options Exchange
Hanson PLC (ADR)	HAN	Chicago Board Options Exchange
Harcourt Brace	HBJ	American Stock Exchange
Harris Corporation	HRS	Chicago Board Options Exchange
Hasbro, Incorporated	HAS	Pacific Stock Exchange
Hecla Mining	HL	American Stock Exchange
Heinz, H.J.	HNZ	Chicago Board Options Exchange
Helmerich & Payne	HP	New York Stock Exchange
Hercules, Inc.	HPC	American Stock Exchange
Hershey Foods	HSY	American Stock Exchange
Hewlett-Packard Company	HWP	Chicago Board Options Exchange
Hilton Hotels Corporation	HLT	Pacific Stock Exchange

Stock	Ticker	Exchange
Hitachi, Ltd.	HIT	Chicago Board Options Exchange
Holiday Corporation	HIA	Chicago Board Options Exchange
Home Depot, Incorporated	HD	Philadelphia Stock Exchange
Home Federal Savings & Loan	HFD	Chicago Board Options Exchange
Homestake Mining	HM	Chicago Board Options Exchange
Honda Motor Company, Ltd.	HMC	Philadelphia Stock Exchange
Honeywell, Incorporated	HON	Chicago Board Options Exchange
Hospital Corp. of America	HCA	Pacific Stock Exchange
Household International Corp.	HI	American Stock Exchange
Houston Industries	HOU	New York Stock Exchange
Humana, Incorporated	HUM	Chicago Board Options Exchange
IC Industries	ICX	Chicago Board Options Exchange
INCO, Ltd.	N	American Stock Exchange
Ingersoll-Rand	IR	New York Stock Exchange
Inland Steel Industries	IAD	Philadelphia Stock Exchange
Int'l Flavors & Fragrances	IFF	Chicago Board Options Exchange
Int'l Minerals & Chemicals	IGL	Chicago Board Options Exchange
Intel Corporation	INQ	American Stock Exchange
Intergraph Corporation	IGQ	American Stock Exchange
International Business Machines	IBM	Chicago Board Options Exchange
International Paper Company	IP	Chicago Board Options Exchange
ITT Corporation	ITT	Chicago Board Options Exchange
James River	JR	New York Stock Exchange
Jerrico, Incorporated	JEQ	Pacific Stock Exchange
Johnson & Johnson	JNJ	Chicago Board Options Exchange
K Mart	KM	Chicago Board Options Exchange
Kaufman & Broad	KB	Philadelphia Stock Exchange
Kellogg Company	K	American Stock Exchange
Kemper Corporation	KEQ	American Stock Exchange Philadelphia Stock Exchange
Kerr McGee Corporation	KMG	Chicago Board Options Exchange
Kimberly-Clark	KMB	American Stock Exchange
Kinder-Care, Incorporated	KNQ	Pacific Stock Exchange
King World Productions	KWP	Pacific Stock Exchange
Knight-Ridder	KRI	Philadelphia Stock Exchange
Kraft, Incorporated	KRZ	American Stock Exchange
Kroger	KR	American Stock Exchange
Lehman Corporation	LEM	Philadelphia Stock Exchange
Lilly, Eli & Company	LLY	American Stock Exchange
Limited, Inc.	LTD	Chicago Board Options Exchange
LIN Broadcasting Corporation	LNQ	Philadelphia Stock Exchange
Litton Industries, Inc.	LIT	Chicago Board Options Exchange
Liz Claiborne	LIQ	Chicago Board Options Exchange
Lockheed Corporation	LK	Pacific Stock Exchange
Loews Corporation	LTR	Chicago Board Options Exchange

Stock	Ticker	Exchange
Lomas & Nettleton Financial	LNF	Philadelphia Stock Exchange
Loral Corporation	LOR	Chicago Board Options Exchange
Lotus Development Corporation	LOQ	Chicago Board Options Exchange
		American Stock Exchange
Louisiana Land & Exploration	LLX	Philadelphia Stock Exchange
Louisiana-Pacific	LPZ	American Stock Exchange
Louisiana-Pacific Corporation	LPX	American Stock Exchange
Lowes Companies	LOW	Philadelphia Stock Exchange
LSI Logic Corporation	LSQ	Chicago Board Options Exchange
Lubrizol Corporation	LZ	Philadelphia Stock Exchange
LyphoMed	LMQ	American Stock Exchange
M/A-COM, Incorporated	MAI	American Stock Exchange
Macmillan	MLL	American Stock Exchange
Manor Care	MNR	Philadelphia Stock Exchange
Manufacturers Hanover	MHC	American Stock Exchange
MAPCO, Incorporated	MDA	Pacific Stock Exchange
Marion Labs	MKC	Pacific Stock Exchange
Marriott Corporation	MHS	Philadelphia Stock Exchange
Marsh & McLennan Companies	MMC	Pacific Stock Exchange
Martin Marietta	ML	Philadelphia Stock Exchange
Masco Corporation	MAS	American Stock Exchange
Masco Industries	MAQ	Pacific Stock Exchange
Mattel	MAT	American Stock Exchange
Maxtor Corporation	MXQ	Pacific Stock Exchange
Maxus Energy	MXS	Pacific Stock Exchange
May Department Stores	MA	Chicago Board Options Exchange
Maytag	MYG	New York Stock Exchange
MCA, Incorporated	MCA	Philadelphia Stock Exchange
McDermott International	MDR	Philadelphia Stock Exchange
McDonalds Corporation	MCD	Chicago Board Options Exchange
McDonnell Douglas Corporation	MD	Pacific Stock Exchange
McGraw-Hill	MHP	Philadelphia Stock Exchange
MCI Communications Corporation	MCQ	Chicago Board Options Exchange
McKesson Corporation	MCK	Pacific Stock Exchange
Mead Corporation	MEA	Chicago Board Options Exchange
Medco Containment Services	MDQ	Pacific Stock Exchange
Medtronic, Incorporated	MDT	Chicago Board Options Exchange
Mellon Bank Corporation	MEL	New York Stock Exchange
Melville Corporation	MES	Pacific Stock Exchange
Mentor Corporation	MNQ	American Stock Exchange
		Pacific Stock Exchange
Mentor Graphics	MGQ	American Stock Exchange
Merck & Company	MRK	Chicago Board Options Exchange
Merrill Lynch	MER	Chicago Board Options Exchange
		American Stock Exchange

Stock	Ticker	Exchange
Mesa Limited Partnership	MLP	American Stock Exchange
Microsoft	MSQ	American Stock Exchange
		Pacific Stock Exchange
Middle South Utilities	MSU	Chicago Board Options Exchange
MiniScribe	MYQ	American Stock Exchange
Minnesota Mining & Mfg.	MMM	Chicago Board Options Exchange
Minnetonka Corporation	MIQ	Pacific Stock Exchange
Mitchell Energy & Development	MND	Pacific Stock Exchange
Mobil Corporation	MOB	Chicago Board Options Exchange
Molex, Incorporated	MOQ	Chicago Board Options Exchange
Monsanto Corporation	MTC	Chicago Board Options Exchange
Morgan, J.P. & Company	JPM	Philadelphia Stock Exchange
Morton Thiokol, Inc.	MTI	Philadelphia Stock Exchange
Motorola, Incorporated	MOT	American Stock Exchange
Murphy Oil Corporation	MUR	Pacific Stock Exchange
Mylan Labs	MYL	American Stock Exchange
National Medical Enterprises	NME	American Stock Exchange
National Patent Development	NPD	Pacific Stock Exchange
National Semiconductor	NSM	Chicago Board Options Exchange
		American Stock Exchange
NCR Corporation	NCR	Chicago Board Options Exchange
Network Systems	NSQ	American Stock Exchange
New York Times C1 A	NYT	Pacific Stock Exchange
Newmont Mining Corporation	NEM	Philadelphia Stock Exchange
Niagara Mohawk Power	NMK	American Stock Exchange
NIKE, Incorporated	NIQ	Pacific Stock Exchange
Nordstrom	NOQ	American Stock Exchange
Norfolk Southern Corporation	NSC	Chicago Board Options Exchange
Northern Telecom	NT	Chicago Board Options Exchange
Northrop Corporation	NOC	Chicago Board Options Exchange
Norton Company	NRT	Chicago Board Options Exchange
Novell, Inc.	NVQ	American Stock Exchange
Novo Industries A/S ADR	NVO	American Stock Exchange
NWA, Incorporated	NWA	Chicago Board Options Exchange
NYNEX Corporation	NYN	New York Stock Exchange
Occidental Petroleum	OXY	Chicago Board Options Exchange
Ocean Drilling & Exploration	ODR	American Stock Exchange
Ogden Corporation	OG	Chicago Board Options Exchange
Olin Corporation	OLN	American Stock Exchange
Owens-Corning Fiberglas	OCF	Philadelphia Stock Exchange
Pacific Enterprises	PET	American Stock Exchange
Pacific Gas & Electric	PCG	American Stock Exchange
Pacific Telesis	PAC	Pacific Stock Exchange
PaineWebber Group	PWJ	Chicago Board Options Exchange
Panhandle Eastern	PEL	Philadelphia Stock Exchange

Stock	Ticker	Exchange
Parker-Hannifin	PH	Philadelphia Stock Exchange
Penn Central	PC	Philadelphia Stock Exchange
Penney, J.C.	JCP	American Stock Exchange
Pennzoil Corporation	PZL	Chicago Board Options Exchange
PepsiCo, Incorporated	PEP	Chicago Board Options Exchange
Perkin-Elmer Corporation	PKN	Pacific Stock Exchange
Petrie Stores	PST	Philadelphia Stock Exchange
Pfizer, Incorporated	PFE	American Stock Exchange
Phelps Dodge Corporation	PD	American Stock Exchange
Philadelphia Electric	PE	Pacific Stock Exchange
Philip Morris Cos., Inc.	MO	American Stock Exchange
Philips Industries	PHL	Philadelphia Stock Exchange
Phillips Petroleum	P	American Stock Exchange
Pic 'N' Save	PIQ	Pacific Stock Exchange
Pillsbury	PSY	American Stock Exchange
Pitney-Bowes, Incorporated	PBI	American Stock Exchange
Pittston Company	PCO	Philadelphia Stock Exchange
PNC Financial	PNC	Philadelphia Stock Exchange
Polaroid Corporation	PRD	Chicago Board Options Exchange Pacific Stock Exchange
PPG Industries	PPG	Philadelphia Stock Exchange
Precision Castparts	PRQ	Chicago Board Options Exchange
Price Company	PCQ	Pacific Stock Exchange
Prime Computer, Inc.	PRM	American Stock Exchange
Prime Motor Inns	PDG	Pacific Stock Exchange
Primerica	PA	American Stock Exchange
Proctor & Gamble Company	PG	American Stock Exchange
Public Serv. Enterprise Group	PEG	American Stock Exchange
Quaker Oats	OAT	Philadelphia Stock Exchange
Quaker State Corporation	KSF	American Stock Exchange
Quantum Chemical	CUE	American Stock Exchange
Ralston Purina Company	RAL	Chicago Board Options Exchange
Raychem Corporation	RYC	Pacific Stock Exchange
Raytheon Company	RTN	Chicago Board Options Exchange
Reebok International	RBK	American Stock Exchange Pacific Stock Exchange
Reynolds Metals Company	RLM	Pacific Stock Exchange
Rite Aid	RAD	Philadelphia Stock Exchange
RJR Nabisco	RJR	Chicago Board Options Exchange
Rockwell International	ROK	Chicago Board Options Exchange
Rohm & Haas	ROH	American Stock Exchange
Rohr Industries	RHR	Philadelphia Stock Exchange
Rollins Environmental	REN	Pacific Stock Exchange
Rorer Group	ROR	American Stock Exchange

Stock	Ticker	Exchange
Royal Dutch Petroleum	RD	American Stock Exchange
RPM, Incorporated	RPQ	Chicago Board Options Exchange
Rubbermaid, Incorporated	RBD	Pacific Stock Exchange
Ryder System, Inc.	RDR	Pacific Stock Exchange
SafeCard Services	SFQ	Pacific Stock Exchange
SAFECO Corporation	SAQ	New York Stock Exchange
Saint Paul Companies	SPQ	Chicago Board Options Exchange
Salomon, Incorporated	SB	Philadelphia Stock Exchange
Sante Fe South Pacific	SFX	American Stock Exchange
Sara Lee	SLE	American Stock Exchange
SCE Corporation	SCE	Pacific Stock Exchange
Schering-Plough Corporation	SGP	Pacific Stock Exchange
Schlumberger, Limited	SLB	Chicago Board Options Exchange
SCI Systems	SSQ	Chicago Board Options Exchange
Scientific-Atlanta, Inc.	SFA	Pacific Stock Exchange
Scott Paper Company	SPP	Philadelphia Stock Exchange
Seagate Technology	SGQ	American Stock Exchange
Seagram Company, Ltd.	VO	Pacific Stock Exchange
Sears Roebuck & Company	S	Chicago Board Options Exchange
Security Pacific Corporation	SPC	Philadelphia Stock Exchange
Service Corporation Int'l	SRV	Philadelphia Stock Exchange
Service Merchandise	SMQ	Philadelphia Stock Exchange
Shaklee Corporation	SHC	American Stock Exchange
Shared Medical Sytems	SDQ	Pacific Stock Exchange
Sherwin Williams	SHW	Chicago Board Options Exchange
Shoney's Incorporated	SHQ	Pacific Stock Exchange
Skyline Corporation	SKY	Chicago Board Options Exchange
SmithKline Beckman Corporation	SKB	Pacific Stock Exchange
Snap-On Tools Corporation	SNA	American Stock Exchange
Sonat, Incorporated	SNT	American Stock Exchange
Sony Corporation ADR	SNE	Pacific Stock Exchange
Southwest Airlines	LUV	Chicago Board Options Exchange
Southern Company	SO	Chicago Board Options Exchange
Southwestern Bell Corporation	SBC	Pacific Stock Exchange
Squibb Corporation	SQB	Chicago Board Options Exchange
Stone Container	STO	Pacific Stock Exchange
Stratus Computer	STQ	Pacific Stock Exchange
Student Loan Marketing	SLM	Philadelphia Stock Exchange
Subaru of America	SBQ	Philadelphia Stock Exchange
Sun Company, Inc.	SUN	Pacific Stock Exchange
Sun Microsystems	SUQ	Pacific Stock Exchange
Super Valu Stores	SVU	Chicago Board Options Exchange
Syntex Corporation	SYN	Chicago Board Options Exchange
Tambrands, Incorporated	TMB	New York Stock Exchange

Stock	Ticker	Exchange
Tandem Computers	TDM	American Stock Exchange
Tandy Corporation	TAN	Chicago Board Options Exchange
		American Stock Exchange
TCBY Enterprises	YOQ	Pacific Stock Exchange
Tektronix, Inc.	TEK	Chicago Board Options Exchange
Tele-Communications, Inc.	TCQ	American Stock Exchange
Teledyne, Inc.	TDY	Chicago Board Options Exchange
		Pacific Stock Exchange
Telerate, Inc.	TLR	New York Stock Exchange
Telxon Corporation	TNQ	Chicago Board Options Exchange
Tenneco, Inc.	TGT	American Stock Exchange
Teradyne, Incorporated	TER	Pacific Stock Exchange
Tesoro Petroleum Corporation	TSO	Philadelphia Stock Exchange
Texaco	TX	American Stock Exchange
Texas Eastern	TET	Philadelphia Stock Exchange
Texas Instruments	TXN	Chicago Board Options Exchange
Texas Utilities	TXU	Philadelphia Stock Exchange
Textron, Incorporated	TXT	Philadelphia Stock Exchange
Tiger, International	TGR	Philadelphia Stock Exchange
Time, Incorporated	TL	Philadelphia Stock Exchange
Times Mirror	TMC	New York Stock Exchange
Torchmark Corporation	TMK	American Stock Exchange
Toys R Us, Incorporated	TOY	Chicago Board Options Exchange
Transamerica Corporation	TA	Philadelphia Stock Exchange
Transco Energy Company	E	New York Stock Exchange
Travelers Corporation	TIC	Pacific Stock Exchange
Tri-Continental Corporation	TY	Philadelphia Stock Exchange
Tribune Company	TRB	Chicago Board Options Exchange
TRW, Incorporated	TRW	American Stock Exchange
Tyco Labs	TYC	Philadelphia Stock Exchange
Tyson Foods	TYQ	Pacific Stock Exchange
U.S. Health Care Systems	HCQ	American Stock Exchange
U.S. Shoe	USR	Philadelphia Stock Exchange
U.S. West, Inc.	USW	American Stock Exchange
UAL Corporation	UAL	Chicago Board Options Exchange
Union Camp	UCC	Chicago Board Options Exchange
Union Carbide Corporation	UK	American Stock Exchange
Union Pacific Corporation	UNP	Philadelphia Stock Exchange
Unisys	UIS	Chicago Board Options Exchange
		American Stock Exchange
United Technologies	UTX	Chicago Board Options Exchange
United Telecom	UT	Philadelphia Stock Exchange
Unocal Corporation	UCL	Pacific Stock Exchange
Upjohn Company	UPJ	Chicago Board Options Exchange

Stock	Ticker	Exchange
USAir Group, Inc.	U	Pacific Stock Exchange
USF & G Corporation	FG	Philadelphia Stock Exchange
USG Corporation	USG	Chicago Board Options Exchange
UST	UST	Chicago Board Options Exchange
USX Corporation	X	American Stock Exchange
V.F. Corporation	VFC	New York Stock Exchange
Valero Energy Corporation	VLO	American Stock Exchange
Varian Associates	VAR	American Stock Exchange
Veeco Associates	VEE	Pacific Stock Exchange
Wal-Mart Stores, Inc.	WMT	Chicago Board Options Exchange
Walgreen Company	WAG	American Stock Exchange
Wang Labs, Incorporated	WAN	Pacific Stock Exchange
Warner Communications	WCI	Chicago Board Options Exchange
Warner-Lambert Company	WLA	American Stock Exchange
Waste Management, Inc.	WMX	Philadelphia Stock Exchange
Wells Fargo & Company	WFC	Chicago Board Options Exchange American Stock Exchange
Wendy's International, Inc.	WEN	Pacific Stock Exchange
West Point-Pepperell	WPM	Chicago Board Options Exchange
Western Digital	WDC	Philadelphia Stock Exchange
Westinghouse Electric	WX	American Stock Exchange
Weyerhaeuser Co.	WY	Chicago Board Options Exchange
Weyerhaeuser Company	WYZ	Chicago Board Options Exchange
Whirlpool	WHR	Chicago Board Options Exchange
Williams Companies	WMB	Chicago Board Options Exchange
Winnebago Industries	WGO	Chicago Board Options Exchange
Woolworth, F.W. Company	Z	Philadelphia Stock Exchange
Wyse Technology	WYS	American Stock Exchange
Xerox Corporation	XRX	Chicago Board Options Exchange Pacific Stock Exchange
Yellow Freight Systems	YLQ	Chicago Board Options Exchange
Zayre Corporation	ZY	Chicago Board Options Exchange
Zenith Electronics	ZE	American Stock Exchange

Appendix B
Major U.S. Stock Markets

American Stock Exchange, 86 Trinity Place, New York, New York 10006

Boston Stock Exchange, 53 State Street, Boston, Massachusetts 02109

Cincinnati Stock Exchange, 205 Dixie Terminal Building, Cincinnati, Ohio 45202

Intermountain Stock Exchange, 39 Exchange Place, Salt Lake City, Utah 84111

Midwest Stock Exchange, 120 South Lasalle Street, Room 1243, Chicago, Illinois 60603

National Association of Securities Dealers, 1735 K Street N.W., Washington, D.C. 20006

New York Stock Exchange, 11 Wall Street, New York, New York 10005

Pacific Stock Exchange, 618 South Spring Street, Los Angeles, California 90014

Philadelphia Stock Exchange, 17th Street & Stock Exchange Place, Philadelphia, Pennsylvania 19103

Spokane Stock Exchange, 225 Peyton Building, Spokane, Washington 99201

Index

203